THE
ROGUE

ALSO BY JOE MCGINNISS

The Selling of the President
The Dream Team
Heroes
Going to Extremes
Fatal Vision
Blind Faith
Cruel Doubt
The Last Brother
The Miracle of Castel di Sangro
The Big Horse
Never Enough

THE
ROGUE

SEARCHING FOR THE REAL SARAH PALIN

JOE McGINNISS

Crown Publishers

NEW YORK

CROWN and the Crown colophon
are trademarks of Random House, Inc.

Library of Congress Cataloging-in-Publication Data
is available upon request.

ISBN 978-0-307-71892-1
eISBN 978-0-307-71895-2

PRINTED IN THE UNITED STATES OF AMERICA

Book design by Elizabeth Rendfleisch
Map on page 10 by Mapping Specialists, Ltd.
Jacket design by Laura Duffy

1   3   5   7   9   10   8   6   4   2

First Edition

For Nancy,

And for the next generation: Chrissy, Suzy, Joe, Matthew, and James

And for the next next generation: Dylan, Lauren, and Carly;
Sebastien, Cecilia, and Samuel; and Julien

And for Kevin, Yves, and Jeanine, without whom there would not be
a next next generation

rogue (rōg), *n.*: An elephant that has separated from a herd and roams about alone, in which state it is very savage.

—WEBSTER'S REVISED UNABRIDGED DICTIONARY

THE
ROGUE

ONE

I MOVED IN next door to Sarah Palin today. It was a dazzling Alaskan spring day: sky blue, air cool, sun warm, the water of Lake Lucille glimmering, mountains standing in bold relief beyond the southern shore, resident grebes tending noisily to their nests.

Sitting on my deck overlooking the lake at 11:00 PM, I consider myself as lucky as a man can be. It has been more than thirty years since I last spent a summer in Alaska, yet here I am. A light breeze blows from the northwest, riffling the lake's surface. The glowing mountains on the far side reflect the day's slowly waning light.

I arrived in Anchorage ten days ago. I stayed with my old friends Tom and Marnie Brennan in their house on Government Hill while looking for a place to rent.

The first possibility was an "executive apartment" in a grubby East Anchorage neighborhood populated mostly by empty storefronts and overflowing garbage bins. (Question: How can the stores be empty and the garbage bins full?) The apartment was in a squat concrete six-plex. The rent was $2,400 per month, utilities not included. I arranged to see it on Wednesday, three days ago.

At 11:00 AM, I pulled into the asphalt lot outside the apartment building to wait for the rental agent. I got out of my car to stand in the warm spring sunshine. Almost immediately, the main door opened and a young woman holding a baby emerged onto a concrete landing a few steps up from the parking lot. The baby was crying. The woman put the baby down on the concrete and sat in a plastic chair. She covered her face with her hands and she, too, began to cry.

A moment later, the door flew open again. A young man in a T-shirt and blue jeans strode out. His head was shaved. He wore a goatee. His arms and neck were covered with tattoos.

"Get back inside, bitch!"

The woman lowered her hands and looked at him. Through her tears, she said, "Can't you understand that I'd rather be dead than stuck here living with you?"

He grabbed her by a bare arm and yanked her to her feet.

The baby continued to cry.

"Listen, bitch—"

"Hey!" I shouted. "Take it easy there."

He let go of the woman's arm and looked down at me from the landing. "Who the fuck are you?"

"Your new neighbor?" I said.

"Let me tell you, mister," the woman said, "you don't want to live here."

"Are you going to be okay?"

She nodded, then went back inside with the man, leaving the baby crying on the landing. The rental agent still had not arrived. I got back in my car and drove off to resume my search.

The next day, Thursday, May 20, I found a "mother-in-law" apartment in a house owned by a schoolteacher in the Hillside district of Anchorage. Hillside wasn't the most convenient area—it was at least a twenty-minute drive from downtown and more than an hour from Wasilla, where I'd be spending most of my working hours—but at $1,650 a month it was better than $2,400 and the need to put the domestic abuse hotline on my speed dial. I arranged to see the apartment at 6:00 PM.

I'd bought a cell phone the previous fall, when I'd spent a month in Anchorage and Wasilla doing research. I turned it off when I left the state and had only just reactivated my account. The missed-calls list showed half a dozen from someone named Catherine Taylor, every three or four weeks, from December through April. My voice mailbox was full because I didn't know how to empty it, so she hadn't been able to leave a message. The phone rang on Thursday afternoon.

"This is Catherine Taylor. I'm so glad I finally reached you. Colleen Cottle told me last fall that you'd be coming back in the spring to work on your book about Sarah Palin and that you'd need a place to stay. I've got a house in Wasilla that's available."

I told her I expected to sign a lease on an Anchorage apartment within hours.

"Oh, that's too bad, because I thought you might find my place convenient. It's actually right next door to Todd and Sarah."

"You're kidding."

"No. In fact, they were renting it themselves until October. Todd renovated the whole upstairs."

"This could be a pretty amazing stroke of luck. Can I come up tomorrow to take a look?"

We arranged to meet at the house at 1:30 PM. Catherine gave me directions: Take the Parks Highway to Wasilla, proceed past all the big-box stores and fast-food outlets to the sign for the Best Western. Turn left, then left again at the stop sign just before the Best Western parking lot. That's called West Lake Lucille Drive, but it's only a dirt road, about a hundred yards long. Turn right at the end, just before the fence. Catherine Taylor's house will be up the short driveway, toward the lake.

At dinner, I tell Tom and Marnie what happened. They find it hard to believe.

"You come back here to work on your book about Sarah and a woman calls up out of the blue and offers to rent you the house right next door?" Tom says.

"Yup."

"It must be a trick," Marnie says.

Tom agrees. "It can't be for real. Nobody could be that lucky."

I DRIVE TO Wasilla the next morning. In good weather it's an easy forty-mile trip on four- and six-lane highways. Halfway up, the Matanuska-Susitna Valley suddenly opens out in all directions, suggestive, even in 2010, of grand dreams and infinite possibilities. It's only when you hit Wasilla that the possibilities shrivel into lost opportunities and the dreams mutate into a nightmare of exurban sprawl.

It used to be said that Wasilla was a trading outpost bounded by two lakes: Wasilla Lake and Lake Lucille. Now it's a city of 7,028 located between Chili's and Wendy's and stuffed to the gills with stores such as Wal-Mart, Sears, Target, Lowe's, Home Depot, and Fred Meyer, and enough small-fry evangelical Christian churches to make Jesus himself weep from the effort of trying to count them all.

I don't exaggerate. There are the Wasilla Bible Church, Wasilla Assembly of God, Church on the Rock (all three of which Sarah Palin

has attended), Sunny Knik Chapel, King's Chapel Alaska, Abundant Life Church, Wasilla Lake Church-Nazarene, Mat-Su Evangelical Covenant Church, Wasilla Christian Church, Wasilla Community Church of God, King of Kings Evangelical Lutheran Church, Fairview Loop Baptist Church, Faith Chapel Pentecostal Church of God, New Life Presbyterian Church, Valley Church of Christ, Apostolic Worship Center, Independent Baptist Church of Wasilla, Glad Tidings Full Gospel Church, Church of Christ at Wasilla, Mid Valley Christian Center, Meadow Lakes Christian Center, Word of Faith Assembly, Frontier Christian Ministries, Big Lake Baptist Church, Pilgrims Baptist Church, Northern Lights Mennonite Church, Trailhead Wesleyan Church, Valley Open Bible Fellowship, Bread of Life Church of Mat-Su, Word of Life International Ministries, Slavic Evangelical Church Nadezhda, Gospel Outreach Christian Center, West Valley Family Church of the Nazarene, Christian Fellowship of Wasilla, Pioneer Christian Fellowship, Independent Baptist Church, Settlers Bay Community Church, Faith Bible Fellowship, Valley Christian Conference, North Bear Street Community Church, Valley Sovereign Grace Baptist Assembly, Birch Harbor Baptist Church, Schrock Road Community Church, and Crossroads Community Church, not to mention another dozen or more Catholic, Presbyterian, Methodist, Seventh-Day Adventist, Mormon, Episcopalian, Lutheran, Russian Orthodox, and Jehovah's Witness churches, and at least another twenty-five or thirty just down the road in Palmer.

There are no synagogues in Wasilla, but there are more than thirty-five chiropractors, or approximately one for every two hundred residents.

Before seeing Catherine, I drive to the other side of Lake Lucille for coffee with Rod and Colleen Cottle, whom I'd first met the previous fall. In its early days, Wasilla's two main business establishments were Teelands general store and Cottles gas station. Colleen was a Teeland. Her marriage to Rod was the Wasilla equivalent of a Cabot marrying a Lodge in Massachusetts.

Colleen knows everything there is to know about Wasilla. She and Rod are lifelong friends of Sarah's parents, Chuck and Sally Heath. Sarah and her siblings grew up with the Cottle children, and Sarah spent many a childhood hour playing in their backyard.

Colleen wastes no time filling me in on all I missed over the winter. Bristol has broken up with Levi, but is practicing abstinence with Levi's best friend, Ben Barber. Ben's mother is manager at the Wells Fargo branch in Wasilla. His father, Jack Barber, is an old-time, oft-married bush pilot. There is also somebody who's the boyfriend of somebody's niece who knows Judy Minnick, who used to work as a hostess at the VFW, who's a friend of Sarah's sister Heather Bruce, in Anchorage. Speaking of Sarah, I should talk to Scott and Debbie Richter, who own land with the Palins—including the cabin at Safari Lake that Todd and Sarah didn't pay property tax on—but they probably won't talk to me because Debbie had an affair with Sarah's former legislative director, John Bitney, and then Todd made Sarah fire him, and Bitney married Debbie after she and Scott divorced, and the Bitneys have a cabin on Big Lake. Also speaking of Sarah, Track is out of the army and still dating Britta Hanson, the daughter of a Lutheran minister, who's not to be confused with Brad Hanson, with whom Sarah had the affair back when Brad and Todd were partners in the Polaris snowmobile store in Big Lake. Angie Johnson, one of the ex-wives of Mike Wooten, whom Todd and Sarah tried to get fired from the state troopers when Sarah was governor after Mike and Sarah's sister Molly divorced, was just killed in a head-on collision on the Parks Highway, along with a couple of her children, but not the ones she had with Mike. If I want to talk to Mike, I can probably reach him through Conrad Holler at Rainbow Pawn, but it's doubtful he'll talk to me because he's keeping a low profile because Todd is still obsessed with getting him fired, even though the whole Palin family ate the moose he shot without a permit because Molly, who had the permit, wouldn't do it.

And speaking of Todd, he's gotten real uptight and suspicious and doesn't trust anyone anymore because, for the first time in his life, he's got money and it's just too much for him, especially because he knows people around here now are fed up with Sarah and him, and besides, he's got Willow to worry about after the vandalism of Audrey Morlock's house in Meadow Lakes.

Whew.

"And Catherine Taylor has been trying to reach you for months. She'd like to rent you the house she owns right next to Todd and Sarah."

"I spoke to her yesterday. In fact, I'm meeting her at the house in half an hour."

"Well, it's practically falling down. It's been vacant all winter. She used to have a bunch of ex-cons and drunks and drug addicts living there, supposedly trying to rehabilitate, although I don't think most of them ever do. They were setting up a meth lab in the basement. Catherine had to call the troopers to get them out. And before that there was a woman living there whose fiancé's son tried to kill her with a machete."

"Sounds like she's due for a tenant who won't cause her any trouble."

"I assured her you were mature and responsible and that you'd be a perfect neighbor for Todd and Sarah."

I TURN LEFT at the stop sign at the entrance to the Best Western and drive down a rutted dirt lane. There are a couple of cabins in the woods on either side. In less than a hundred yards the lane ends at a clearing marked with DO NOT ENTER and NO TRESPASSING signs. There's an abandoned delivery truck and three abandoned cars and an abandoned boat and three unused sheds in weeds at the edge of the clearing. The weeds stop at a ten-foot-high wooden fence, the uglier, back side facing Catherine Taylor's property.

Close to the lake is a dilapidated ranch house that looks at least fifty years old. The wood siding has started to rot, some of the exterior glass is broken, and the steps leading up to the front door sag. The fence runs alongside the house, only six feet from it. On the other side, built smack-dab up against the fence, looms Todd and Sarah's much newer, bigger house.

Catherine arrives twenty minutes late. She tells me she's older than me, but I don't believe it. She looks at least ten years younger, with dark hair and a dramatically expressive face. She carries herself like an actress and speaks in a manner that suggests familiarity with soliloquy. "I used to be quite photogenic," she says. She's so exuberant that I feel it's only with difficulty that she's resisting the impulse to reach out and pinch my cheek.

"What do you think?" she says.

"I think it's right next door to Todd and Sarah."

When I was in Wasilla last fall, I'd stopped by the Palin house to drop off a copy of *Going to Extremes,* my book about Alaska in the

1970s. I'd inscribed it, "To Sarah Palin—from one author who loves Alaska to another." Track came to the door and we had a brief, pleasant chat as I gave him the book. "You wrote this? Wow! That's awesome." I told him I was glad he'd made it back safely from Iraq. He thanked me and said he'd give the book to his mother.

As we stand outside, Catherine, who lives in Settlers Bay, a residential enclave ten miles west of Wasilla, tells me she received title to this house, and to the vacant lot adjacent to it, in a divorce settlement with Clyde Boyer. Clyde is an accountant who was the father of five children before Catherine married him. They had no children of their own. He was chairman of the Mat-Su Valley hospital board when they illegally banned abortions. He took up with the marriage counselor Vivian Finlay after Vivian's husband died of a stroke. Clyde and Vivian are now married and live in Homer.

You don't simply conduct a business transaction in Wasilla, or anyplace else in Alaska. Even in preliminary discussion, you become a member of the other party's extended family—more often families—to a degree that can leave you reeling from intimate information overload.

Catherine got the Lake Lucille house in 1997. It was surrounded by woods on both sides until the Palins built on the adjacent lot, which they bought after Sarah became mayor. The Palin lot was landlocked, meaning they had no vehicular access to it (see diagram, next page).

The seven two-acre lots in what is known as the Snider subdivision are long and narrow, offering a hundred feet of lake frontage and extending from the lake back almost to the railroad tracks. Catherine's house is on Lot 2. The Palin property is Lot 3. West Lake Lucille Drive, the dirt road leading from the Best Western, provides road access to Catherine's property. The private Nevada right-of-way that extends from South Hallea Lane to Lot 7 is where Charlie Nevada built the first house in the subdivision.

When you cross the railroad tracks on South Hallea Lane you

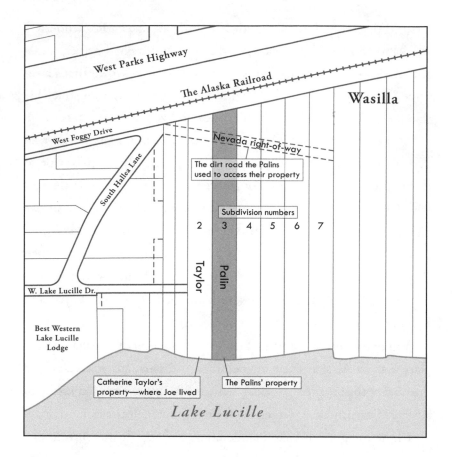

immediately see a dirt track on the left with an old wooden sign that reads NEVADA. That's the right-of-way that goes to Lot 7. It cuts across the back of Catherine Taylor's property, providing the only land access to Lot 3. I used it in the fall when I dropped off a copy of my book at Sarah's house.

The Palins had no road access to their new property, but Todd didn't consider that a problem. Instead of asking for permission or offering a modest payment, he simply told Catherine that they'd be building next to her and cutting across her property in order to do so.

Catherine didn't like being bullied. She told Todd he had no right to cut across her property to get to his own. Todd told her, very plainly, that Sarah was mayor and they could do whatever they wanted, and it would be a mistake for her to try to stop them. Catherine called Sarah, who at least pretended to be more reasonable. Todd then called Catherine and said, "I don't want you calling my wife again."

"He was angry," Catherine tells me. She recalls that he also said, "If you do anything to make it more difficult for me to build my house, I'm going to be very unhappy."

She asked if he was threatening her. After a long pause, he said no, in a manner that did not convince her. It left her, in fact, with a "creepy, creepy, creepy feeling." She went to her lawyer. Her lawyer said, "Todd's right: Sarah is mayor. Do you really think you can fight city hall?"

So the Palins cut through her land without her permission in order to build their new home. They moved in during the summer of 2002. Todd had the house built to within ten feet of the property line, as close as he could get legally, and put up a ten-foot-high fence, the back side facing Catherine's house, which is not the way good-neighbor Alaskans usually do it.

"They tortured that woman," a friend of the Palins later told me. "I'd be with them when they were just laughing at her. I'd say, 'Why are you being so mean?' Sarah said, 'Because we can.' Todd said, 'I want her to get the message: we're here now.'"

Because she was already settled in Settlers Bay, Catherine never intended to live in the Lake Lucille house. Her first thought had been to use it as a shelter for battered women, but once Mayor Palin and her family moved next door she realized the house couldn't be as private as such a shelter needed to be.

Instead, starting in 2005, she rented it to the Oxford House organization. Oxford House is a national network of group homes for recovering drug addicts and alcoholics, with particular emphasis on those who've just been released from prison. Their motto is "Self-Help for Sobriety Without Relapse." The residents themselves run the houses. There are more than six hundred Oxford Houses throughout the United States. Catherine's was one of five in Alaska.

The Palins never complained about their neighbors. Neither Todd nor Sarah seemed bothered by having six ex-cons and recovering addicts living in such close proximity to them and their children. "Sarah was very pleasant to the men," Catherine tells me. "She'd say hi when she was down at the lake, and sometimes she'd send over a plate of cookies."

Catherine ran into problems in 2008, when the resident who'd been de facto manager of the house decided he was well enough to live on his own. Without his supervision, standards declined—to the point where two new arrivals began to build the meth lab in the basement, and Catherine had to call the state troopers to evict them.

And, yes, before that there was a woman named Elann "Lenny" Moren, whose fiancé's son tried to kill her with a machete. The man did succeed in killing his father with the machete, and less than twenty-four hours later he killed a complete stranger in Anchorage before he was arrested, convicted, and sentenced to 498 years in prison. His name was Christopher Erin Rogers, Jr.

Because Lenny moved out before the Palins moved in, Todd and Sarah just missed having him for a neighbor.

ONCE INSIDE the house, I'm pleasantly surprised. Down a flight of stairs from the front entrance is a finished basement in need of attention, but on the main level the dining area, living room, kitchen, and bathroom have been newly renovated, with brand-new appliances and fixtures.

"Todd had this done last year," Catherine tells me. "He and Sarah rented the house from May through October. He said he wanted to fix it up for a special guest who would be coming for an extended stay. Instead of paying rent, he renovated. I think Bristol and her baby were living here.

"In October, when he was supposed to start paying three thousand dollars a month, he left me a message saying the guest wasn't coming and they didn't need the house anymore. I said, 'Todd, you're leaving me in the lurch. There's no way I can rent this house through the winter.' He said, 'Don't worry about it, you'll find someone.' I said, 'Yes, but I don't want to rent to anyone you wouldn't feel comfortable having next door.' He said, 'Don't worry about it. That's why we built the fence.'

"Colleen told me you were coming back," Catherine says to me, "and I thought, 'How perfect!' I tried to reach you for months."

"And now you have."

"Well?"

"It's more than perfect. But I can't pay three thousand a month."

"What can you pay?"

"Fifteen hundred? And only for the next few months. Once I've finished talking to people, I've got to go home and write."

"It's a deal."

No need for any formalities, such as a lease. I write her a check and we seal the deal in the old-fashioned Alaskan way: with a hug.

"You've never been in prison, have you?" Catherine asks me as we walk back to our cars.

"Nope."

"Have you ever been convicted of a felony?"

"Not yet."

"In that case, you'll be the first neighbor Todd and Sarah have ever had here who didn't have a criminal record."

MARNIE LOANS ME a duvet, and Tom puts some fresh-caught salmon and halibut into a cooler. I buy a Traeger grill. Traeger is an Oregon company that makes grills that use wood pellets instead of charcoal or gas. I've always been a charcoal man. I'd as soon cook indoors in an electric oven as use a gas grill outside. On the other hand, I don't want to burn down Catherine's house by cooking with charcoal on a wooden deck. The Traeger seems to offer a path between the horns of my dilemma.

I buy the Traeger Junior, the smallest model, taking the one already assembled because I'd never have the patience or skill to put a grill together myself and I don't want to have to ask my new neighbors to help me. It's not polite to ask for a favor on the day you move in.

I head up the Parks Highway and get to the house in time to set up the grill and cook some of Tom's salmon, which I eat on my deck overlooking the lake. It's the best salmon I've ever eaten.

Except for a dining room table, four chairs, two plastic deck chairs, one horribly saggy mattress on a broken box spring, some old dishes, and a mix of plastic and metal utensils, Catherine's house is unfurnished. If Bristol and her baby were living here, they were living rough.

But furnishings are a problem for tomorrow. Right now I'm still trying to come to terms with my amazing stroke of good fortune.

Admittedly, Lake Lucille is dead: not fit for either fishing or swimming. Even before Sarah became mayor in 1996, the lake was listed as "impaired" by the state Department of Environmental Conservation. The runaway growth Sarah encouraged during her six years in office worsened the problem. Leaching septic systems and fertilizer runoff, combined with pollution caused by the heavy automotive traffic through Wasilla, have killed off the fish population. "It's basically just a runway for floatplanes," one resident says.

Even so, it sure is nice to look at on a fine spring evening. I play music on my laptop and enjoy a glass of wine on my deck, listening to the grebes squawk and the Alaska Railroad trains whistle in the dimming light of midnight as they race along the tracks that run parallel to the highway, less than fifty yards behind my house.

As a red-and-white floatplane lands on the lake and taxis toward the Best Western dock, I can't help but feel that I've never been off to a better start researching a book.

Did Catherine rent me this house because, as she says, she wanted a tenant who she knew would respect the Palins' privacy? Or was she motivated, at least in part, by lingering raw feelings over the way Todd steamrollered her when he wanted to build? I don't know. I'm just glad to be here. I move to a state two and a half times bigger than Texas and I wind up living fifteen feet from the subject of my next book. Forty years in the business and I've never had a piece of luck like this.

It's not that my proximity to Sarah will enable me to learn anything about her that I wouldn't discover if I were living in Anchorage, as I'd planned to: I'm not going to spy on her, or crouch in the backyard with my ear pressed up against the fence. But being here will certainly give my book a sense of place.

At first, Sarah probably will be less than thrilled to learn I'm here. I wrote a cover story for *Condé Nast Portfolio* magazine in 2009 that was highly critical of her proposal for a natural gas pipeline, and she expressed irritation about it at the time. I also wrote a piece for The Daily Beast that pointed out that while she was claiming to tour the country by bus to promote her book *Going Rogue,* she was actually doing most of the tour by private plane. Now I'm here to work on a book about her.

So, no, she won't be happy to learn that I'll be living next door for the coming few months. And who can blame her? Nonetheless, once she understands that I'm not here to hassle her, or to invade her family's privacy in any way, maybe we can become, if not friends, then at least reasonably cordial summer neighbors. She got along fine with the Oxford House guys, so why not with me? All things great and small seem possible on a magnificent night such as this.

TWO

SARAH WAS BORN February 11, 1964, in Sandpoint, Idaho, then a town of fewer than five thousand people, almost all of them Caucasian, about fifty miles from the Canadian border.

Her father, Chuck Heath, grew up there. In *Going Rogue,* Sarah describes his childhood as "painful and lonely." Chuck's father, Orville Wayne "Charlie" Heath, earned a living taking photographs of boxers and wrestlers in Los Angeles. In 1948, when Chuck was ten, his father abandoned photography, uprooted the family to Idaho, and opened a fishing lure shop, while his wife, a Christian Scientist, taught school.

Sarah writes, "Dad doesn't talk much about his childhood." This is peculiar, because in Wasilla, Chuck Heath is known as a raconteur. Why no stories of growing up in northern Idaho in the 1950s? Sarah doesn't say, but *Going Rogue* contains this striking passage: "Through the years I heard enough muffled conversations between my mom and dad to know that his parents' acceptance of pain must have translated beyond the physical."

What can a reader make of that? Or of this: "Sports and the outdoors were Dad's passion, but his parents thought they were a waste of time."

Chuck's father, a sports photographer who left L.A. to sell fishing lures in an area of the United States where hunting and fishing were almost sacred parts of communal life, thought sports and the outdoors were a waste of time?

Whatever the case, as a teenager, unable to tolerate what Sarah calls "his family's brokenness," Chuck moved out. "He went from couch to couch," Sarah writes, "staying with different families . . . and was virtually adopted by a classmate's kind family, the Mooneys."

The adoption may have been more than virtual. A 1992 obituary of eighty-year-old Dorothy Mooney, of Sandpoint, lists among her survivors "an adopted son, Chuck Heath of Wasilla, Alaska."

Sarah's mother, Sally Sheeran, grew up—less traumatically, it appears—in Richland, Washington. Sally's father worked at the nearby Hanford nuclear plant.

Chuck and Sally met at Columbia Basin, a junior college in Pasco, Washington. They married in 1961.

Chuck began to teach school in Sandpoint. Chuck Junior was followed by Heather the next year, and by Sarah a year later. Molly arrived two years after Sarah.

SARAH WAS three months old when the family moved to Skagway, a historic gold-mining town in southeastern Alaska. After five years they moved to south-central Alaska, living in Eagle River, just north of Anchorage, for two years before settling in Wasilla in 1972, when the town's population was less than five hundred.

Chuck taught at Iditarod Elementary School. Sally found part-time clerical work. She also left the Roman Catholic Church and joined the Assembly of God, soon becoming a committed evangelical.

Paul Riley, the founding pastor of the Wasilla Assembly of God church, remembers Sarah first attending services when she was in second grade. In addition, she became active in a church program for girls called Missionettes. By the time she was twelve, Riley says, "She began to have a strong desire for the Lord."

The major event of Sarah's childhood occurred that summer, the summer of 1976. Immersing themselves—or being immersed—in the waters of a nearby lake, she and her mother were baptized together by Pastor Riley. "Sarah loved the Lord with all her heart," Riley says, adding, "I know that she did receive an experience of the Holy Spirit, and that she received a calling on her life."

The baptism also affected Sarah's mother. She seemed to lose interest in both husband and children. "These days," an old friend says, "we'd call it a dysfunctional family. Primarily because Sally never really functioned as a mother. Once she got caught up in Assembly of God, all her energy went into the church and none of it into raising her children.

"Sarah's older sister, Heather, was the mom. She cooked, cleaned, took care of everything in the house. Sally was always off doing something with the church. You'd go there any time of the day when school was not in session and Heather was baking or cleaning, making sure that everything was ready for everybody.

"The kids were not tended to as children. The house was run-down. Where the kids slept upstairs, they had a room with a wood-stove in it, and the girls had an attic where they slept, and there was no heat, so if they didn't leave the door open it was cold." Another childhood friend of Sarah's says, "I spent the night over there a couple of times and I remember Sarah and Molly and I all sleeping in the same bed because it was that cold."

A longtime Wasilla acquaintance recalls that "Chuck Heath was a good teacher and a terrific track coach, but he had a mean streak, and very high expectations for the kids. They were forced to do sports. Sarah liked playing basketball, but she only did cross country and track because her dad made her. She did it to appease him. She didn't want that meanness turned on her.

"Chuck was definitely not a nice dad with Chuck Junior. I remember one summer he actually threw him out of the house for not cutting firewood when he was supposed to. And whenever anybody got involved in any sport, they had to win. There was no such thing as losing. Being competitive is one thing, but Chuck carried it way beyond that.

"Bottom line, there was not a lot of tenderness or loving in that household, mostly because Sally never really was a mom. She just wasn't a nurturing person. Sarah's not either, of course, but maybe that's because she never received any nurturing as a child."

As Sarah entered adolescence, her religion seemed to define her. She liked boys and hard rock and heavy metal—Molly Hatchet and Lynyrd Skynyrd being particular favorites—but she loved the God she learned about from Pastor Riley.

Not that this was unusual in Wasilla. "In high school, if you wanted to play on a varsity team, you had to join the Fellowship of Christian Athletes," J. C. McCavit, a classmate of Sarah's, says. Sarah became a leader of the Fellowship. A former basketball teammate recalls, "Her group was always making us pray before games. I hated that. They'd start talking over each other, saying, 'Lord Jesus protect us' and 'Praise Jesus,' and on and on. Why should I be forced to do that if I didn't believe that way? But if I didn't, I'd be blackballed."

When the boys' and girls' basketball teams took long bus trips to away games, the girls would sit in the front, leaving the back to the boys. But Sarah didn't sit still. "She'd come back there with these Assembly of God pamphlets," McCavit says, "and start preaching to us all about 'the Rapture.' We'd be like, 'Yo, Sarah, go back and sit down. We're playing cards.' I remember even way back then she kept talking about how the Bible said the Middle East was going to be a bloodbath and that the end-times were upon us or drawing nigh or some such shit. Nobody paid her any attention, not even Todd."

One idiosyncrasy recalled by another schoolmate was Sarah's propensity for sleeping naked on athletic trips. "We'd all sleep on the floor of a classroom, on little mats about an inch thick," the schoolmate recalls. "The boys would be in one classroom and the girls would be across the hall. The girls were amazed: there would be these pictures of Abraham Lincoln looking down, and Sarah would be walking around naked. It was a little bit weird. They said they'd all be getting ready for bed, wearing T-shirts and pajama bottoms, and Sarah would be naked. She said it wasn't healthy for girls to sleep with clothes on because you needed to, more or less, air it out after having had clothes on all day. I don't know where she got that from. Maybe it was something her father taught her."

Sleeping nude in a room full of girls did not indicate promiscuity. In Sarah's case, quite the contrary. "I know a few who took a swing at the plate and came up empty," a classmate recalls. "She didn't have any boyfriends until Todd. John Cottle used to call Sarah and her little gang The Nunnery."

Not many Wasilla High boys considered Sarah attractive. "She wasn't remarkable at all," one says. "Round features, big, heavy-rimmed glasses, a goofy haircut, and that goofy voice. All the guys were after her sisters. Heather was a nice-looking blond girl, and Molly was also a blonde, cute as a button. Sarah was the homely brunette in the middle. She could never quite compete with either of her sisters for attractiveness."

One who did find her attractive was Todd Palin, who arrived in Wasilla at the start of senior year and immediately created a stir. He was good-looking and he drove a classic Ford Mustang Mach 1, blue with a white stripe. He also owned a Datsun four-wheel-drive truck with a lift kit, which he quickly upgraded to a Toyota pickup with oversize tires and chrome alloy rims with gold centers.

J. C. McCavit remembers going with Todd to pick up the new truck. "He paid, I think, twelve thousand five hundred dollars cash, in hundred-dollar bills. That blew me away. Todd had a lot of spending money from working in his grandmother's fishing business every summer in Dillingham. Most of us didn't even have a job. I worked for minimum wage at the Carrs grocery store."

"Todd instantly fit in with the cool guys," says Bitney. "At that time, the cool guys were on the basketball team. Hockey was for the renegades, the stoners, the misfits. They called themselves the Mob. The basketball team was the Beaver Patrol. Molly Hatchet's 'Flirtin' with Disaster' was the song."

Adding to Todd's panache was the fact that his mother, Blanche Kallstrom, was one-quarter Yup'ik Eskimo, making Todd one-eighth Native. (The word *Native* is used in Alaska to describe the state's indigenous people.) Given the racism rampant in Wasilla—then and now—it was a tricky thing to be just Native enough to seem glamorous, but not so Native that it was obvious. Todd could easily pass for all white. But the first day he met McCavit and John Cottle, Rod and Colleen's son, he got drunk on beer. "When he gets drunk he starts talking like a Native," McCavit says, "so we all knew right away. A part-Native with wheels like he had and with all the money he had— it was just one more thing that made him cool."

But there was another side to Todd that wasn't so cool. Racism had come to the Valley with the influx of right-wing Southerners who arrived to work on the oil pipeline in the seventies. Wasilla was so white that there was only one African American in the entire school system. He was Clyde Boyer's adopted son. Catherine Taylor was his stepmother.

One day, when the boy was in junior high school, Todd, then a senior, and two friends waylaid him by the gravel pit adjacent to Wasilla High and beat him up, simply because he was black. It was far from the worst beating he endured. "Not even in the top ten," he would tell me. "Once, I wound up with seventy-seven stitches in my head after some guys kept banging it against the curb. Sure, Todd was a racist bully, but that just made him one of the guys. Growing up black in

Wasilla was hell, and I'd never have made it without the love and support I got every day from my dad and from Catherine."

Sarah and Todd graduated from Wasilla High in 1982. Instead of the usual well-wishes or humorous remarks, Sarah inscribed Bible verses in her friends' yearbooks. After graduation, she and Todd went separate ways—Sarah to the Hilo campus of the University of Hawaii, and Todd to a junior college in Washington State. Todd didn't last long: college was not for him. He'd barely managed to graduate from Wasilla High. Not even his best friends would say he had an aptitude for the classroom or an interest in the life of the mind. Todd liked machines. He could fix things. In Alaska, this was a coveted attribute. But *Mechanix Illustrated* was as deeply as he delved into literature.

Sarah was hardly an intellectual herself. In her high school yearbook she declared that her ambition was one day to broadcast major sporting events alongside Howard Cosell.

She left Hilo after three weeks, without formally enrolling, because the many people of color there made her nervous. "They were a minority type thing and it wasn't glamorous," Chuck Heath later explained. Sarah and her closest Wasilla High friend, Kim "Tilly" Ketchum, enrolled instead at Hawaii Pacific University in Honolulu. They shared a condo at the high-rise Waikiki Banyan on Ohua Avenue, less than two blocks from the ocean.

There were people of color, however, even on Waikiki Beach. Sarah and Tilly soon transferred to North Idaho College in Coeur d'Alene, less than fifty miles from Sandpoint. Then Sarah transferred to the University of Idaho in Moscow. She dropped out and returned home to take classes at Mat-Su Community College before returning to Moscow for three more semesters. She finally graduated in 1987.

The one constant through all the fits and starts was Tilly Ketchum. From the locker room at Wasilla High to Hilo to Honolulu to Coeur d'Alene to Moscow, wherever Sarah went, Tilly followed, or vice versa. For five years, the two were inseparable. They remain close friends today.

Sarah also grew close to Tilly's father, Kerm Ketchum, a professor at Mat-Su Community College. "He became her surrogate father," Bitney says. "He's the first person Sarah ever smoked pot with—the old professor, a good man. He loved Sarah, still does. And she inhaled. She's never denied it. Kerm Ketchum got Sarah good and stoned."

After her graduation, Sarah returned to Alaska and worked on the sports desk of Anchorage television station KTUU. On weekends, she'd sometimes appear on camera, delivering sports reports during the 10:00 PM newscast.

Her attitude toward people of color was evolving. In Anchorage, she even dated black men. A friend says, "Sarah and her sisters had a fetish for black guys for a while."

Each year, over Thanksgiving weekend, the University of Alaska hosted a basketball tournament called the Great Alaska Shootout, featuring some of the country's best teams. In 1987, one of the top squads to visit Anchorage was the University of Michigan, led by six-foot-eight junior Glen Rice, number 41.

Rice would lead Michigan to the NCAA Championship in 1989, appearing on the cover of *Sports Illustrated* and setting a scoring record for the NCAA tournament that stands today. After graduating from Michigan as the school's all-time leading scorer, he starred in the NBA for fifteen years.

Whether in her professional capacity as a sports reporter or simply as a basketball groupie who'd begun to find black men attractive, Sarah linked up with Rice during the weekend tournament. One friend recalls, "They went out. I suspect it was more than that. I can't say I *know* they had sex, but I remember Sarah feeling pretty good that she'd been with a black basketball star."

In one version of the story, Sarah's encounter with Rice took place in her sister Molly's dorm room at the University of Alaska Anchorage.

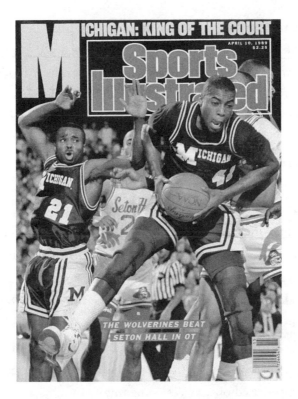

MICHIGAN: KING OF THE COURT

APRIL 10, 1989
$2.25

Sports Illustrated

THE WOLVERINES BEAT
SETON HALL IN OT

"She hauled his ass down," a friend says, "but she freaked out afterward. Hysterical, crying, *totally* flipped out. The thing that people remember is her freak-out, how completely crazy she got: *I fucked a black
man!* She was just horrified. She couldn't believe that she'd done it."

Glen Rice remembers the weekend quite differently. When I spoke
to him by telephone in March 2011, he said, "I remember it as if it
was yesterday. She was a sweetheart. I met her almost as soon as we
got out there."

Rice does not recall being in a university dorm room. "We hung
out mostly at the hotel where the team was staying," he told me. "We
just hit it off. In a short time, we got to know a lot about one another.
It was all done in a respectful way, nothing hurried."

"So you never had the feeling she felt bad about having sex with a
black guy?" I asked.

"No, no, no, nothing like that," Rice said. "Even after I left Alaska, we talked a lot on the phone. I think right up until the time she got married. She was a gorgeous woman. Super nice. I was blown away by her. Afterward, she was a big crush that I had. I talked about her for a long time. Only good things. She was a well-rounded young lady. It's amazing the way that's stayed with me. I think the utmost of her and I felt that way from the start."

Todd, meanwhile, was living the happy bachelor life in Wasilla. "They were pretty wild times," McCavit says. "We were young and single and making enough money to have fun."

The group included Todd, McCavit, Bitney, Tim Smith, Dan Fleckenstein, Joey Austerman, Ted Knutson, Casey Williams, Jim Spain, and Howard Tresham. In later years, some fared better than others. Todd was arrested for a DUI in the mid-1980s, but avoided further brushes with the law. Austerman wound up working in Sarah's gubernatorial campaign. Bitney became her legislative director after she was elected governor. McCavit became a successful executive with an Anchorage-based oil services company.

Ted Knutson, however, went to prison following "a short foot chase" in April 2008, after which, as the state police report said, "He was arrested for DUI, Eluding, Misconduct Involving a Controlled Substance 6th Degree, and Driving with a Revoked License."

And then there was Howard Tresham, who in January 2010 was charged with stealing thirty thousand feet of copper wire, valued at $114,500, from the Matanuska Telephone Authority, where he had worked for twenty-five years.

"Coke was everywhere in Wasilla," Bitney recalls. "What's now the Mug-Shot used to be called Huppie's. Its motto was 'Ain't No City Bar.' They were dealing coke right out in the open. Sometimes they'd lock the front door and start chopping lines on the bar. It was a pretty rough joint. Those were great days."

Huppie's changed its name to the Mug-Shot Saloon when management announced a plan to put mug shots—either real or staged—

of frequent patrons on the wall. In the face of opposition from the clientele, most of whom did not want to be known as frequent patrons, the plan was abandoned, but the name change stayed.

"What's now the Sports Bar used to be the Kashim, a twenty-four-hour diner," Bitney says. "It was the closest thing Wasilla ever had to an institution. Huppie's stayed open till five, then we'd all go over to the Kashim. Sure, Todd did coke with us all. He was on the end of the straw plenty.

"The thing about Todd is, he doesn't sleep. He's one of those people, he might not sleep at all one night and the next night get three hours. A long night's sleep for him is five or six, and that's rare. He's an all-nighter. You see that a lot with emotionally unstable people, guys notorious for their temper, like Todd is. When they fly off, it's like, wow! When Todd is on a temper bender you don't want to be anywhere close."

"I'll tell you this about Todd," McCavit says. "He has the most amazing beer-drinking capacity I've ever seen. He can consume ten times the quantity of a normal person and still not seem drunk. And he's the fastest drinker I've ever seen. He says, 'Hey, you want to split a six-pack?' and you say, 'Yeah,' and by the time you've finished your first, he's already chugged the other five.

"Normally this doesn't affect him, but if he's already wound up about something—watch out. I had to fight him sometimes when he was drunk, because it was the only way to get him out of my face. And I wasn't the only one; any of his friends will tell you the same."

One fistfight McCavit recalls involved Sarah. "No, no, it wasn't jealousy, nothing like that. Matter of fact, in regard to Sarah, all of us felt he was welcome to her. Nobody envied him, that's for sure. But this one time, he was going on and on, he wouldn't shut up, he kept saying Sarah wanted to get serious but he didn't think he could give up all the other girls. 'What should I do? What should I do?' he kept saying. I finally said, 'I don't give a damn what you do, but just shut up about it, all right?' Next thing I know he's swinging at me."

• • •

WASILLA WASN'T ALL fun and games in those days. In December 1983, state troopers arrested George Koenig, a music teacher at Iditarod Elementary School, and charged him with having molested seventeen third-grade girls.

For months, parents had been complaining to the school principal, Ray Carter, about Koenig. He refused to act on the complaints. After Koenig's arrest, a new superintendent of schools fired Carter. By a 6–0 vote, the school board supported his decision. At that point, Chuck Heath swung into action. Carter was an old friend of Heath's from Sandpoint. Chuck wanted his pal Carter reinstated and he wanted the three women on the school board recalled.

Chuck and his friends set up an RV in the parking lot of Wasilla's shopping center (there being only one at the time) and spent Saturdays and Sundays urging Wasillans to sign recall petitions against the three women. As one of the women, Pat O'Hara, recalls, "Chuck Heath created a lynch mob mentality about a horrific crime that should have been handled with great sensitivity."

Meetings were held at Cottonwood Creek Elementary School. Chuck and his crowd denounced the board members who'd voted to uphold Carter's firing. "The good old boys could do nothing wrong, and we had no right to challenge their power," O'Hara says. "Chuck Heath led an ugly, violent mob that quickly grew out of control. There was always the threat of violence in the background."

O'Hara recalls Chuck spreading rumors that the women on the board were having affairs with the new superintendent. "The tactics were violent and dangerous," she says. "I was alone much of that winter, with a five-year-old and a newborn and no near neighbors. I lived in a constant state of fear. My husband had to leave his job in Valdez and fly home. No matter how ugly the threats, we could never get police protection. It was the custodian at Cottonwood Creek school who walked us through the gauntlet of hate and shouts and threats after meetings and made sure we got to our cars safely. And then we'd find death threats written in the snow on our cars.

"There was a willful ignorance of inappropriate sexual behavior in the Wasilla community," O'Hara says. "The Iditarod school staff and most of the community, including the local papers, seemed unconcerned about what occurred with Koenig and his victims. The furor was focused on protecting Ray Carter, and Chuck Heath was largely responsible for that."

Eventually, a compromise was reached: the recall petitions would be withdrawn, and a hearing officer would conduct an independent, noncriminal investigation of Carter. On July 16, 1984, after the hearing officer delivered her findings, the school board controversially re-hired Carter, but not as a principal. The board issued a statement that said: "We have placed him in . . . the correspondence area, where students pursue lessons at home rather than in schools."

Koenig pleaded guilty and was sentenced to forty years in prison. The new superintendent of schools quit and left town. Pat O'Hara was reelected to the school board. Chuck Heath returned to teaching sixth grade.

"Chuck Heath and a few others created such a maelstrom that nobody was safe for a while," O'Hara says. "They were bullies, pure and simple, and essentially that's what Sarah and her cohorts are today. They bully the most vulnerable parts of the society—young women, children, gays, the poor.

"Sarah learned from her father: if someone disagrees with you or does something you don't like, annihilate first, ask questions later. Like Chuck, she's all about intimidation and fear. 'Don't retreat, reload.' Veiled threats, verbal violence, complete disregard for the welfare of victims—these all came from Chuck and they are all inherent in the current persona of Sarah Palin."

THREE

Sunday, May 23, 2010

I INVITE A COUPLE of friends from Anchorage for dinner on the deck. It's been another splendid spring day. One friend has brought her children, who play in the yard and on the somewhat decrepit dock. I cook salmon and halibut on the Traeger. I'm quickly falling in love with my grill. I even like the sound of the name.

"Traeger," one of my friends says. "The Palins could name their next kid that: Track, Tripp, Trig, and Traeger."

"Laugh now," the other friend says. "This is going to get a lot less funny very soon."

"What do you mean?" I ask.

"How do you think they're going to react when they find out you're living next door?"

"Todd and Sarah?"

"Yes, and the millions who adore her from afar."

"I don't know. I'd like to think Todd will take me for a ride in his floatplane and Sarah will bring me over a housewarming gift and welcome me to the neighborhood."

"Are you serious? This is no neighborhood: it's a compound. And you've breached the wall."

"It's a fence, not a wall. And I haven't breached it. Nor will I. I'm only kidding about the housewarming gift. Frankly, I expect them to be annoyed. But once they see I'm going to mind my own business, things should be fine."

"You're dreaming. Sarah's the most paranoid person on earth, and Todd's now apparently a close second. It's their perception. They'll see this as an aggressive act by a wise-guy writer who's out to get her. She always has to play the victim. Wait till you hear her squeal about this."

"But I'm not going to bother her. I'm not the *National Enquirer.* I'm not going to take pictures over the fence or write about what they're cooking on their grill—if they even have a grill. As a matter of fact, once Todd gets a whiff of the Traeger, he'll probably be over here cooking on mine."

"Do you know who's going to be over here? A gang of vigilantes, armed. Todd and Sarah are not going to just sit back and let this happen."

"That's ridiculous. This is Alaska: live and let live."

"No. That is Alaska, starting at the end of your driveway. This is Palinland. And uninvited visitors are not welcome."

Monday, May 24, 2010

THE WEATHER CONTINUES to be perfect. It's the sort of day when the mountains beckon, when you want to pull on the hiking boots and head up a trail toward the tree line, leaving the cares of low altitude behind.

Not me. I head for Target and spend $250 on household supplies and groceries. In the late afternoon I call my wife, Nancy, in Massachusetts. She'll be coming out for ten days on June 3. She hasn't been here since 1976, when she worked as a reporter at the *Anchorage Daily News* while I researched *Going to Extremes.*

Then I call Levi Johnston's mother, Sherry, and arrange a meeting for tomorrow. It's just after 5:00 PM when I take my laptop outside. I listen to music while I go through my list of appointments. I'm about halfway through a run of a dozen Hank Williams songs when somebody walks around the end of the fence. I look up.

"Who are you?" the guy says. "What are you doing here?"

"I'm renting this place. I just moved in."

I think it's Todd Palin, but I can't be sure. In the pictures I've seen, Todd had a moustache and small goatee. This fellow is clean-shaven. Then I notice his T-shirt. It says, in block letters across the front, FIRST DUDE. Yup, must be Todd.

"How long are you going to be here?" he asks.

"I'm not sure yet. Probably four months, maybe five."

"What for?"

"Hold on. Let me come down and talk to you." I don't see any point in carrying on a Romeo-and-Juliet balcony scene. I walk down the steps from the deck to the yard. First Dude meets me at the bottom.

"I'm Joe McGinniss," I say, extending my hand. He shakes it briefly and says, "Todd Palin."

Then he says, "Wait a minute. You're that guy that wrote that bunch of crap in that magazine about AGIA."

He is referring to the cover story I did for the April 2009 edition of *Portfolio* that pointed out that, contrary to what she'd claimed at the 2008 Republican convention, Sarah's Alaska Gasline Inducement Act (AGIA) had not brought about "the largest private-sector infrastructure project in North American history," and that construction had not begun on "a nearly $40 billion natural gas pipeline to help lead America to energy independence."

"That story was a bunch of lies," he says. "It was a bunch of bullshit. And you were wrong. AGIA is working. That pipeline is going to get built."

"I think reasonable people still disagree about that."

"Bullshit. What are you doing here now?"

"I'm writing a book about your wife."

"What for?"

"Because she's a phenomenon. Whether you agree with her politically or not, she's unlike anything seen before in American political history. She's probably the most famous woman in the world. And a lot of people think she's going to run for president in 2012. I've been writing about politics since 1968. I'm fascinated by what's happening now. Why wouldn't I want to write about her?"

Todd considers this. Then he says, "So what can we expect? Telescopic lenses hidden in the trees and secret microphones stuck under the fence?"

"No. As a matter of fact, that's exactly what won't happen as long as I'm here. That's not my style, Todd, as anyone who knows my work can tell you."

He shakes his head. "I don't like this," he says.

"Listen, I'm a good neighbor. Ask anybody. Ask Roger Ailes at Fox News. Your wife is working for him now. Roger and I disagree about everything political that it's possible to disagree about, but we've been friends for more than forty years. Have Sarah call him and ask what kind of a neighbor Joe McGinniss is going to be. He'll tell you that you're lucky it's me renting this house and not somebody who would do the kind of stuff you're afraid of."

But the more I talk, the angrier he looks. Finally, he waves a finger toward my face and says, "We'll just see how long you stay here." Then he stalks back across my yard and around the bottom of his fence.

I return to the deck. Standing at the end farthest from the Palin house and facing away from it, looking at the woods on the other side, I call Nancy.

"I just met Todd."

"How did that go?"

"Not real well. He remembers my *Portfolio* piece and he seems to think I'm here to snoop on Sarah."

"And you told him you weren't."

"Of course."

"What do you think he's going to do?"

"What can he do? I'm here. I told him if he was worried about me, he should have Sarah call Roger Ailes. Roger can put her mind at ease. Obviously I don't want any fuss. I hope they don't either."

In retrospect, it's amazing that at the age of sixty-seven, having been a professional author and journalist for more than forty-five years, I could have been so naïve.

I'm heading for bed at 11:00 PM when my phone rings. It's one of my Anchorage friends.

"You'd better check out Sarah's Facebook page."

"How come?"

"You'll see. And if you smell smoke tonight, it's probably your house on fire."

At 10:17 PM, Sarah posted this on Facebook:

Just When Ya Think It Can't Get Any More "Interesting"—Welcome, Neighbor!

Spring has sprung in Alaska, and with this beautiful season comes the news today that the Palins have a new neighbor! Welcome, Joe McGinniss!

Yes, that Joe McGinniss. Here he is—about 15 feet away on the neighbor's rented deck overlooking my children's play area and my kitchen window. Maybe we'll welcome him with a homemade blueberry pie tomorrow so he'll know how friendly Alaskans are.

We found out the good news today. Upon my family's return this morning from endorsement rallies and speeches in the Lower 48 states, I finally got the chance to tackle my garden and lawn this evening! So, putting on the shorts and tank top to catch that too-brief northern summer sun and placing a giddy Trig in his toddler backpack for a lawn-mowing adventure, I looked up in surprise to see a "new neighbor" overlooking my property just a stone's throw away. Needless to say, our outdoor adventure ended quickly after Todd went to introduce himself to the stranger who was peering in . . .

Joe announced to Todd that he's moved in right next door to us. He's rented the place for the next five months or so. He moved up all the way from Massachusetts to live right next to us—while he writes a book about me. Knowing of his many other scathing pieces of "journalism" (including the bizarre anti-Palin administration oil development pieces that resulted in my Department of Natural Resources announcing that his work is the most twisted energy-related yellow journalism they'd ever encountered), we're sure to have a doozey to look forward to with this treasure he's penning. Wonder what kind of material he'll gather while overlooking Piper's bedroom, my little garden, and the family's swimming hole?

Welcome, Joe! It'll be a great summer—come borrow a cup of sugar if ever you need some sweetener. And you know what they say about "fences make for good neighbors"? Well, we'll get started on that tall fence tomorrow, and I'll try to keep Trig's squeals down to a quiet giggle so we don't disturb your peaceful summer. Enjoy!

—Sarah Palin

Along with her post is a photograph, taken from her yard, showing me at the far end of my deck, looking into the woods while talking to Nancy on my cell phone.

Beneath the picture, she wrote, "Hi, Neighbor! May I Call You 'Joe'?"

"Todd went to introduce himself to the stranger who was peering in . . . "?

Peering in?

"Overlooking Piper's bedroom . . . "?

Assuming Piper's bedroom is one of the second-floor rooms that looks down upon my house, it would be she who was overlooking me.

"My little garden and the family's swimming hole"?

What garden? What swimming hole? Does she mean Lake Lucille?

Fortunately, I have enough Splenda so that I won't have to borrow a cup of sugar anytime soon. But whatever tomorrow brings, I don't think it will include Sarah's "homemade blueberry pie."

Tuesday, May 25, 2010

THE STRING of impeccable spring days continues. Daylight arrives before 4:00 AM, so I'm up early. It's four hours later in the East, and I discover that the media carnival triggered by Sarah's Facebook post has begun. By the time I'm back from breakfast at the Mat-Su Family Restaurant at 9:00, I'm being called everything from a pedophile to a spy secretly employed by Barack Obama.

Politico writes that Sarah has suggested I'm "really there to peep at her young daughters, noting that his property overlooks Piper's bedroom."

It doesn't, of course, but it's clear that facts are not going to matter for a while. After posting on Facebook last night, Sarah wrote to her Fox News colleague Glenn Beck, who read her e-mail on his morning radio program: "Unbelievable continued harassment. The reporter/writer who continually writes hit pieces from the east coast just moved in next door. He's twelve feet away from me right now. Todd approached him on the deck of the neighbor's house as he announced he'd just moved in. He's our new neighbor. He's also here to write a book about me. I spotted him while I started mowing the lawn with Trig in my backpack. Things like that now are not going to happen until the guy moves out. This is a nightmare for my family."

Beck called me "creepy" and "a stalker" and said Todd "should receive a medal for restraint." He continued, "If your wife was treated the way she is being treated—if your wife was under constant attack like this . . . what would you be feeling? I think a guy who wrestles bears . . . with his bare hands, in a territory that is unlike anything in the Lower Forty-Eight—these are real people. I got news for you. In Alaska, you hassle my wife, you do these things, you just keep hounding my wife, you get your ass kicked. And I think you should." He went on to say that until Random House "reined" me in and got me "under control," he'd never again plug a Random House title on his show.

Anonymous commenters on various websites are urging violence against me, imploring someone to burn down my house and using Beck's words *creepy* and *stalker* over and over again.

What I find remarkable is how Sarah's overreaction and false statement (that I am "overlooking Piper's bedroom") and blatant sexualization ("shorts and tank top") of a distinctly nonerotic event (my renting the house next door) has played into the fantasy lives of those who idolize her, triggering torrents of filthy comments and accusations.

Lunacy reigns. The photograph that Sarah posted clearly shows me at the end of my deck farthest from the Palin property, facing in the opposite direction as I talk on my cell phone. Yet some commenters claim I'm looking into bedroom windows with binoculars.

All day I hear hammering and sawing. Todd has about twelve guys throwing up a new fence that's roughly twice the height of the old one. I'm all in favor of the fence. Maybe once it's up, Sarah will chill and we can both get on with our business.

· · ·

I VISIT Levi's mother in the afternoon. I have to go to her home because she's under house arrest, having pleaded guilty to selling Oxycontin in the parking lots of Fred Meyer and Target during the 2008 presidential campaign.

Her story is simple and sad. For years she'd been disabled by pain resulting from a botched hysterectomy and several subsequent surgeries. She couldn't work. Then her husband left her. Then she got into a snarl with her insurance company, and coverage of the Oxycontin she received by prescription was suspended. By the fall of 2008 she was running out of money for food and electricity. On three occasions she sold ten Oxycontin pills to an old family friend named Junior Latocha, who had become an undercover police informant in return for a reduced sentence on his own drug-dealing conviction. She served several months in prison and was now a few months into a three-year term of house arrest.

Levi's sister, Mercede, is at the house. She has to stay there in case Sherry is called for a random drug test. The testing facility is sixteen miles away, and Sherry must get there within an hour of being called. She can't drive herself because of the pain medications in her bloodstream.

"It kind of sucks," Mercede tells me. "I graduated from high school a couple of weeks ago, but I can't even think about going away to college. I can hardly even go out on a date. Sometimes they call my mom for testing three or four times a week."

"Doesn't Levi help?"

"Levi? Forget it. He's too busy being a star. I don't even speak to him anymore. He'll come to the house and I'll be in my room and he won't even bother to say hi. The Palins—especially Bristol—have ruined our relationship. Bristol tells him not to talk to me, so he won't. He has to do what she says, or she won't let him see his son."

Mercede is a stunningly attractive young woman, all blond hair and white teeth and tanning-salon skin. And Sherry, for all her problems, has kind eyes, a genuine smile, and the sort of resigned tranquility that can come from living with chronic pain.

Neither has anything very helpful to tell me, but I find them utterly without guile. I like them and I'm sorry about their circumstances. I leave, after two hours of conversation, wanting to find Levi and give him a good hard shake and tell him to forget about his sputtering career for half a second and go home, because his mother needs him.

This is what happens in Alaska. People are so open and giving and trusting, and eager to help you in any possible way, that you quickly come to care about them and to want to help them in return.

Sherry Johnston will be confined to her home for three years for selling thirty Oxycontin pills for $800, after having been set up by a police informant. But in January, Todd Palin's thirty-six-year-old half sister, Diana, received a suspended sentence and was released into a residential rehab program after pleading guilty to multiple break-ins at a Wasilla residence from which she stole more than $2,600. And she'd brought her four-year-old daughter along for the crimes.

Diana Palin used the child as part of her MO. As the *Mat-Su Valley Frontiersman* reported in January 2010, "Investigators found that Palin had been doing similar things before in her own neighborhood, sometimes using her daughter as cover. For instance, the girl would ask to use a person's bathroom, which would give Palin a pretext to get into the house and find prescription medications and other things to steal."

It looks like there may be two standards in the Valley: Johnston justice and Palin justice.

Prior to her sentencing, Diana Palin had been in court twice, both times as a victim of domestic abuse. In addition, she'd first sought treatment for her methamphetamine addiction in 2007. In January 2010 her husband (who was not accused of domestic abuse) filed for divorce, seeking custody of the four-year-old child who'd been used in the burglaries.

"I really love dysfunctional families," Diana wrote on her MySpace page in 2009. "Especially mine."

Sarah certainly seems to have married into one. Before his current marriage to Faye, Todd's father, Jim, was married to Todd's mother, Blanche Kallstrom, and, before that, to Diana's mother, Elayne Ingram. Kallstrom and Ingram, both part-Native, were from Dillingham, the largely Native town in western Alaska where Todd grew up.

Elayne Ingram was married three times. In a 2001 interview with the Center for Alaska Native Health Research, she said, "I got married at age nineteen and had my first daughter at age twenty . . . I still don't feel like I was an alcoholic at that point in time, but I was definitely a battered wife. The beatings were so bad that I weighed ninety-six pounds, I couldn't sleep, I couldn't eat, my mind was racing. We finally divorced after three kids."

Then she married Jim Palin. "He could provide better financially and I was looking for security. And I found it. Then I worked on the pipeline. When I became financially secure, I left him. By then, it was alcoholic drinking for both me and him." It was during her alcoholic marriage to Jim Palin that Elayne gave birth to Todd's half sister, Diana.

Jim later married Todd's mother, Blanche. He divorced her and married Faye, who was not a Native. Blanche wound up in court after accidentally serving a child a lye-based detergent that she said she thought was fruit juice. Meanwhile, Todd's full brother, J.D., was involved in a hit-and-run accident after a drinking binge.

"Crazy thing is," Diana Palin wrote on MySpace, "the more you go through—the better it gets."

And Todd and Sarah are worried about having *me* for a neighbor?

Wednesday, May 26, 2010

THERE'S A POUNDING at my door. I sit up in bed. Seven thirty AM. The pounding continues. I walk through the living room, into the kitchen. I see somebody filming through my window with a television camera. It's ABC News. I tell them to leave or I'll call the police.

I check my e-mail and the Internet. The world has gone mad. Sarah called Glenn Beck's radio show at 6:00 AM Alaska time.

"He's stalking you," Beck says.

"He's an odd character, yeah, if you look at his history and the things that he's written and the things that he's been engaged in."

Beck asks why the owner of the house rented it to me. "Todd was trying to get ahold of her all winter long," Sarah says, "because the house was vacant and we were going to rent it and even ask if we could purchase it, for fear of something like this happening, and couldn't get ahold of the neighbor, and next thing you know there are new tenants in it—a new tenant."

"Shame on Random House," says Beck. "Do you feel, as a woman, do you feel violated?"

"I feel more protective than ever in terms of my kids. Any mom would. Just wantin' to bring your family even closer and wrap your arms around 'em and not let the infringement on their rights and privacy be so overwhelming as to make us not enjoy our life up here."

In a warning tone, she adds, as if speaking to me, "You better leave my kids alone."

Beck is starting to choke on his outrage. "Here's a guy doing a book on your family who is now able to look into Piper's bedroom! He's a voyeur! The only reason why he moved there is to be either a Peeping Tom and watch your family over the fence or (b) watch the comings and goings of your family. This is harassment! This is stalking and harassment! Leave my family, leave people's families alone!"

"A very classless thing that Random House is doing," Palin says, "and if I find out that Random House is the one actually renting this place for their author to be able to sit here over our shoulder for the next five or six months, that would be pretty disturbing, too.

"Let me tell you something practical that happens in Alaska. We don't have air-conditioning, so you leave your windows open all summer long, it's the only way to keep cool under the midnight sun, because the sun essentially doesn't set for many of the days in the summer. Leaving the windows wide open—well, now that's gotta change, because the guy's sittin' right there; we're not going to let him overhear our children's conversation or anything else, so, practically speaking, a real pain in the butt, a real inconvenience and disturbing thing, but—"

"I don't wish anybody harm," Beck interrupts, "but I think Todd deserves a medal for why he doesn't go over there and punch that guy in the face. I mean, that is not the way to handle things, but as a man, and you are screwing with my wife and my children . . . it would take everything in me not to do that."

"Well, amen, yeah, but that's what he wants. He so wants a reaction like that from Todd so he can jot it down or he can call the cops and jot that down as a chapter in his book."

It doesn't matter that Alaskan mosquitoes pose more of a threat to Sarah's children than I do. In Palinland, as in war, truth is the first casualty.

I HEAD FOR Wasilla City Hall to have coffee with the mayor. In 2008, Verne Rupright succeeded the woman who succeeded Sarah in the office.

A Vietnam vet, Verne grew up as a blue-collar brawler from the hard-nosed Saugus/Lynn/Revere area of Boston's North Shore. He came to Alaska with the military in 1972. After returning to Massachusetts to acquire an associate of science degree in law enforcement management and administration from North Shore Community College, he came back to Alaska to stay. He received a bachelor of arts in justice from the University of Alaska Anchorage and embarked on a career as a state prison corrections officer. Ten years later he got a law degree from Creighton University in Nebraska. He worked as a criminal defense attorney in Wasilla until his election as mayor.

He doesn't mention it in his official biography, but Verne once served as recording secretary of the Alaska Independence Party, the secessionist group to which Todd Palin belonged before his wife's career required him to change his voter registration to Republican.

He's a thrice-married pack-a-day smoker, and is seldom the first man to leave a saloon. His office uniform most days is blue jeans, running shoes, and a polo shirt.

I met Verne last fall. I think the world of him and I'm glad to see him again. He's a hall-of-fame bullshitter, but there's something genuine behind the façade, which can't be said of all recent mayors of Wasilla.

"Do you want a gun?" is the first thing he asks me.

"Do you think I need one?"

He considers. "Mmmm, probably not. I think most of the threats are coming from Outside. People around here don't give a shit about Sarah anymore. They're burned out on all her drama. Do you have much experience with handguns?"

"None at all."

"Then I think you're better off without one. You'd be more likely to hurt yourself than anyone else. You're probably not in serious danger, but I just hired a new police chief, brought him up from Texas, and I'll talk to him this afternoon. I don't care who you are, you move into my town, you're entitled to feel safe, and you're entitled to respect until you show you don't deserve it. You pay your rent on time and you don't violate any city ordinances, you have a right to live wherever you want.

"Even so, you should put a chain across the end of that road so if somebody does shoot you, at least it won't be a drive-by. And if you change your mind about a weapon, let me know."

I'M BACK AT the house when Nancy calls. Fox News is having a discussion about whether I can be criminally prosecuted for stalking and harassment. They show the picture of me talking on my cell phone while facing toward the woods and away from the Palin property.

"Looks like he might have binoculars there," one of Fox's legal experts says.

"He'll be watching her children, watching her gardening, on and on it goes. She will have no privacy now," says another.

Regrettably, says a third, I cannot be arrested for stalking, because under Alaska law "stalking" means "to recklessly place another person in fear of death or personal injury," and, as she concedes, "We're probably not there yet."

But how about a civil suit for invasion of privacy? All that takes is evidence of "intentional intrusion on someone's solitude, seclusion or private affairs," to a degree that "a reasonable person would find highly offensive."

Even that is a stretch, one of the legal experts says, "unless he points those binoculars in her direction."

"Which he will."

"Well, we think he's going to."

I have not held a pair of binoculars in my hands since I watched a horse race at Saratoga in 2004. But hysteria does much more for ratings than the unexciting truth.

"She should go forward and say to a court, 'I need an order of protection, this is getting absolutely insane.' If they have pictures of him using the binoculars, peering into these children [sic], I think a court would take that extra step and say, yes, here's an order of protection against him."

"The children add a whole new element to it," says another.

They sure do. Suppose I kidnap one? And who's to say that's not what I'm plotting? Once you've cut the cord that tethers you to reality, anything goes.

Comments on right-wing websites show how far things already have gone:

"I hope this 'reporter' understands that Palins are hunters by hobby and will use loaded weapons to defend themselves from harm to their family."

"Any bets that McGinniss disapears in the Alaskan wilderness?"

"If I was Todd, I'd take my family on a hike and squirt fish oil and beaver castor on the thick brush after they pass through so that the stalker would pass through and get some fish oil on his trousers. Walk toward a salmon river when the salmon are running and the bears are fishing. Have a boat waiting, take off and leave him with the Grizzlies and smelling like a ripe salmon. To a Grizzly, a journalist that smells like fish oil and beaver castor is just dinner."

"Todd could also have a beaver carcass stored in a five gallon can and drag it on a rope so the 'journalist' walks over the scent. Grizzly attacks are nearly always fatal. A crime that is difficult to prove if the Grizzly eats all the evidence."

"I'd be looking for line of sight, fire lanes, etc. That guy would have trouble getting out of the house in the morning, being his tires were flat, engine full of sugar and some masked guy with a oak limb, whittled down for a hand grip, keeps beating him."

"You know the sound you hear when you rack a round into a shotgun? That's what I am hearing right about now. Loudly & clearly. Make my day M.F. This dumbass obviously has no idea of gun law in Alaska and how it is almost obligatory to shoot first and ask questions later when threatened."

I have lunch with a friend at a Thai restaurant on the Parks Highway. (Note to self: don't let anyone persuade you that a Thai restaurant in Wasilla is "really not that bad.") After lunch, we go to Lowe's and buy a chain to put across my driveway.

Catherine Taylor calls to suggest I change the locks because Todd still has keys from when he rented the house.

"I'm sure he's a gentleman," I say. "I'm sure he'd never use those keys now that there's someone else living in the house."

"I've known him a long time," Catherine says. "I've had dealings with him. Change the locks."

I GO OUT to the store in early evening. As I'm relocking the chain upon my return, my nearest neighbors from the other side come over to introduce themselves and to apologize for the way the Palins have treated me. They say they're pleased that I'll be living next door and that if there's anything I need, all I have to do is ask. A very typical—and welcome—Alaskan gesture.

I spend a pleasant evening on my deck. A few voices of sanity have emerged. In the *Washington Post,* Dave Weigel writes, in regard to Sarah's Facebook post, "Can somebody explain to me how this isn't a despicable thing to do?" He points out that "no one has ever challenged the facts" in my *Portfolio* piece about Palin's AGIA initiative, adding, "not that this has prevented every other media outlet from typing up Palin's Facebook post like some lost Gospel. But assuming he's rented the house near the Palins for some period of time, assuming the Palins know he's there and that he's writing a book, then what, exactly, is wrong with this?"

Weigel writes, "It's incredibly irresponsible for [politicians] to sic their fans on journalists they don't like. And that's what Palin is doing here—she has already inspired Glenn Beck to accuse McGinniss of 'stalking' and issuing a threat to boycott his publisher . . . No one in the media should reward Palin for this irresponsible and pathetic bullying."

Also in the *Post*, Greg Sargent asks, "At what point do Sarah Palin's attacks and smears become so vile and absurd that they no longer merit attention? Is there such a point?"

In the Huffington Post, Alaska blogger and radio/TV personality Shannyn Moore points out that my house used to be an Oxford House. "The tenants were men recently released from prison, who were recovering addicts. What? No fence to protect sexy Sarah in her tank top? Dear God! Who was lurking in that house watching her children play?"

And in *Salon,* Alex Pareene notes that I "wrote a critically respected book on Alaska 30 years ago" and that my "one reported story so far on Palin was factual and responsible. There's nothing even remotely tabloidy about McGinniss' Portfolio story on the years Palin wasted not getting a gas pipeline built." Nonetheless, writes Pareene, Palin knows that "she can, through sheer force of will and the devotion of her cult, make this into the story of a creepy gotcha journalist stalking her, and threatening her children."

JUST OFFSHORE, a mother grebe is sitting on her nest. She and her mate are my summer neighbors, too. Grebes are fascinating, besides being noisy. With a bit of online research, I learn that they're members of the *Podicipedidae* family of freshwater diving birds, notable for their floating nests, made of plant material, and for how the newborn chicks ride on the mother's back before starting to swim on their own.

Their chicks hatch in late spring. Right now, at 10:00 PM, I've got a mother grebe sitting on her eggs no more than ten feet offshore. I can't quite tell how many eggs there are. If only I had a pair of binoculars.

FOUR

THERE HAS BEEN much speculation that Sarah was pregnant with Track when she and Todd married in 1988. "It was essentially a shotgun-type wedding," a friend of Todd's confirms.

After briefly sharing Heather's apartment in Anchorage, Todd and Sarah moved to a townhouse across from Wasilla High. Todd, taking advantage of the special status afforded him for being one-eighth Native, obtained a blue-collar job with BP on the North Slope. Sarah's pregnancy proceeded uneventfully, though—in contrast to her 2007–2008 pregnancy with Trig—quite noticeably. "I've got pictures of Sarah being very, very, very, very pregnant with Track," an old friend says.

In either April of 1989 or March of 1990—Todd used different dates on separate voter registration and absentee ballot applications—they bought a starter home in the Mission Hill subdivision. Their address was 825 Arnold Palmer Street. They were surrounded by neighbors on such thoroughfares as Sam Snead Loop, Lee Trevino Avenue, Jack Nicklaus Drive, Ben Hogan Avenue, Tom Watson Place, and Byron Nelson Drive.

Some say the marriage proved rocky from the start. "They don't have a marriage," Sarah's brother, Chuckie, confided to a friend in Anchorage. "I don't know how they live together."

"It's never been a happy marriage," someone who's known Todd and Sarah since high school told me in 2010. Part of the problem was Sarah's lack of domestic skills. "She can't cook shit," the old friend said. "She couldn't do grilled cheese. She'd burn water."

Another sticking point was her lack of enthusiasm for child rearing, a trait she shared with her mother. "From the start," a friend recalls, "Todd was the parent. When he was home, he changed the diapers. He fed the kids. Sarah never lifted a finger."

With her father providing financial help, Sarah and Todd bought a home on the western shore of Lake Wasilla, at 1018 Westpoint Drive. There were three children by then: Track, Bristol, and Willow. Sarah had not worked since her brief stint as a sports announcer for an Anchorage TV station before her marriage.

IN 1987, Wasilla elected a new mayor: John Stein, a lifelong Alaskan, born in Sitka, and the holder of a degree in city planning from the University of Oregon.

Stein had arrived as city planner in 1984. Given the appearance of the city today, the notion of a Wasilla city planner may seem oxymoronic, but Stein says things could have been worse. "Those old forty-acre homesteads were being subdivided into one-acre lots," he told me when I visited him at his home in Sitka during the summer of 2010. "Anchorage was overflowing, and people were flocking to the Valley because it was cheap. And it was cheap: cheap, cheap, cheap. There were essentially no building codes and no minimum standard for borough roads."

Speaking of his first term in office, Stein says, "It was the first time they'd had a planner as mayor. I tried to bring things under control. It was the first time anybody there had ever heard the phrase 'comprehensive plan for development.' Until then, it was still the frontier. You could say I'm responsible for the commercial strip on the Parks Highway, and I'll plead guilty. But by allowing that, I protected the city's residential neighborhoods."

John Stein was reelected, uncontroversially, in 1990. By then Wasilla was a city in chaos, plagued by both substance and spousal abuse—the two not being entirely unrelated. Homeschooling was on the rise, and not only because parents feared exposing their children to the evils of secular education. A child who went to school could talk about how daddy had beaten up mommy the night before, or display his or her own bruises.

Intact nuclear families were a minority. One year, a fourth-grade teacher attempted a genealogy project. The first step was for the students to list their grandparents. He had to abandon the project because many students literally did not know what a grandparent was. Indeed, many, while knowing the woman they lived with, were unsure if she was their birth mother; nor were they certain if the man in the house was their father.

Young mother Sarah remained active in the Assembly of God and made a first gesture in the direction of politics by working to get a creationist majority elected to the Wasilla school board. It was also through her church affiliation that she found the cause that would inspire her for years to come: abortion.

The Valley Hospital was the only one in Alaska in which doctors performed second-trimester abortions, which had been legal since *Roe v. Wade.* This did not sit well either with Catholics, such as hospital board chairman Clyde Boyer, or with the Valley's exploding evangelical Christian population.

The hospital was controlled by a fifteen-member governing board, which in turn appointed seven members to an operating board that made policy decisions. Members of the governing board were chosen by an annual vote of the membership of the hospital association. Membership was open to any Valley resident who filled out an application and paid a five-dollar fee.

Until 1992 there had been only about four hundred members of the hospital association. But in the months leading up to the April 1992 election, in which five governing board seats were up for grabs, more than two thousand new members joined the association, almost all recruited by evangelical churches, foremost among them the Assembly of God.

No one recruited more enthusiastically than Sarah. The two thousand new voters were given a slate of five antiabortion candidates to support. All five won, receiving more than twice as many votes as the leading pro-choice incumbent, Sarah's stepmother-in-law Faye Palin. The five new members gave the antiabortionists a majority on the governing board, which quickly translated into a majority on the operating board, which quickly translated into a vote to prohibit all abortions at the hospital.

Her contribution to the winning side whetted Sarah's appetite for politics. "If it wasn't for the abortion fight, she would never have run for any kind of office," says Reverend Howard Bess, the only one of more than forty Valley ministers to oppose the antiabortionists.

At the same time, Mayor Stein had come to believe that Wasilla could no longer rely on state troopers for law enforcement, but needed its own police department. Merchants were reporting appalling rates of theft and robbery, and residents of the city's new senior housing project were under constant threat of break-in by youths, who stole painkillers and other prescription drugs.

A police department, however, could be funded only by new taxes, and, as Stein recalls, Wasilla was populated largely by "libertarians who hate two things: cops and taxes." Nonetheless, with the help of a city councilman named Nick Carney, a member of one of Wasilla's oldest and largest families, Stein formed Watch on Wasilla, a group whose purposes were to educate the public about the need for a police department and to find a means to pay for it. Jim and Faye Palin joined, and Faye, having recently lost her seat on the hospital board, was named president.

The city's businesses were all for the creation of a police department, but Watch on Wasilla felt it also needed an advocate more attuned to the city's growing number of young families—someone with the time and energy to run for and win a city council seat. They interviewed a number of potential candidates, including a young Wasilla Lake housewife named Sarah Palin.

After their first choice said she wasn't interested, Carney and Stein took a second look at Sarah. "She wasn't the brightest star on the horizon by any means, but at least I'd known her all her life," Carney says. "She'd even gone to school with my daughter."

Four years earlier, at the age of twenty-four, Sarah had joined a Wasilla prayer group led by a woman from Ketchikan named Mary Glazier. "God began to speak to her about entering politics," Glazier told attendees at a religious conference in Everett, Washington, in June 2008. "We began to pray for Sarah. We felt she was the one God had selected." Sarah viewed the invitation to run for city council as God's answer to Mary Glazier's prayers.

At twenty-eight, Sarah had three children, she belonged to the Iditarod Elementary School PTA, she'd played basketball at Wasilla High, and she was Chuck Heath's daughter. "She also told us she was a born-again Christian, a lifetime member of the NRA, and a 'hockey mom,' which was not a phrase I'd ever heard before," Stein says.

"The evangelicals had been storming into Wasilla—we even

rented the city council chamber to one of those groups for Sunday services—so I figured she'd have a strong base of support," Stein says. "I didn't care about her religion or her views on guns or abortion. All that mattered to me was that she'd vote for the police department and the sales tax. After all, what did you really have to know to serve on city council? You need gravel for roads, and sewage runs downhill—that's about it."

Stein mentored Sarah, and Nick Carney took her campaigning door to door. In October 1992, as the sales tax initiative passed, she easily won election to the council. Thus did John Stein open the gates of the city to the mother of all Trojan horses.

Knowing he could pay for a police department with revenue from the sales tax for which Sarah had campaigned, Stein hired Wasilla's first chief of police. Irl Stambaugh was another lifelong Alaskan, and a Vietnam vet who had more than twenty years of experience with the Anchorage police department. Within six months, Stambaugh had an eight-man force up and running. The following year, after his officers arrested more than two hundred drunk drivers, he was named municipal employee of the year.

Stein was elected to a third three-year term in 1993, but a backlash was starting to develop. No small number of those two hundred drunk drivers were Wasilla voters. And while there were more jobs with the city—year-round jobs (with benefits) not dependent on the weather or on an oil company's whim—they were government jobs. Many Wasillans saw them as evidence of government encroachment on private life. The bureaucratic mentality was incompatible with the free spirit of the frontier.

"Your typical female employee who had a job with the city as a secretary or clerk," a former city official told me, "was married to a man who had only seasonal work. So the city job was necessary for the year-round income that could provide family stability. There hadn't been a middle class here. There were slopers—guys who did shifts on the North Slope—and other construction guys and disabled vets with drug and booze problems. And a bunch of teenagers learning how to be thieves. We were the imbecilic stepcousins of Palmer, which had been settled by the Midwestern farmers in the thirties, thanks to the New Deal. This was a rough-and-tumble place, not a good place to raise young children."

Another longtime resident said, "There were a lot of people here who prided themselves on their misfit status. They had contempt for the stable middle class. They didn't want to be citified. Suddenly we had a police department. Wal-Mart and the seniors in subsidized housing liked that, but the libertarian base didn't. What did city cops mean to them? Suddenly you got busted for growing pot in your back shed. You got a ticket if you had a hole in your muffler. You got a ticket if your dog barked too loud. For a place that prided itself on being outside the conventional lifestyle, this was a lot to swallow, and it did not go down very well."

Sarah was among those picking up on the vibrations of discontent. She'd been reelected to city council in 1994. During her first term, she'd sat silently in meetings, sometimes chewing gum, never asking questions, never reacting to proposals, never contributing ideas. "It was almost as if she wasn't there," Stein told me.

That began to change during her second term, when—in one of the weirdest alliances in the history of Alaskan, if not American, politics—the dopers and boozers combined with Wasilla's evangelical Christians to form Sarah's first political base.

On the secular side, she fell under the sway of two of Wasilla's most outspoken and extreme right-wingers, Steve Stoll and Mark Chryson. They became friends with Todd through membership in the Alaska Independence Party, which advocated that Alaska secede from the United States and become an independent republic. Sarah attended the AIP's biennial convention in 1994 and told friends she liked what she'd heard.

On the religious side—while continuing to attend Glazier's prayer group—Sarah grew even more involved in the ongoing legal struggle over banning abortions at Valley Hospital. In 1993 a state judge issued a temporary injunction that prevented the hospital board from enforcing its abortion ban. On September 20, 1995, Superior Court judge Dana Fabe made the injunction permanent. Only an appeal to the Alaska Supreme Court could vacate the judicial order. In the meantime, despite the decision of its operating board and the wishes of a majority of its membership, Valley Hospital would have to continue to offer second-trimester abortions.

On one level, the whole fight was a very large tempest in an extremely small teapot. On average, no more than ten second-term abortions were performed at Valley each year, all for medically valid reasons, such as, in the opinion of a doctor, that the fetus was badly damaged and would be born dead or would result in a seriously deformed child, or because of knowledge of the mother's heavy drinking and the likelihood that the child would suffer from fetal alcohol syndrome.

To abortion opponents, "medically valid" did not mean morally valid. Abortion was murder. To deliberately cause the death of a four-month-old fetus was as reprehensible as to cold-bloodedly murder a four-year-old child. A significant number of Valley residents, including Sarah, believed this.

She felt she had to do more to save the unborn. Her ministers and fellow worshippers at the Assembly of God told her she had to do more. Other fundamentalist preachers told her the same. The Ministers' Prayer Group, a network of right-wing evangelical pastors in the Valley, urged her to run for mayor in order to "bring Christianity to city hall."

Through Mary Glazier's prayer group, Sarah was also hearing the voice of God directly. Years earlier, God had spoken to Glazier, she says on her website. He called her "Wind Walker," and, she says, "revealed to me that he was teaching me to ride the wind with him."

Glazier was no two-bit local prayer group leader. She was a member of the Apostolic Council of Prophetic Elders of C. Peter Wagner's Global Harvest Ministries, based in Colorado Springs, an organization whose mission was "to train Christian leaders in prayer, spiritual warfare . . . prophetic ministries, signs and wonders [and] social transformation."

Global Harvest Ministries was part of an extreme Pentecostal Christian movement called the New Apostolic Reformation, known also as the Third Wave of the Holy Spirit. Although the general council of the Assemblies of God, parent body of the Wasilla church, had declared the Third Wave a heresy, Sarah's local Assembly of God remained closely linked to it and supported Glazier in her wide range of activities, one of which was to free Alaska from the spell of demonic witchcraft.

Glazier had already claimed one scalp. She said God had advised her that a particular applicant for a chaplain's job in Alaska's state prison system was a demon. She organized an "intercessory" prayer group that called upon the Holy Spirit to destroy the witch.

The result? "Her car engine blew up, she went blind in her left eye, and she was diagnosed with cancer," Glazier told *SpiritLed Woman* magazine in 2003, adding that the chaplain/witch was forced to leave Alaska to seek medical treatment for the ailments Glazier had inflicted upon her in the name of God.

Having accomplished that, how hard could it be to make Sarah mayor of Wasilla?

Stoll and Chryson promised covert support from the Alaska Independence Party, while Larry Kroon, who had succeeded Paul Riley as pastor of the Assembly of God church, guaranteed an equivalent under-the-table effort from evangelicals.

By then, Sarah was occupying her time at city council meetings with doodling that turned out to be far from idle, as a reporter for *The New Republic* discovered in 2008:

Sarah was getting so antsy that one day in early April she actually drove to Anchorage just for a glimpse of Ivana Trump. She told Todd she was going to Costco to buy groceries. Instead, she went to JCPenney to see Ivana, who was peddling a line of perfume. She told the *Anchorage Daily News* that she was simply the wife of a commercial fisherman and she'd come to see Ivana "because we are so desperate in Alaska for any semblance of glamour and culture."

Sarah realized that even in Wasilla she couldn't mount a viable campaign against John Stein as the candidate of only secessionists and religious extremists. She needed a link to a more established political organization. The powerful right-wing Republican state senator from Wasilla, Lyda Green (a native of Texas), provided it.

Green offered Sarah the services not only of her son-in-law, Tuckerman Babcock, a Republican political strategist, but also of her staff member Laura Chase, whom she recommended as campaign manager.

A graduate of the University of Idaho, like Sarah, Chase had gained experience in public relations while working for Alyeska, the oil company consortium that built and operated the Trans-Alaska Pipeline. She'd also worked for the Wasilla Chamber of Commerce.

Chase liked and respected John Stein. Senator Green, however, urged her to work for Sarah instead. "She'll bring fresh energy," Green said. "She's innovative. After nearly a decade of Stein, it's time for a change." Green also stressed that the job would be "great experience" for Chase.

At their first meeting, according to Chase, Sarah said her main goal was to build more bike paths in the city. That was it. No greater vision, and certainly no covert Christian extremist agenda. "Bike trails are my baby," Sarah said.

She invited Chase to a meeting at her home. "Tuckerman Babcock was there," Chase recalls, "with a big city map and a laminated Republican playbook. They knew I wasn't comfortable, because John Stein and Nick Carney were my friends."

Sarah eventually persuaded Chase to take the job by offering a personal inducement. "I can visualize you being deputy administrator," she said. "You and I will run the city together. We can make it the kind of place we've always wanted it to be."

Chase recalls no mention of any affiliation with the evangelical right. "She was very careful not to let me see that," Chase says, "because if I'd gotten the slightest whiff of it, I'd never have gotten involved. For one thing, I'm very openly and actively pro-choice."

Having assembled her campaign staff, Sarah announced her pro–bike path candidacy, making no mention of her real platform, an amalgam of Assembly of God and Alaska Independence Party ideals.

John Stein was in his office when a friend from the chamber of commerce told him that Sarah planned to run against him. "I was stunned," he recalls. "I was astounded. Not just because I'd been her mentor, but because in her four years on city council she'd never said a word. She had not put forward a single idea."

Stein now admits to having been naïve. "Municipal races in Wasilla had always been about sewers and roads," he says. "The Mat-Su Borough, not the city, controls the fire department and the school system. The city is strictly nuts and bolts. It never occurred to me that a city race could be the vehicle for advancing extremist ideology."

Until the 1996 race, not even party affiliation had been an issue. Stein was a Republican, but nobody had noticed or cared. What mattered, as a former city official recalls, was that "John Stein commanded loyalty, allegiance, and respect because he would carefully listen to people and actually consider what they had to say. You never came away from a meeting with John feeling you'd had anything less than a fair hearing."

Nonetheless, after nine years in office, Stein was vulnerable to charges of cronyism. "Once I confirmed that Sarah was serious, I did some soul-searching," he says. "I think most politicians succumb to arrogance eventually, and I certainly don't exempt myself. I'd get together with my staff and socialize after council meetings, and that led to the charge that we were conducting business on the sly. I didn't pay enough attention to appearances.

"In addition, there was a hard-core residue of anger about the police department and the sales tax. These extremists like Stoll and Chryson were looking for an excuse to detonate. And Chuck Heath was hooked up with them from the start."

Even so, Stein wasn't overly worried. Wasilla was growing according to plan: not the way urban aestheticians such as Jane Jacobs might have liked, but the old slogan "We Don't Give a Damn How They Do It Outside" still resonated strongly in the Valley.

Ignoring the bike paths, Sarah focused the secular aspect of her campaign on two issues: closing hours for local bars and liberalization of Alaska's already lenient gun laws.

In regard to the bars, the issue was whether to allow them to remain open until 5:00 AM or require them to close at 2:00, as did the bars in Anchorage. Both Stein and Wasilla's first police chief, Irl Stambaugh, advocated the earlier closing.

"What was happening," Stambaugh told me during the summer of 2010, "was half the drunks in Anchorage would drive up here at two AM and get drunker for another three hours and then try to drive home. We were getting kind of tired of scraping them off the Parks Highway. I was also concerned with the number of women who were calling our domestic abuse hotline just after five o'clock in the morning saying, 'Help, quick, my husband just came in and he's trying to kill me!'"

To Stein, a 2:00 AM closing "seemed like a no-brainer, what with the epidemic of drunk driving plaguing us, and especially in a city with such a strong Baptist and fundamentalist presence."

You'd think an evangelical Christian mother such as Sarah would have agreed. You'd be wrong. The bar owners argued that the hours between 2:00 and 5:00 AM were particularly lucrative and that city government didn't have the right to interfere with free enterprise. Sarah wholeheartedly agreed. She saw the bill that would mandate a 2:00 AM closing as a classic example of government interference with personal freedom.

The bar owners rivaled the right-wing Christian churches as the largest donors to Sarah's campaign. Big jars into which Palin campaign donations could be placed appeared on all Wasilla bars and were filled to the brim nightly. In the same saloons, pictures of incumbent mayor Stein were placed inside the urinals.

The proposed changes to the state's gun laws, which would allow the carrying of concealed weapons in bars and banks and on school grounds—they were already permitted everywhere else—seemed even less relevant. "It simply wasn't a municipal issue," Stein said. "The state legislature would decide that, and it didn't matter how Irl Stambaugh or I felt about it."

But it mattered to Sarah and her supporters. She accused Stein, a longtime member of the National Rifle Association, and Vietnam vet Stambaugh of being "anti-gun." In Alaska—especially in the Valley—this was a more serious charge than pederasty.

Sarah's campaign operated on two levels. On the surface—the Laura Chase level—she was the bubbly, energetic "hockey mom," Chuck Heath's daughter, a Wasilla High grad, and a member of the team that won the girls' state basketball championship in 1982, which, even fourteen years later, was no small thing in Wasilla. She was a personification of the change long overdue at city hall.

But there was also the secret underbelly: the doper/boozer–charismatic Christian coalition, which spread rumors that because John Stein's wife still used her maiden name professionally the two of them weren't actually married, and—far worse—that Stein was a Jew!

"I'd been a Pennsylvania Dutch Lutheran all my life," Stein told me when I talked to him during the summer of 2010. "I'd lived in Wasilla for twelve years and had been mayor for nine. Where was this suddenly coming from? I actually had to say in public, 'I am not a Jew.' As for not being married, my wife and I laughed. But the whispers grew louder, and pretty soon they weren't whispers anymore. I actually had to produce a marriage license, and even then Stoll and Chryson said it was probably forged."

Sarah also introduced innuendo about sexual harassment into the campaign. She encouraged gossip about Stein and Stambaugh acting inappropriately during an early-morning step-aerobics class that she occasionally attended. The two men, being less than svelte, had signed up for the class, along with the head of the department of public works, Jack Felton.

"It was a small room," Stambaugh said, "and there were maybe twenty people in the class. Us big guys stood in the back so nobody would have to look at us, because, to tell you the truth, it wasn't a pretty sight. One day Sarah shows up. She goes right to the front and she puts on this incredible demonstration—three risers, double steps, I don't know what all, but it was a hell of a routine. Afterward, I complimented her on her incredible stamina."

Before the next class, the instructor approached the three men. "Sarah Palin says she's uncomfortable," the instructor said, "because she thinks you guys are ogling her butt. She wants me to move you to the front of the room so you won't be able to watch her during class."

The men agreed. But that didn't work either. "You guys are so big," the instructor said, "that when you're in the front of the room you block everybody's view of me."

And that was that. Neither the mayor nor the police chief nor the superintendent of the department of public works wanted to make Sarah or any other woman in Wasilla uncomfortable in exercise class. So they stopped going. Too late: Sarah's supporters had something else to whisper about.

A friend offered a different perspective. "One morning," she told me during the summer of 2010, "Sarah came back in her workout stuff—her outfits were very provocative—and she's singing, 'I like big butts and I cannot lie,' and she's dancing around the kitchen. Todd comes in from the garage, and Sarah starts going on about how the guys are checking her out at the workout place. The way she's saying it is totally antagonizing Todd, and he finally says, 'Well, why don't you put some fuckin' clothes on?'"

. . .

AT ONE POINT in the campaign, Sarah claimed her tires had been slashed and implied that Stein supporters had done it.

"If it happened, which I doubt," Stein says, "it was probably related to the domestic turmoil she was going through at the time. We were hearing a lot of scuttlebutt, and Todd was certainly notable by his absence. He and Brad Hanson broke up their snow machine business in Big Lake and we were hearing that was because Sarah was having an affair with Brad. She was apparently telling people, 'I'm not sure Todd's my man.' And I do remember that her wedding ring was coming off and on a lot."

Sarah's affair with Hanson, which was revealed nationally by the *National Enquirer* during the 2008 campaign, was apparently common knowledge in Wasilla. Hanson was a property developer and businessman whose parents were friends of Chuck and Sally Heath's. He would go on to become a Palmer city councilman and coach of the Palmer High School hockey team.

"It was known," a friend of Todd's told me in 2010. "For example, Todd knew that I knew. He was embarrassed. It wasn't something he talked about a lot."

Both Sarah and Hanson have denied that they ever had an affair. People who claim to be aware of the affair—six months is a common estimate of its duration—believed that Sarah was using Hanson to show Todd that two could play the game she suspected he'd been playing for years in Dillingham.

"Todd was basically spanked and put back in his box," a friend of his says. "The marriage was never right before and it was never right after."

. . .

IT WAS NOT in Stein's nature to fight dirty. "I didn't want any part of any of that," he told me. "In fact, when I heard that Sarah was afraid I'd get nasty, I actually called her and went to her house to assure her that if any information about her personal life came my way I would not use it in the campaign. That didn't stop her, of course, but I stuck to my promise and I don't regret it. No office is worth holding if you have to win it by spreading slime. I will tell you, though: right up to Election Day, they were really afraid."

Campaign manager Chase recalls no fear. Indeed, her biggest shock came from learning the extraordinary nature of Sarah's ambition. "We were sitting at my kitchen table at about eleven o'clock one night, and I said, 'Sarah, you'll be governor in ten years.' And she said, 'I don't want to be governor, I want to be president.'"

She ran as if she truly believed she was God's chosen candidate. "I'll never forget a speech she gave to the chamber of commerce," a Wasilla lawyer recalls. "She was so nervous her voice was quavering, but she said, 'Anyone who thinks faith has no place in government has no place in government himself.' I said, 'Where in the hell did that come from?' I'd never known her to be religious. But then it all started: guns and God and abortion-is-evil and all gays are perverts on one hand and man's divine right to drink himself into roadkill until five AM on the other. Sarah was off to the races."

For at least ten years, since first learning about it at Mary Glazier's prayer group and at the Assembly of God, Sarah had subscribed to an evangelical Christian ideology frequently referred to as dominionism. The goal of dominionists is to put Christian extremists into positions of political power in order to end America's constitutionally mandated separation of church and state. Dominionists believe that America was founded as a specifically Christian republic and that Christians should control all levels of government.

Although she'd been reluctant to discuss her beliefs with Laura Chase at the start of the campaign, before it was over, Sarah grew so open about her dominionist affiliations that she even bused in members of right-wing extremist Jerry Prevo's Anchorage Baptist Temple to go door to door campaigning for her.

And just as her father had used threats to try to get his way in his fight against the women on the school board, Sarah and her supporters did not shy from intimidation.

"I was renting an apartment," Carolyn Johnson, a former resident of Wasilla now living in Texas, recalls, "and I put a Stein sign in the window. My landlord told me to take it down. He had the vending machine account at the Wasilla Bar and he was told he'd lose it if anyone saw a Stein sign in his building. I said no. Then the threats started, late at night, always by phone. 'Watch what you're doing . . . it's gonna get ugly . . . you'd better watch your back . . . it would be too bad if something happened to your daughter.' My daughter was a small child at the time, and I was living alone with her. I took down the sign."

Although Stein was also a Republican, the party fervently supported Sarah. Republicans sponsored fund-raising dinners for her, and she appeared in newspaper ads and on television commercials alongside Republican state legislators.

"I just don't get the big full-court press that the Republicans are pushing," Stein told the *Frontiersman*. "I find it pretty offensive in a local election."

He ran on the slogan "Protect the Progress" and emphasized his experience. He stressed that under his stewardship Wasilla had created a police force, had attracted new business, and, because of the 2 percent sales tax, now had not only a balanced budget but more than $3 million in reserves.

Sarah stuck with the not particularly original slogan she had first doodled at a council meeting: "Time for a Change."

Given the intensity and acrimony of the campaign, one might have expected massive voter turnout, but on Election Day, October 1, 1996, fewer than one third of Wasilla's eligible voters cast ballots.

It would not be unreasonable to suppose that among the more motivated were those who favored keeping the bars open until 5:00 AM and/or those whose Pentecostal ministers told them that failure to vote for Sarah would invite perdition. Puritanical oldster John Stein had no such threats in his arsenal.

In what the *Anchorage Daily News* called "an upset victory," Sarah won 661 to 440.

As vote totals were posted at the Mat-Su Borough offices in Palmer, she shouted, "We won! We won!" and jumped up and down. The next day, she told the *Daily News* that the lessons she'd learned playing basketball for Wasilla's state championship team in 1982 had carried her to victory.

"This really sounds hokey, but that was a turning point in my life," she said. "We were supposed to be the underdogs big-time. You see firsthand anything is possible and learn it takes tenacity, hard work, and guts."

She gave no credit to either the Alaska Independence Party or Mary Glazier, or, for that matter, to God himself. To be fair, she didn't credit the owners of the Mug-Shot or the Wasilla Sports Bar either.

She was sworn in on October 14. Within hours, she launched what many Wasillans today remember as nothing short of a reign of terror.

FIVE

SARAH'S OLDER BROTHER, Chuckie Heath, who lives in Anchorage, tells The Daily Caller that because I am living next door, Sarah fears for the safety of her children. I make a cup of coffee and take it onto the deck to greet yet another brilliant spring day. By midafternoon, the temperature might even hit seventy. I realize I need to buy sunblock.

The new fence is up, and I'm grateful for it. I feel not quite so exposed to prying eyes. Chuckie says my deck "looks right down into her kitchen and into the bedrooms and the upstairs, too." He's wrong on all three counts. Even before the new fence went up, no one sitting on my deck—or sitting anywhere inside my house—could see into any of the rooms next door.

How did my living next door get to be about the safety of Sarah's children? And why do the mainstream media, which treat every other utterance out of Sarah's mouth as preposterous, deceitful, or meretricious, now accept her allegations about me as factual?

A right-wing radio commentator broadcasts my e-mail address. I'm inundated with thousands of threats and pieces of hate mail. I create a new account and share it with everyone I need to stay in touch with, and delete all the messages from the old one unread. But it's another sign of how a wink from Sarah gets the attack dogs slavering.

Greta Van Susteren calls me "the Wasilla stalker." Movie actresses on *The View* say I'm going through the Palins' garbage. In *Slate*, Christopher Beam addresses the question of whether Palin could get a restraining order against me. The piece is headlined "The Stalker Next Door." The threats continue to pile up. From Craigslist:

> *The Woods are lovely,*
> *Dark and Deep.*
> *But I have promises to keep,*
> *and miles to go before I sleep.*
> *But the woods can also be very dangerous if you go around fuck-*
> *ing with people. You never know when Wolves, a pack of Feral*
> *Dogs, a Bear or Moose might decide to kill you, then have a little*
> *snack. That goes triple for pesky writers. I wonder who will write*
> *the Murder Mystery when this guy turns up dead in the Woods?*
> *Best Seller!*

Mayor Rupright assures me that Wasilla police are keeping a round-the-clock watch on my house. I call Catherine Taylor and advise her to increase her fire insurance. At 10:30 PM a friend calls from the stop sign at the Best Western to say she's about to drop off the television set I'm borrowing in order to watch the World Cup. I go down to unlock the chain. Her car approaches. Right behind it is a state police car that has apparently been sitting in the Best Western lot, alert to anyone heading in my direction.

The wind dies down at dusk. At 1:00 AM—not quite total darkness even yet—there is the most extraordinary full moon shining on the lake from over the mountains, its light reflected brilliantly by the still waters. I bask in the moment. Just sitting here in this magical light and silence—except for the grebes, who squawk round the clock—makes me fall in love with Alaska all over again.

Friday, May 28, 2010

NORMALLY, FOR A news story to continue beyond the first twenty-four-hour cycle, something newly newsworthy must occur. A story pertaining to Sarah is the exception to this rule. It's now been four days since she first took to Facebook, and absolutely nothing has happened. I've exchanged neither a word nor a glance with anyone across the fence. So by today, Friday, maybe things will start to calm down?

Twenty minutes on my laptop kills that hope. In this Internet age, when anyone with an opinion, however ill-informed, can broadcast it to a worldwide audience within seconds, news-cycle projections become irrelevant.

At some point we reached critical mass. Now the fission process has blown us into an alternate universe. Maintaining what I'd considered a prudent silence has led only to slander, and some highly specific and graphically expressed threats on my life, as well as threats against my family, even my grandchildren.

So today I respond. I talk by phone to David Carr of the *New York Times* and to Dave Weigel at the *Washington Post* and in person to a *Wall Street Journal* reporter who's been sent up from San Francisco. I also talk to a producer at the *Today* show to arrange a live interview from my deck at 3:45 AM next Tuesday.

I've known David Carr for several years. Therefore, I listen when he warns me to get out. "What's the upside compared to the downside," he asks, "when the downside is you get killed?"

He has a point. He continues: "Some of these people she's inflaming are certifiable lunatics who've got guns. All it takes is one who thinks he's proving his love for Sarah by blowing you away. I'm serious. Your life is in danger. Go somewhere else. You don't need to be there to write your book."

"If I leave, she wins. And the crazies win."

"And they lose if you're dead?"

Carr is a savvy guy who has been around a few different blocks. He's not a hysteric. I don't like what he says, but I take it seriously. I resolve to think about it as soon as I get the chance.

On the other hand, the cable guy comes to hook up my TV for World Cup viewing. Mayor Rupright stops by, just to check in. He's still not worried. He says his cops have my back. A Wasilla Police Department sergeant calls to say that while I might not be aware of it, they are having regular patrols check on my house throughout the night. And I know the state police are involved.

Screw it, I'm not going to leave. Caving in to bullies only emboldens them further. How far would I have to retreat? To the Best Western? To Anchorage? Back to Massachusetts? If I'm actually in danger, the only way to protect myself fully would be to abandon the book. Is that what America has come to? That someone who ran for national political office and who is known to be considering running for national office again can silence critics by instigating a campaign of threat and intimidation against them?

My position is simple: if I actually do something intrusive, then you have the right to react. Wait for me to take a picture, or peer over the fence with binoculars, or pass along to the public something I heard while eavesdropping. Then you'll have every right to be apoplectic. But as I told Todd, that's not going to happen. So let's proceed, as the Italians say, *con calma*.

In the evening, I'm looking out my kitchen window, into my front yard. A car pulls up to the chain. Two women get out and walk around it. I step outside to ask them to leave.

"Don't shoot!" one of them yells and holds up a wooden sign that reads WELCOME. The other woman unfurls an Alaskan flag. "We come in peace," she says.

They are just two residents of Wasilla offended by the Palins' behavior.

"Real Alaskans don't act that way," one says. The other says, "Here's a sign for you, and here's an Alaskan flag you can fly from your deck. And I've got six different handguns in the cab of my truck. You can borrow any or all."

I thank them for the sign and flag but say I'll pass on the guns. They leave me their phone numbers in case I change my mind. We all hug, and they leave. A sign, a flag, and your choice of six guns: it's the Wasilla Welcome Wagon.

Saturday, May 29, 2010

NOT ONLY am I not leaving, I'm throwing a housewarming party. I put the WELCOME sign on the mantelpiece and hang the Alaskan flag and an American flag from the deck. I've got friends coming up from Anchorage and down from Talkeetna, an hour and a half to the north.

In the *Washington Post,* Dave Weigel quotes me accurately: "Look, this is a pain in the ass for them. I understand that. If I were her, I'd be upset. I'd be annoyed. But I'd be an adult about it, and I would figure out, okay, how can we resolve this in a way that's not going to make it into something that everybody gets obsessive about?"

Sarah's inability to do that has taught me something important about her: she has no sense of proportion, no ability to modulate her response. She's over the top in all directions: rah-rah cheerleading for those whom she supports, spewing vitriolic condemnation of anyone who challenges her.

This strikes me as a potentially dangerous character flaw in some- one seeking a position of national leadership. If this is how she reacts, as a private citizen, to an unwelcome neighbor next door, what would she do as president if the Iranian government suddenly irked her?

This is not an idle question. An unchecked emotional response could cost millions of lives. Such a notion becomes considerably less unthinkable when you consider that Palin herself has said that she believes us to be in the "end-times," awaiting the rapturous return to earth of Jesus Christ, an event she has predicted will occur during her lifetime.

Here's something else: as I said to Weigel, "By being here, I've gotten an insight into her ability to incite hatred that before I only knew about in the abstract." Isn't it strange that the supporters of someone who so brassily proclaims her devotion to Jesus are so prone to expressions of hatred and violent threats, rather than tolerance and respect? I guess "Love thy neighbor" isn't a precept they teach at the Wasilla Bible Church or Assembly of God.

I DIDN'T SEE the ABC piece that resulted from the network's early-morning wakeup call, but Alex Pareene did, and in *Salon* he calls it "the worst non-Fox coverage of the Sarah Palin/Joe McGinniss feud that I have seen so far."

He writes: "Reporter Neal Karlinsky quotes Palin calling McGinniss an 'odd character' without pointing out to his audience that McGinniss is a respected, longtime reporter, who has written about Palin and Alaska before."

Pareene also notes that "Karlinsky repeats the weird and completely over-the-line accusation by Palin that McGinniss is spying on Piper's bedroom," and says, "In the most audacious and bizarre portion, Karlinsky harasses McGinniss at the house he is renting—an actual intrusion onto his private property—in the process of reporting a story on how creepy it is that this reporter is 'violating' Sarah Palin's privacy. At no point does Karlinsky acknowledge the irony."

Like truth, I'm afraid, irony does not fare well in Palinland.

KITTY FELDE of Southern California Public Radio posts a blog item called "Gentleman Joe McGinniss," in which she writes, "I worked alongside Joe McGinniss for nine long months during the O. J. Simpson trial. It was an intense time, when reporters spent more time together than with their families. While Dominick Dunne and Joe Bosco loved the limelight, McGinniss was quiet, standing off to the side, but always watching and thinking—an intelligent guy with a wry sense of humor. I wouldn't mind having him move in next door to me."

But the Internet never lets you feel good for long.

The first comment in response to Felde's piece reads, "Joe McGinniss is an idiot. I wish he lived next door to you, too. You two would get along splendidly."

The second reads, "Joe McGinniss is a STALKER! I wish he lived next door to you, too."

I sometimes wonder why anyone bothers to blog. Almost nothing anyone writes ever changes anyone else's mind. Most people who read a blog already agree with the writer's point of view. The others read so they can write quick, nasty comments in response. The whole blogosphere sometimes seems like one vast game of verbal paintball.

MY PARTY is a great success. Tom Kluberton, who runs the Fireweed Station Inn in Talkeetna, brings burgers made from Herman the Ill-Tempered Yak.

Most of Tom's guests at Fireweed are climbers on their way to or from ascents of Denali guided by Alpine Ascents International. Todd Burleson, perhaps best known for the heroism he displayed on Mount Everest in 1996, recounted by Jon Krakauer in *Into Thin Air,* founded Alpine Ascents. In addition to guiding Denali ascents, Burleson, who has led eight Everest expeditions and who has himself climbed the Seven Summits twice, has been seeking to re-create the Himalayan trekking experience at Denali, complete with sherpas and yaks.

But every once in a while a yak goes rogue. Such was the case with Herman, an eight-hundred-pounder, last fall. I was staying at Fireweed Station when Burleson announced (over a dinner of roadkill

black bear tacos expertly prepared by Tom and his longtime companion, Hobbs) that Herman's days were numbered. The number, in fact, was one. He'd be killing Herman in the morning. Then he and Tom would spend the day butchering, wrapping, and freezing the meat.

I'd already been back to Fireweed Station this spring and enjoyed a hearty meal of yak loaf, with an *H* for "Herman" written in chili sauce on top. Now all that was left of Herman were the dozen or so burgers that Tom brought. The Traeger cooked them to perfection. Earthier than moose, slightly hairier than caribou was the consensus.

Of the nine people at the party, only four bring handguns to loan me. We wrap things up in the early evening when APX Alarms arrives to install the new home security system that Catherine Taylor has insisted on. It's an excellent system, although I'm slightly concerned that the interior motion detector will go off when I get up to use the bathroom in the middle of the night.

Sunday, May 30, 2010

SUNDAY BREAKFAST at the Mat-Su Family Restaurant, which the old-timers still call the Country Kitchen, is one of the few non-religious experiences that offers a glimpse of the essence of Wasilla. The Mat-Su is the place in town to see and be seen, at least between 6:00 AM and 6:00 PM. After that, the Mug-Shot Saloon and the Sportsman's Bar vie for the honor. Sunday morning is when most of Wasilla is there, either before or after church services.

The Mat-Su does the basic diner breakfast as well as it can be done. The service is never less than competent, and the portions are Alaska-size. A storm may be raging all around me, but at the Mat-Su I'm just another customer, entitled to good food, good service, and the opportunity to eat in peace.

I'm enjoying breakfast until I turn to the editorial page of the *Mat-Su Valley Frontiersman.* An editorial begins, "We don't really care if the Palins want some privacy from what they worry might be prying eyes." It ends by saying, "Finally, those who are fond of Joe McGinniss might remind him (if he doesn't already know) that Alaska has a law that allows the use of deadly force in protection of life and property."

Satchel Paige once warned, "Don't eat fried food, it angries up the blood." A *Frontiersman* editorial that all but puts me in the crazies' crosshairs does the same.

I BUY two armchairs at a garage sale, but I need to get them delivered. A friend of a friend, a Mat-Su Borough assemblyman named Mark Ewing, calls to say he can pick them up and bring them over. Then he calls back: "I just can't take the chance. Todd or Sarah might recognize my truck."

Then someone named Dewey Taylor calls. "I'll get your chairs for you, and I don't give a damn if Todd or Sarah recognize my truck. I don't know how people can walk around living in fear of the Palins."

Dewey, a retired schoolteacher and principal who's now a Democratic Party activist, delivers the chairs in midafternoon. A couple of friends come with him. One of them brings a freshly baked homemade blueberry pie. She says, "I figure Sarah might not have got around to it yet."

The chairs are perfect: now I can watch the World Cup in comfort. The pie is perfect, too.

Monday, May 31, 2010

NANCY CALLS TO tell me our new home phone number. We had to change it after she started getting threats. My son, Joe McGinniss, Jr., the novelist, is receiving threats against his wife and two-year-old son. People in my agent's office and at Random House report hate mail and threats. Then I hear that at about four o'clock this morning somebody shot out the driver's-side window of Dewey Taylor's truck, which was parked in his driveway.

The smaller house, on the left, is mine.

I call him and offer to pay for a new window. "Don't be ridiculous," he says, "it was probably just a coincidence."

"How long have you lived there?"

"About twenty years."

"Ever had a problem with a vehicle parked in your driveway before?"

"Nope."

"I don't think it was a coincidence."

"Maybe not, but screw 'em. I'm already on my way to get it replaced."

That's an Alaskan.

THE REST of the day is dominated by the *Today* show crew, which arrives in force. The cameramen and soundmen were here last fall, when they did a Thanksgiving special with Sarah in the kitchen of the house next door. I do some "B"-roll footage for them. When they leave at 8:00 PM I go to bed, because they'll return at 1:00 AM to prep for the show.

When I can't fall asleep, I go out for a Dairy Queen chocolate sundae at 11:00 PM. During this, the last hour of May, even on the Parks Highway, the chain-store clutter recedes and the glory of the mountains presses close. From somewhere long ago and far away, lines from an e.e. cummings poem spring to mind. I can't remember the poem's title (I later find that it's "when faces called flowers float out of the ground") but the lines are as clear as when I first memorized them in high school fifty years ago:

> —it's spring(all our night becomes day)o,it's spring!
> all the pretty birds dive to the heart of the sky
> all the little fish climb through the mind of the sea
> (all the mountains are dancing; are dancing)

Tuesday, June 1, 2010

NBC'S BIG TRUCKS roll in at 1:00 AM and light up the neighborhood like Times Square on New Year's Eve. We do the four-minute interview at 3:45 AM, 7:45 in New York.

Afterward, I decide that the *Today* interview will be my last about living next door to Sarah until I'm ready to leave. I came out here to ask questions, not answer them. As with blogging, nothing anybody says at this point is going to change anyone else's mind. It might not be the end of the story, but it's the end of my participation in it.

Chris Matthews says, "Palin has issued a fatwa against McGinniss."

New York magazine asks, "Will Sarah Palin Kill Joe McGinniss?"

A Huffington Post story based on the *Frontiersman* editorial—headlined "Newspaper Reminds Journalist: Palins Can Shoot to Protect Property"—leads their home page, just beneath a banner headline about the BP oil spill. Even more incredibly, the story has received more than ten thousand comments in twenty-four hours. I've written whole books that sold fewer copies than that.

The worst of the filth is coming from commenters on the website of Andrew Breitbart, a right-wing digital media entrepreneur deemed so significant in these times that the May 24 *New Yorker* devoted a full-length profile to him. Here are some typical remarks:

> "This is one psychotic liberal. I hope someone mistakes him for a moose and puts an end to his publicity stunt. It would be nice if he ends up at the bottom of Lake Lucille."

> "If trapped in a house and not able to get out for food, does anyone know how long a freaky marxist fanatic can survive on a diet of KY Jelly?"

> "I hope someone knocks his teeth down his throat."

"What a spineless creepy bordering on sex-predator freak. I hope he tries to break into the Palin's yard and gets a gut full of shotgun shell."

Those are just about me. They get worse:

"hey, Joe, sleep with one eye open, you POS. can't wait for your grandkids to show up and play in the woods and water."

And, after publishing my home address:

"Joe's lonely wife needs mail, phone calls and other assurances of concern and good will in Joe's absence."

I can't help but wish that my friend the late William F. Buckley were around to witness this spectacle. He would have reduced it to size in a hurry. Even more, I wish Bill were still with us and able to skewer the Palinista phenomenon, as he surely and adroitly would have done.

At least Nancy is arriving the day after tomorrow. Maybe together, despite everything, we can enjoy what's left of this resplendent Alaskan spring. As cummings wrote,

> *sweet spring is your*
> *time is my time is our*
> *time for springtime is lovetime*
> *and viva sweet love*

Wednesday, June 2, 2010

SARAH CAN'T BEAR not to have the last word. She turned down an invitation from the *Today* show to appear in the same segment as me—sharing a screen as we were interviewed on opposite sides of the fence. Instead, she had her PR people prepare a statement that she wanted NBC to read. NBC didn't. Sarah quickly twittered her displeasure:

> Any wonder why public can't trust mainstream media? I'll facebook our latest incident w/NBC unbalanced/sensational "reporting";Don't trust'em

Facebook it she did, painting herself, as usual, in the black and blue of victimhood, as well as in red, white, and blue:

> It's a shame that Todd and I had another disappointing encounter with the media on Memorial Day of all days. It was time that we could have spent with our kids and on a day when we honor those who have died in defense of our Constitution, including our free-dom of the press.

Colleen Cottle tells me Todd wasn't even in Wasilla on Memorial Day. He and Track were in Texas, visiting Colleen's son, John.

NBC broadcast her statement this morning, but even that isn't last word enough. Todd calls Kathleen Parker at the *Washington Post* to say my presence next door has ruined their summer.

Like Glenn Beck, Parker thinks Todd deserves high praise for "trying to keep his cool." She quotes him as saying, "Coming from me, people twist and turn [what I say] and before I know it, I've threatened someone. The media would love for me to go out and hit somebody." Guess who?

FOR ME, it's back to work. I drive to Palmer, fifteen miles across the Valley, for a 3:00 PM meeting with Zane Henning, a Christian con-

servative and former North Slope oil worker who filed an ethics complaint against Sarah in November 2008, charging that she was using
state property to promote her national political career.

He based that complaint mostly on an interview Sarah did with
Greta Van Susteren of Fox News on November 11, 2008, from her
governor's office in Anchorage. When asked about her plans for 2012,
Sarah said, "Faith is a very big part of my life. And putting my life in
my creator's hands—this is what I always do. I'm like, okay, God, if
there is an open door for me somewhere, this is what I always pray,
I'm like, don't let me miss the open door. Show me where the open
door is. Even if it's cracked up a little bit, maybe I'll plow right on
through that and maybe prematurely plow through it, but don't let
me miss an open door. And if there is an open door in '12 or four
years later, and if it is something that is going to be good for my family, for my state, for my nation, an opportunity for me, then I'll plow
through that door."

Henning later filed a second complaint, charging that Sarah had
improperly billed the state per diem costs for days when she worked
out of her Wasilla home.

A stocky man who's obviously spent a lot of time outdoors, Henning
meets me at Vagabond Blues, the downtown coffee and sandwich shop
where just about everybody meets everybody in Palmer. He's known
Sarah since childhood. Chuck Heath was his sixth-grade teacher. He
remembers Chuck coming in the first day and telling the students to
forget the curriculum for the year: they weren't going to waste time on
stuff like English and history and math. They were going to study the
only subject that really mattered—the great Alaskan outdoors.

"If you were an outdoorsy kid, he was the greatest teacher you
could have," Henning says. "But if you were any kind of bookworm,
it must have been a very long year. He didn't hesitate to make fun of
boys he didn't think were manly enough, and the only girls he paid
attention to were the pretty ones."

Henning was friends with Sarah's younger sister, Molly, but as for Sarah herself, he says, "She gave me the willies from the get-go. She was always standoffish, and if she didn't get her way she was a bully."

Moving back to Wasilla in 1989, after several years in southwestern Alaska, Henning found the adult Sarah not much different from the child. "Todd and I hit it off okay—we were both fishermen and we could talk about snow machines—but Sarah still had this clique-y high-schoolish thing going, and my wife didn't like her, so we never really socialized."

Even so, Henning voted for her for mayor. "I had joined the Last Frontier Foundation, which was all about more conservative, smaller government, and I was a Christian and I knew she was, too, so it was a pretty easy choice."

It was also one he soon regretted. "She didn't know what she was doing. She didn't know the first thing. She had to hire a business manager to run the city because she didn't know how. And then she spent fifty thousand dollars remodeling her office without getting city council approval."

Henning approached her one night at a social gathering. "It was at Harry and Whitney's house—they live in Utah now—and I asked her about the remodeling. She said how dare I ever question her! Just like that. Boom. From that point forward the door was closed for conversation."

With increasing dismay, Henning watched Sarah spend $15 million to build a new sports center on land the city didn't own. "She wanted to prove she was a hockey mom, but to me that wasn't being conservative."

Once she became governor, Henning turned into an outright gadfly, requesting copies of state e-mails that, he said, showed Sarah was doing state business on private accounts to avoid public scrutiny.

"She'd promised open and transparent, but that was just another of her lies. And Todd was copied on everything. He was supposed to be working for BP, a company with which the state is doing business. But she's copying him on confidential documents regarding oil and gas. How can you say that's ethical?

"Listen, I used to see Todd up on the slope. Even after I filed my ethics complaints, he never pointed a finger at me. He's a wimp. He makes me sick. People say he's a man's man? I'd love to grab him by the neck and beat the shit out of him."

"That doesn't sound very Christian," I say.

Henning laughs. "I know. Todd and Sarah bring out the worst in me. I've got to be careful to not let myself grow too spiteful. But she's the one who gets the Christian perspective all wrong. Look at this hatred for Obama. Is that being a true Christian? I'm a conservative and I oppose his big-government policies, but I don't try to incite hate. And her so-called family values? After the way she's neglected her own kids? She's too narcissistic to care about her kids. It's always 'me, me, me,' and everybody else is always wrong. She's so narcissistic she couldn't even care for a pet. And that's true. Linda Menard gave her a puppy named Agia. She got rid of it because she couldn't be bothered to care for it.

"Name one thing she's done—just one—that reflects a truly caring, Christian heart. She's never volunteered for charity. Habitat for Humanity? The United Way? Even Christian-sponsored charities. Take a look at her tax returns. Do you see any donations? Do you see even a dime? No, what you see is them trying to get out of paying property tax on that cabin they built on Safari Lake."

These are strong words to be uttered in a venue as mellow as Vagabond Blues on such a spirit-lifting spring afternoon.

"It's time for strong speech," Henning says. "She's running for president. And I need to find a way to make the religious-right hard core understand that she's not what she says she is. I used to go to Assembly of God. When I was a kid, I watched them speak in tongues. I don't know what Sarah has taken away from her experiences there, but it's twisted. She's twisted. And you've managed to show that already, without having written a word."

Henning has to leave. He's heading for the Gulf of Mexico to work on cleaning up the BP oil spill. I walk him out to his truck. He unlocks it and takes two guns off the front seat. One is a Glock. I don't recognize the other one.

"Take your choice," Henning says. "Or take them both, if you want."

"No, thanks," I say. "I walk in peace."

"So do I," he says, "but you're living next door to the Palins."

Thursday, June 3, 2010

I'M AWAKENED by an unfamiliar sound. Rain on the roof. First rain in the twelve days I've been here. In other ways, the climate seems to be improving.

A woman I don't know, who got my e-mail address from a friend, writes to say that I am welcome to stay at her house on Knik-Goose Bay Road. "You can see the neighbors' porch lights in the distance at night and hear a bunch of howling dogs, but otherwise it's pretty quiet and my house is down a long driveway so nobody would know you are even here. Got an extra house key ready for you. If anyone asked, I'd just tell them you're my cousin Joe from New Jersey."

It's not the first such invitation I've received, though it is the first from someone I've never met. It's not long before the second arrives.

In preparation for Nancy's arrival, I'm washing the dishes at 11:00 AM when I see a big black truck pull up to the chain and stop. A large man gets out and starts walking toward the house. I cannot tell if he's armed.

I open the front door and step out. "Can I help you?"

He grins. He's got a voice like a bear. "I came to see if I could help you."

His name is Jay Cross and he lives out beyond Big Lake, twenty miles to the west. He's a part-Native lifelong Alaskan, a retired air force mechanic with a wife, grown children, and grandchildren. In 2006 he ran as a centrist independent for state senate against Republican incumbent Charlie Huggins and lost. I invite him in, telling him not to bother taking his shoes off.

"I won't stay long," he says, "and I'm sorry to show up unannounced. But I've been reading about this bullshit you're having with these people next door and it pisses me off. They're not behaving like Alaskans. You know that. You've been here before."

"Thank you. It may start to die down."

"Well, I hope so. Now, I know everybody and his brother has been offering you guns, and I've got a whole bunch I could give you, but what I want to give you this morning are these."

He holds out a set of house keys. Then he unfolds a piece of paper.

"These are the keys," he says. "And this is the map. It's got my address on top. It's a little hard to find, so pay attention. Look, you turn down Big Lake Road and then on your right you're gonna come to Beaver Lake Road. You take a right there and you go down to where you see a sign for Ryans Creek Drive, and you take a right there and you go over the little bridge and start up the hill and—"

"Excuse me, but where am I going?"

"You're going to my house. Anytime you want. Whether I'm there or not. It don't matter. Anytime this bullshit here starts to get on your nerves. Actually, most of the summer I'm not going to be there. My wife's father is pretty sick down in Phoenix, and I'll be going down to help her take care of him, but that don't matter. If I am there, you're not going to bother me. You'll have your own entrance and a whole floor to yourself. You don't even have to call me. That's why I'm giving you the keys. You just head up whenever you want, and it don't matter if I'm there or not."

"These are the keys to your house?"

"That's right."

"But you don't know me."

"Sure I do. We just met."

"But I can't stay in your house."

"You can if you want to. I just gave you the keys."

"This is incredible. I mean, thank you."

"Don't think nothing about it. And by the way, if I'm heading Outside, I'll leave you some guns on the counter. Hell, I've even got an AK-47 you might like."

I stammered.

"It just pisses me off," Cross repeats. "A man comes up here to do a job, and people like them next door make life difficult. It ain't right. It's not the way Alaska ought to be."

Blogger and political commentator Shannyn Moore has an expression she uses when something particularly inexplicable by Outside standards occurs: TIA. "This is Alaska." As Jay Cross climbs back in his truck and turns around, that's all I can say. TIA. And God bless it.

PERHAPS EVEN MORE remarkable is that the new edition of the *Frontiersman* contains an apology, of sorts, from T. C. Mitchell, who wrote the "deadly force" editorial. He writes, "In an effort to find a catchy ending, I was a bit too creative with the last paragraph. If I had it to do over again, I would have left off the last sentence . . . I certainly did not mean to suggest that McGinniss would or should be the victim of violence. For that matter, I didn't mean to suggest that the Palins would do such a thing. All of which points to the power of words. I misused them on Saturday. I'll try to have more respect for that power next time around."

Maybe sanity is regaining a foothold. Through drizzle, I drive to Anchorage in early evening. It's my first time out of the Valley in twelve days.

Nancy arrives at the Anchorage airport at 8:00 PM. In and of itself, that means the worst is over.

SIX

O N THE NIGHT of October 1, 1996, after learning she'd been elected mayor, Sarah thanked the dozens of people who had helped her. The one person she did not thank was Laura Chase, who had been led to believe she'd be appointed deputy administrator. "She never mentioned me," Chase recalls. "Not the night she won and not even in interviews over the next few days."

Four days after the election, Sarah called Chase to say she wanted to meet for coffee. "Who do you think I should appoint as deputy administrator?" she asked.

"You've been telling me all along it would be me," Chase said.

"Oh, I can't do that. It wouldn't look right if I appointed a friend."

And that was that. Chase learned only later that Sarah's real reason for not following through with the promised appointment was that the religious right would not approve of a city official who was pro-choice. She also learned only later that Sarah had already filled the deputy administrator position by choosing John Cramer, an evangelical Christian who'd also worked as an aide to state senator Lyda Green.

On her first day in office, Sarah changed the screen saver on the mayor's official computer to read GOD LOVES YOU SARAH PALIN.

Then—as a local radio station proclaimed, "Wasilla has a Christian mayor!"—she set about firing non-evangelicals or forcing them to resign. The first head to roll, on the morning of her first day in office, was that of John Cooper, the head of Museum and Recreation Services.

"As soon as I was summoned to appear," Cooper recalls, "I warned my museum staff as to what probably was up." Museums were not a priority for Sarah, but getting rid of Cooper was, because her ardent supporter Steve Stoll wanted him gone.

Cooper was suspected of being "progressive." To Sarah and Stoll, this meant he might use museum exhibits to contradict the version of the history of the earth, mankind, and Wasilla preached by ministers at the Assembly of God and other right-wing evangelical churches in the Valley.

As the new deputy administrator Cramer looked on, Sarah told Cooper she wanted his resignation. "I told her I refused to comply until I knew what my rights were." She told him to consult a lawyer. When he did, Cooper was advised that department heads were "at will" employees and served at the pleasure of the mayor. He typed a resignation letter and delivered it to Cramer. As he accepted the letter, Cramer said sheepishly, "I have a family, too." It turned out that the money used for Cramer's salary had come from Sarah abolishing Cooper's position. A few days later, Cooper saw Steve Stoll in a parking lot. Stoll made a pistol-firing motion with his thumb and forefinger and said, "Gotcha!"

In the months that followed, Cooper was unable to find a new job. Wherever he turned he was told that to hire him would be to risk the wrath of Sarah, and no Wasilla employer was willing to do that. Eventually Cooper and his wife moved to Hawaii.

At her first city council meeting as mayor, Sarah attempted to appoint Stoll—who belonged to the John Birch Society as well as to the Alaska Independence Party—to her vacated city council seat and to appoint another political ally to a second open seat. Nick Carney's "no" vote stopped her that night. The city attorney, Richard Deuser, stopped her permanently, pointing out that the mayor had no authority to appoint council members. She wrote Deuser's name in her little red book.

The *Frontiersman* was not amused. "Wasilla found out it has a new mayor with either little understanding or little regard for the city's own laws . . . Sarah Palin failed in a blatant attempt to confuse and circumvent the law Monday night in order to pack the city council with candidates favored by her and her supporters."

At the end of that first council meeting, a friend of Sarah's who had voted for her but who worried that her lack of knowledge—especially in the field of economics—might pose a problem, stepped up to hand her a copy of *The Worldly Philosophers: The Lives, Times and Ideas of the Great Economic Thinkers*, by Robert L. Heilbroner. Sarah would not even look at the cover of the book. The friend tried to hand the book to her, but she would not take it. When he put it on the table in front of her, she pushed it to the edge with the back of her hand, saying, "I never read anything that might conflict with my beliefs."

She didn't want to *hear* anything that conflicted with her beliefs, either. One of her first acts was to institute what the *Frontiersman* called a "gag order," demanding that department heads get her approval before speaking to reporters.

Without council approval, Sarah used city money to lease a new gold Ford Expedition ("The Mayormobile," as it came to be known) and took $50,000 that had been budgeted for road improvement and repair and used it to redecorate her office at city hall. She favored a red wallpaper motif that left the office looking, in the words of Nick Carney, "like a bordello."

Carney, though no longer a political ally, didn't want to see Sarah make needless trouble for herself. He thought she actually might not understand that a mayor cannot appropriate portions of the city budget for her own use without council approval. "I told her it was against the law," he told David Talbot of *Salon* in 2008. "She said, 'I'm the mayor and I can do whatever I want until the courts tell me to stop.'"

Having disposed of John Cooper, Sarah began to operate the city's parks herself. "One of the first things she did," a former city employee told me in the summer of 2010, "was give Assembly of God complete access to any park in the city to sing the Gospel and give out flyers. I received many, many calls from irate mothers who didn't want their young children exposed to this at a city park. And, of course, at Christmas the parks department was instructed to set up a nativity scene in the park, along the Parks Highway coming into town."

Someone who left her city job and moved out of Wasilla told me, "Every day, department heads and secretaries feared for their jobs. If anyone had shown open support for John Stein they were fired immediately, and Sarah brought in her high school friends to fill those positions."

On October 24, on the advice of Todd's father, Jim Palin, Sarah requested letters of resignation from the four department heads who remained in the wake of John Cooper's dismissal. She said it was a test of their loyalty and that she'd decide later which resignations to accept. Police chief Irl Stambaugh refused. His contract with the city, he said, made it clear he could only be fired for cause.

On the afternoon of her first day in office, Sarah had reassured Stambaugh that despite his support of John Stein and their differences on issues such as bar closing hours (which remained at 5:00 AM) and the right to bear arms inside a school, bank, or bar (the bill passed the state legislature but was vetoed by Governor Tony Knowles), she would retain him as chief as long as he agreed to support her. He agreed.

Two days later she told Stambaugh she was dissolving Wasilla's Liquor Task Force, a group formed to combat the epidemic of drunken driving in the city. Her bar-owner supporters, such as Ted Anderson, who owned the Mug-Shot, considered the group a nuisance. Sarah agreed: it was just one more example of a quasi-governmental agency inhibiting the constitutionally guaranteed freedoms of Americans.

But when the *Frontiersman* asked her, on October 23, if she had disbanded the group, she said no. The newspaper then presented her with Stambaugh's description of the meeting six days earlier. "Confronted with these conflicting stories Wednesday afternoon, Palin dropped the denials she had made earlier in the day," the newspaper wrote.

Sarah was furious that Stambaugh had given the press an account of their meeting about the Liquor Task Force that conflicted with her own. In late October she told him that the NRA, which had supported her, did not like him. "They want change," she said, "and I was elected to bring change." She also said she'd heard that he and the city librarian, Mary Ellen Emmons, were "acting sad and unhappy" at a post-election chamber of commerce meeting and that she did not intend to surround herself with unhappy faces, because unhappiness indicated lack of support.

"I knew she'd promised the bar owners she'd get rid of me," Stambaugh told me, "but I was with her at a chamber of commerce breakfast at the Windbreak and she said, 'I've decided not to fire you.' I said thank you. A couple of days later, in the hallway at city hall, she said the same thing." Stambaugh trusted these face-to-face assurances. That would turn out to be a mistake.

Sarah spent November tending to other matters. Having made short work of museum director Cooper, she wanted to get rid of the museum itself.

THE DOWNTOWN building that housed the museum was built in 1931 as a community hall. For more than thirty years it was home to dances, political meetings, and basketball games. After extensive renovation, it became Wasilla's first museum in 1967. In 1989 it was renamed the Dorothy Page Museum in memory of the former Wasilla mayor who helped create the 1,161-mile Iditarod Trail Sled Dog Race from Anchorage to Nome, first run in 1973.

The museum's home page states, "It has preserved and shared a growing collection of treasures with the people of Wasilla and the Matanuska-Susitna Borough. Today, the Museum continues to educate and inspire through exhibitions, programs and lectures, while preserving an expanding collection representing the most comprehensive assemblage of Wasilla artifacts in the region."

To Sarah, this was a bunch of hooey. She'd never been a museum kind of gal. She saw few lessons to be learned from the past. God had created the earth six thousand years earlier and had populated it with mankind and dinosaurs. Mankind had survived, dinosaurs had not. End of story.

She considered the museum a blight on downtown Wasilla, a rebuke to her values, and an affront to her vision of the future, which seemed to be mostly about better shopping. If she couldn't demolish it outright, she could do the next best thing: move it away from the center of town. She proposed just that to the city council in early November. The outcry in response was immediate, long, and loud. Linda Beller, a member of the Wasilla Historical Society, later remembered her reaction as "Oh my God, who is this little punk?"

When she saw she couldn't surmount the opposition, Sarah retreated, reloading only to the extent of announcing that the museum's hours would be drastically curtailed and its staff reduced. Her people wanted roads and sewers and commercial development, she said, not museums.

With Cooper gone and Stambaugh on the ropes, Sarah turned her attention to a third thorn in her side, the city librarian, Mary Ellen Emmons. One of Wasilla's most respected and popular civil servants, Emmons had been librarian since 1989. Sarah's distaste for Emmons dated from her second term on city council, when she learned from fellow Assembly of God members that the library had a copy of a book about gay parents, called *Daddy's Roommate,* illustrated and written by Michael Willhoite.

When the book was published in 1990, *Publishers Weekly* said, "This picture book is an auspicious beginning to the Alyson Wonderland imprint, which focuses on books for and about the children of lesbian and gay parents. [The] text is suitably straightforward, and the format—single lines of copy beneath full-page illustrations—easily accessible to the intended audience (Ages 2–5.) . . . Willhoite's cartoony pictures work well here; the colorful characters with their contemporary wardrobes and familiar surroundings lend the tale a stabilizing air of warmth and familiarity."

Sarah was outraged that the library had a copy and she told Emmons she wanted it removed. Emmons brought a copy to the next council meeting and suggested that Sarah look at it. Averting her eyes and pushing it away, Sarah said, "I don't need to read that kind of stuff."

Wasilla's evangelicals already had an ad hoc censorship mechanism in place: They would scour the library shelves looking for materials they considered objectionable. Then they would check the books out, sometimes returning them with pages torn out and other offensive passages blacked out with Magic Marker, and sometimes not returning them at all.

This informal policing was not good enough for Sarah. Within days of her election, even before assuming office, she told Emmons she expected cooperation in censoring books that some Wasillans found objectionable. Emmons said she opposed censorship in any form and would not remove books because of citizen complaints.

Sarah raised the issue again at the close of a city council meeting on October 28, a few days after she'd requested letters of resignation from all department heads. She said there were books in the library that should not be there. "What would your response be if I asked you to remove some books from the collection?" Sarah asked. Emmons, who in addition to being Wasilla librarian was president of the Alaska Library Association, said she would refuse.

"So you would object to my censorship?"

"Yup," Emmons replied, "and it wouldn't be just me. It would be a constitutional question, and the ACLU would probably get involved."

"But suppose people were circling the library protesting about a book?"

"I will fight anyone who tries to dictate what books can go on the library shelves," Emmons said. "And if people are circling the library in protest, then the ACLU would definitely get involved."

For Sarah, the issue was far from hypothetical. *Daddy's Roommate* had been bad enough, but that was only a picture book for preschoolers. Now a more dangerous threat lurked: *Pastor, I Am Gay* by Howard Bess, pastor of the American Baptist Church of the Covenant in Palmer.

Bess was a leader of the pro-choice movement that had successfully sued to force Valley Medical Center to continue to perform legal abortions. A graduate of Wheaton, the Christian liberal arts college in Illinois, he came to the Valley in the mideighties after his uncompromising support of gay rights wore out his welcome even in Santa Barbara, California.

Bess was a happily married heterosexual and the father of three grown children, one of whom was head of the graduate school of architecture at Notre Dame. He began to focus on the difficulties of gays in Christian churches in the 1970s, after a member of his Santa Barbara congregation came to him and revealed his anguish as a closeted gay man and a Christian. Bess's thinking evolved to the point where, in *Pastor, I Am Gay,* he posited a special position for gays in the Christian hierarchy: "Look back at the life of our Lord Jesus. He was misunderstood, deserted, unjustly accused, and cruelly killed. Yet we all confess that it was the will of God, for by his wounds we are healed . . . Could it be that the homosexual, obedient to the will of God, might be the church's modern day healer-messiah?"

That kind of talk didn't go over well at the Assembly of God or Wasilla Bible Church or, in fact, at any other church in the Valley. Homosexuality was a perversion and gays were evil, seeking to undermine the moral fabric that—along with military might—made America such an exceptional nation.

For seven years Bess wrote a weekly column for the *Frontiersman.* When the book was published, in 1995, they fired him. In addition, they printed a cartoon of a church with a sign in front that said: WASILLA CHURCH OF THE COVENANT, HOWARD BESS, PASTOR. ALL SINNERS WELCOME. BIBLE INTERPRETATIONS TO SUIT YOUR "LIFESTYLE." Standing next to the sign was a grotesquely ugly, drooling man holding a little girl's doll in his hand, saying to himself, "Hmmm . . . They welcome gays—how about pedophiles?" Perhaps embarrassed by it today, the *Frontiersman* was not willing to make a priority of my request for permission to reprint the cartoon.

Waldenbooks, the only full-service bookstore in Wasilla, refused to stock *Pastor, I Am Gay.* One Saturday, Bess rented space in the mall corridor outside their doors and sold more than a hundred copies.

Although Sarah never mentioned by name any of the titles she wanted banned from the Wasilla library, Emmons and many others knew that *Pastor, I Am Gay* was at the top of her hit list. In a mid-December interview with the *Frontiersman,* Emmons said it didn't matter what books Sarah had in mind. "The free exchange of information is my main job and I'll fight anyone who tries to interfere with that," she said.

It would soon become apparent that Sarah wanted to rid herself of Emmons almost as much as she wanted to dispose of Stambaugh.

• • •

SHE STARTED in on Stambaugh again the week before Christmas. She sent him a memo saying his officers were not friendly enough while on patrol. "Most businesses would enjoy having them stop in, visit with patrons, drink a cup of coffee, eat a meal, in general spread some sense of belonging and real down-home community," she wrote. The fact that she put this in writing suggested that, despite what she told him to his face, she was laying the groundwork for his dismissal.

She sent another note to all department heads on December 26. "What a wonderful time of year! As we enter 1997, let's take this opportunity to start the new year off on a positive note." Henceforth, she wrote, she expected weekly reports from each department head, with "at least two positive examples of work that was started, how we helped the public, how we saved the City money, how we helped the state, how we helped Uncle Sam, how we made operations run smoother, or safer, or more efficient. Please use numbers when appropriate."

She made it clear she wanted only good news. "I believe if we look for the positive, that is what we will ultimately find," she wrote. "Wasilla has tremendous assets and opportunities and we can all choose to be a part of contributing to the improvement of our community . . . or not. I encourage you to choose the prior because the train is a'moving forward!"

Stambaugh tried to comply with Sarah's demand for "good news" bulletins. His first weekly report, delivered in January, said that his officers had "assisted 14 individuals by giving them rides or helping them with their vehicles during the cold spell we experienced," and that "Officer Sonerholm was able to return to full duty—even though he is still having some problems with his knee."

This was apparently not cheery enough. Stambaugh was at his desk on the afternoon of January 30, 1997, when John Cramer handed him an envelope. Inside was Palin's notification that he was fired, effective in two weeks.

Cramer dropped a similar letter on the desk of librarian Emmons.

She was shocked. Both she and Stambaugh had supported Stein's re-election bid, but, as she told the *Frontiersman,* "After the initial roller coaster, we were ready to work for Mayor Palin. I think we were both fired for politics."

At first Sarah denied that politics had any part in the firings, but declined to go into detail. "I'm going to get myself in trouble if I keep talking about it," she said to the *Frontiersman.* Then she denied that she'd even fired them. "There's been no meeting, no actual terminations," she said.

Stambaugh pointed out that his letter said, "Although I appreciate your service as police chief, I've decided it's time for a change. I do not feel I have your full support in my efforts to govern the city of Wasilla. Therefore I intend to terminate your employment. . . ."

"If that's not a letter of termination, I don't know what is," Stambaugh said.

After meeting with Stambaugh and Emmons the next day, Sarah announced that she'd changed her mind about Emmons, saying that the librarian supported Sarah's intention to merge the library and museums into a single operation. She didn't mention the issue of banning books. As for Stambaugh, Sarah said only, "You know in your heart when someone is supportive of you."

Nick Carney had had enough. After receiving calls at home from irate constituents, he said there might be no alternative to a recall petition. "I've been telling people to hold off," he said to the *Frontiersman,* "but now all bets are off."

On February 7, Concerned Citizens for Wasilla, a group headed by Carney, met to discuss a recall motion. About seventy people showed up. The meeting was typical Wasilla. As the *Anchorage Daily News* reported, there were "two hours of sometimes raucous debate, which was occasionally interrupted by an incoherent man in his socks threatening to sue Carr's [supermarket] and the local fire marshal." In the end, the group decided to wait on a recall until after Sarah had

had the chance to respond directly to their concerns. They developed a list of twenty-five questions and asked the mayor to meet with them within two weeks.

She had no intention of doing so. She said her critics were "the same few disgruntled citizens" who had always opposed her, and added, "I don't remember any past mayors having to face a firing squad."

By now the *Frontiersman* was in high dudgeon. "Palin seems to have assumed her election was instead a coronation," one editorial read,

> Welcome to Kingdom Palin, the land of no accountability. . . . Wasilla residents have been subjected to attempts to unlawfully appoint council members, statements that have been shown to be patently untrue, unrepentant backpedaling, and incessant whining that her only enemies are the press and a few disgruntled supporters of Mayor Stein. . . . Palin promised to change the status quo, but at every turn we find hints of cronyism and political maneuvering. We see a woman who has long since surrendered her ideals to a political machine. . . . The mayor's administration has been one of contradiction, controversy and discord. While she will blame everyone but herself, we see mostly Sarah at the center of the problem. . . . [and] we still don't understand how someone can be claiming to keep her campaign promises when she pooh-poohed the complexities of city government, then hired a deputy city administrator to help her.

The deputy administrator, John Cramer, advised the Concerned Citizens that they could fax their questions to city hall. The *Frontiersman* noted that Sarah "doesn't intend to face the hostile group," adding that "Palin continues to lose public faith sticking by her philosophy that either we are with her or against her." An editorial said, "Wasilla is led by a woman who will tolerate no one who questions her actions or her authority."

It also said, "Mayor Palin fails to have a firm grasp of something very simple: the truth."

Recalling those days, a former city employee told me in 2010, "Sarah Palin ruined the lives of many dedicated, hardworking people who loved the city of Wasilla. There were . . . houses lost and families separated as wage earners had to leave Wasilla to make a living. She had no sympathy for those families; there was no Christian charity on her part."

IN JANUARY 2011 I spoke to someone who offered a different perspective on Sarah's early days as mayor. Soon after her election, Sarah approached a woman named Catherine Mormile in Carrs supermarket. Mormile was a forty-three-year-old physical therapist who lived about fifteen miles west of Wasilla, beyond Settlers Bay on Knik-Goose Bay Road.

In 1991, Mormile had finished fifty-eighth in the Iditarod, Alaska's most famous sporting event. Competing again three years later, she almost died from carbon monoxide poisoning when she and three other mushers were stricken by exposure to toxic fumes from a propane heater installed inside an airtight tent used as a rest stop along the trail. Mormile suffered significant brain damage, from which she was still recovering in 1996. She'd angered members of Alaska's close-knit dog-mushing community by filing suit against the Iditarod in 1995. As her suit proceeded through the legal system, Mormile found herself shunned and reviled in Wasilla. It was during this darkest period of her life that she met Sarah.

"I felt this little hand on my shoulder," Mormile told me, "and I turned around and there was a woman smiling at me. 'You don't know me,' she said, 'but you're my hero. You're the strongest, bravest person I know. Your courage is an inspiration to me. I wish I could be like you.' Then she walked away and said, kind of over her shoulder, 'By the way, I'm Sarah Palin.'

"I was hooked. I went home and told my husband, 'I've just met the most wonderful woman: Sarah Palin, the new mayor.'"

Sarah approached Mormile several more times over the next few months. "She'd say, 'Remember me? I'm Sarah. Is there anything I can do for you? I want to help. Just know that I'm here for you, whatever you need. You're my hero and my role model. I wish I could do what you've done.'"

Mormile was a Republican, like Sarah. The two women began to attend meetings of the Mat-Su Women's Republican Club together. Almost everywhere else in Wasilla, Mormile remained an outcast, so Sarah's support was something she cherished and felt strengthened by at the time.

Later, in retrospect, she would view it in a very different light.

SEVEN

NANCY CAME to Alaska with me in the winter of 1975—when Sarah Palin was twelve years old—and became an award-winning reporter for the *Anchorage Daily News* while I researched *Going to Extremes* throughout the following year.

On her twenty-ninth birthday, September 8, 1976, we awakened in our tent near Wonder Lake, in Denali National Park, to find our drinking water frozen and our butane cooking stove needing to warm in the sun before it would ignite.

A couple of hours later, hiking in open country on a bright, clear day, and having walked past several piles of still-steaming, berry-rich bear skat, Nancy saw what looked like a boulder rolling downhill in our direction.

I looked through my pocket monocular, a lighter, more compact alternative to binoculars.

"Looks pretty hairy for a boulder," I said.

"Let me see," Nancy said.

It was still coming downhill, toward us.

"It's not a boulder," she said, "it's a bear."

"What color?"

"It's not black."

"Oh, fuck."

"And it's not rolling, it's running."

"Oh, fuck!"

There was nowhere to hide. There were no trees to climb. And neither of us had a weapon.

A few years earlier, in Vietnam, where she'd been taking pictures to illustrate the columns I was writing for a national newspaper syndicate, Nancy and I had come under mortar and rocket fire. But this was peacetime, it was her birthday, and there wasn't even a bunker to dive into.

The month before, while on a two-week hike through the Brooks Range, also undertaken without firearms, I'd seen twelve grizzlies, including—in a surprise encounter at alarmingly close range (about twenty yards)—a mother and two cubs. I'd also slept through a grizzly sniffing my tent, which I discovered the next morning when I saw its paw prints.

Seasoned by these experiences, I took command of the situation. "Back downhill slowly," I said in my most authoritative voice, "but do not break eye contact with the bear."

"What did you say?" Nancy asked. "I couldn't hear you over your shoulder because you were running."

Oh. I was apparently not as seasoned as I thought.

"It doesn't matter," I said. "It's not up to us, it's up to him."

"Or her."

Having closed the distance from perhaps two hundred to less than fifty yards from us, the bear slowed, stood to sniff the air, then veered ninety degrees to its left.

Once again, I came face-to-face with the fact that in the Alaskan wilderness it's the bear, not the man, who makes the choice.

Now Nancy is back, almost thirty-four years later, with me living next door to a self-proclaimed mama grizzly.

"Whatever you do," I say, "don't come between her and her cubs."

"Please. Just for tonight, let's not talk about Sarah Palin."

Later, she asks, "Do the grebes ever shut up?"

"Only in the presence of true love."

It was the quietest night since my arrival.

OVER THE NEXT few days, Nancy and I make social calls on a bipartisan group of Valley luminaries. We have coffee with Lyda Green and her husband. Green, a conservative Republican from Wasilla, was president of the Alaska state senate when she chose not to run for re-election in 2008. A major factor in her decision was knowing how far Sarah would go to see her unseated.

Ideologically, Sarah and Lyda were Siamese twins: it was Green who'd introduced the bill that would have permitted the carrying of concealed weapons in banks, bars, and schools that Sarah championed in 1996. But ten years later Green declined to endorse Sarah in the Republican gubernatorial primary against incumbent governor Frank Murkowski. She knew Sarah would never forgive her for that.

Sarah revealed the depth of her continued antipathy toward Green in a radio interview with Anchorage broadcasters Bob Lester and Mark Colavecchio in January 2008. As governor, Sarah called in to their show.

Speaking of Green, Lester said, "Governor, you can't say this, but we can. She is a cancer." Alaskans were well aware that Green was a cancer survivor, having undergone a radical mastectomy ten years earlier. Three minutes later, Lester, a particularly noxious specimen of the shock-jock species, said it again: "I'm going to say what I wish you could say: Lyda Green is a bitch, and she needs to go away because she is a cancer on the progress of the state of Alaska."

Sarah laughed delightedly at the comment. She laughed equally loudly on two other occasions when Lester insulted Green. As Green related to the *New Yorker* after John McCain chose Sarah as his running mate, "Sarah can be heard in the background tittering, hee-hee-ing, never saying, 'That's not appropriate, let's not talk like that, let's change the subject.' Sarah certainly knew I had breast cancer, because she sent me flowers when I was ill."

A friend of Green's tells me that not long after the radio program, Chuck Heath approached her at the Fred Meyer store in Wasilla. He said, "Why don't you resign now, you fat old cow?"

Green leaves no doubt about her feelings: "Sarah becoming governor was an insult to educated women," she says. "Sarah was a know-nothing idiot who hadn't paid her dues. I think she's utterly without morals, as well as being paranoid and narcissistic."

NANCY AND I have tea with Katie Hurley at her home on Wasilla Lake. At eighty-nine, Katie is as focused and vigorous as she was more than fifty years ago, when she served as secretary to territorial governor Ernest Gruening and chief clerk to the Alaska Constitutional Convention. She later served in the Alaska legislature, as president of the state board of education, and as chairwoman of the Alaska State Commission for Human Rights.

She has a life-size cardboard cutout of Barack Obama in her living room. You look at pictures on the wall that show her as a young woman and it's easy to see why John F. Kennedy, visiting Alaska as a U.S. senator in 1959, made a pass at her. She laughs out loud at the thought of Sarah in national office.

We have dinner at the Palmer home of recently retired superior court judge Beverly Cutler and her husband, a former state trooper who now farms potatoes. She's the daughter of the late Lloyd Cutler, the Washington, D.C., attorney who served as White House counsel to both presidents Carter and Clinton and who also chaired a commission for Ronald Reagan. As a judge last year, she granted Levi's mother, Sherry Johnston, the right to a public defender. In her on-the-record comments about Sarah, Beverly exercises judicial restraint, but it's not hard to sense the feelings that she is too prudent to express.

JOHN WOODEN has died and Sarah commemorates the passing of the former UCLA basketball coach on Twitter: "You shall be missed dearly, and we shall remember your lessons."

This brings to mind Sarah's paean to Wooden's wisdom as recounted in *Going Rogue.* "Ever since we were kids, Todd and I have looked at Coach John Wooden as a true hero. His quotes plastered our bulletin boards, school notebooks, and locker doors." She gives an example: "Our land is everything to us . . . I will tell you one of the things we remember on our land. We remember our grandfathers paid for it—with their lives."

It's not clear where Sarah had that particular quote "plastered," but it is clear that John Wooden never uttered those words. They come from a 1960 essay entitled "Back on the War Ponies," written by Native American activist John Wooden Legs and reprinted in 2003 in *We Are the People: Voices from the Other Side of American History.* This can happen when your ghostwriter gets careless while Googling inspirational quotes.

NANCY AND I have dinner at the home of J.C. and Brenda McCavit on Wasilla Lake. J.C. was the Palins' high school classmate. He's now an oil services executive, a world-class water skier, and one of the finest amateur chefs in Alaska, but back in the day he was best known for throwing parties at his bachelor pad on Melanie Avenue in Wasilla.

"Dan Fleckenstein and I rented the apartment," he says. "We shared it with all our friends. We were like the first guys to have their own apartment. We had lots of parties. Todd visited frequently and even Sarah once or twice during the holidays."

After dinner he takes out an old photo album and starts to flip through it: standard-issue stuff of guys in their early twenties acting silly, often with alcohol involved. What you might see on MySpace or Facebook today.

He turns to a new page. I get a quick glimpse of unclothed bodies. "Oops!" he says. "I didn't think these were still in there. Sorry, there are a few I can't let you see."

"Which ones are those, Dad?" asks J.C. and Brenda's son, Chase, who is eighteen and has just graduated from high school.

"Never mind," J.C. says, clearly embarrassed. "Why don't we talk about something else?"

So we talk about how J.C. gradually grew disaffected with Todd and Sarah. He didn't like her Assembly of God–driven, right-wing political agenda, and he didn't like who she was becoming personally as she grew more consumed by ambition. He also lost respect for Todd for selling out his own values in the service of Sarah's career. "I was surprised he wanted to be a player in politics," J.C. says, "but I guess that power trip can be seductive."

An open rupture occurred in 2007 when Sarah fired her legislative director, John Bitney, another close friend of J.C.'s from the Wasilla High class of '82.

Bitney had separated from his wife and was dating Debbie Richter, the estranged wife of Scott Richter, a building contractor who was Todd's best friend at the time. Richter had built a cabin for the Palins on twenty acres of land they owned on Safari Lake, about twenty-five miles northwest of Talkeetna and accessible only by floatplane or snow machine. The structure was so inordinately lavish for its rustic surroundings that it was commonly referred to as the Todd Mahal.

John Bitney served as de facto manager of Sarah's gubernatorial campaign; Debbie Richter was treasurer. After Sarah won, Debbie became head of the Permanent Fund Dividend Division at the State Department of Revenue, which each year sends a check for thousands of dollars to every man, woman, and child in Alaska as a reward simply for living in the state. Sarah named Bitney her legislative director.

But postelection, Scott Richter complained to Todd about Bitney's ongoing relationship with his soon-to-be ex-wife. "By now Todd was the king," J.C. tells me, "so he had to do something." He promised Richter that he'd have Sarah fire Bitney. And she did, in the most graceless and humiliating way possible, waiting until he was out of the office, then turning off his state BlackBerry and shutting down his state e-mail account, leaving him unable to communicate with the governor's office. Neither Todd nor Sarah ever spoke directly to Bitney about his dismissal.

The Palins didn't stop there. When Speaker of the House John Harris hired Bitney for his staff, both Todd and Sarah pressured him to rescind the appointment. Harris stood firm, Bitney married Debbie, life went on. The lasting casualty was J.C.'s friendship with Todd.

In *Going Rogue,* Sarah shows how vicious she could be toward a lifelong friend with whom she'd fallen out. She writes that as she and her staff prepared her first budget for presentation to the legislature, Bitney "would wander in and out, plop down in the chair at the end of the table, nibble cookies, and absently thumb his BlackBerry." She accused him of playing video games when he should have been working.

Later in the book, she describes Bitney "slouching against the wall," and writes, "The fact that his shirt was buttoned one button off and his shirttail was poking through his open fly didn't exactly inspire confidence."

And then one more twist of the knife: "Later we learned the legislative director had been too busy with his personal affairs to attend to much state business."

"The way they treated Bitney was obscene," J.C. says. "And Todd was behind it; he was the moving force. He wanted to punish Bitney for having an affair with Debbie Richter. Not because Todd doesn't approve of affairs—let's not even get into his private life—but because

Bitney had the gall to have an affair with the wife of one of Todd's buddies. It was purely personal, it was vindictive, and it was a betrayal of a thirty-year friendship. I have no use for either Todd or Sarah anymore and, unlike a lot of people you're going to run into, I'm not afraid to say that on the record. I don't know how anyone can walk around Wasilla afraid to say what they think of Todd and Sarah. Life's too short to live it in fear of schoolyard bullies like them."

J.C. invites us back for a boat ride around the lake.

THE MORNING AFTER dinner at the McCavits', I read that a Wasilla soldier, Jeremy Morlock, has been charged with murder in the deaths of three Afghan civilians. This must come as a terrible shock to my neighbors. Jeremy and Track were hockey-playing friends throughout high school, and Palin ties to the Morlock family go back years.

Acquaintances I've made in Wasilla explain the connections. Jeremy's mother, Audrey, played high school basketball with Sarah. Even before that, in Dillingham, Todd was close to Audrey's twin sister, April. A generation later, not only did Track and Jeremy play hockey together, but Jeremy's sister, also named April, became—and remains—one of Bristol's best friends, even joining her in Los Angeles when Bristol competed on *Dancing with the Stars*. In addition, Jeremy's older brother, Alex, was coached by former Palin in-law Mike Wooten when he played Pop Warner football in Wasilla.

Jeremy first got in trouble with the law at age fifteen, when he was charged with "leaving the scene of an accident involving an injury or death." He received a deferred prosecution. He was known in high school for his violent temper. A former hockey coach recounted one incident to the *Anchorage Daily News*. "Booted off the ice for bad behavior . . . Morlock went into a locker room and assaulted a younger player. Morlock punched, squeezed the player's jugular and slammed the younger boy's body against the wall, narrowly missing a coat hook," the newspaper reported. Morlock's assault on the younger boy was so violent that Wasilla police were called to the scene.

Morlock graduated from high school in 2006 and enlisted in the army soon afterward. While in the army, he got married. In 2008, when he was twenty, his wife sought a domestic violence protective order against him. The *Anchorage Daily News* reported that he "was charged . . . with fourth-degree assault for allegedly throwing a beer glass at his wife and pressing a lighted cigarette against her chest." A year later he was again charged with assault.

During the winter of 2010, Audrey Morlock moved out of her home on Joes Drive in Meadow Lakes, just west of Wasilla. Fifteen-year-old Willow Palin and two dozen friends got together at the vacant house for a vodka-fueled party that degenerated into vandalism that caused at least $20,000 worth of damage. The incident was reported by the *National Enquirer.* In the end, only the boys involved were charged with vandalism. The girls were cited as witnesses. Many in Wasilla believe that it was only Sarah's intervention that spared Willow from criminal charges.

The vandalism seems inconsequential compared with Jeremy Morlock's alleged crimes. The army charged him with murdering the three civilians earlier this year. He is one of a group of five soldiers accused of killing civilians for sport and keeping body parts as souvenirs. He was brought back from Afghanistan in custody on June 3 and is currently confined at an army base in Washington State, awaiting court-martial.

Bristol's friend April, Jeremy's sister, is quick to spring to his defense, writing on Facebook: "Please please everyone pray for my brothers release . . . Love you Jeremy Morlock I am so proud of you no matter how much shit ppl want to talk . . . You were doing your fucked up job that our country tells you . . ."

In March 2011, Morlock pleaded guilty to charges that he'd murdered three Afghan civilians. In return for his agreement to testify against other soldiers in future legal proceedings, he was sentenced to only twenty-four years in prison. He'll be eligible for parole in 2018.

Obviously, military service doesn't always solve the problems of a troubled teenager. But it seems to have helped Sarah's son Track, whose behavior during his high school years paralleled in many ways that of his friend Jeremy Morlock.

Like Morlock, Track was known for his violent temper, often displayed during hockey games. Palin friend Curt Menard told the *New York Times* in 2008 that if you wanted to watch Track play you had to be present at the start of the game. "Track has a temper," Menard said. "Get there late and he'd already be out."

The degree to which "hockey mom" Sarah involved herself in Track's playing career is a matter of debate. The *New York Times* reported in 2008 that she "would drive to rinks at all hours, children in tow. She sometimes ran the scoreboard, let hockey players from other cities sleep on the floor of her home and got involved in the management of her eldest son's teams."

I don't find anyone in Wasilla who confirms this. Instead, I'm told that Track's biggest problem with regard to hockey was getting to the rink. "Track was always finding his own way," a team parent tells me. Others recall that it was not Sarah, but state trooper Mike Wooten, when he was married to Sarah's sister Molly, who would most often drop off and pick up Track. "I almost never saw Sarah at a game," another parent says. When Sarah did attend, spectators recall that she cheered loudest not for goals, but on those occasions when Track knocked an opposing player down and hit him repeatedly with his stick.

His temper was a problem off the ice, too. "He's always been out of control," an old family friend tells me. "He ran over Sarah. He'd shout, 'Fuck you, don't tell me what to do!' and she'd be like, 'Okay.' Then she'd run to Todd and say, 'He's your son: do something!' Todd and Track never had a relationship. Zero. I remember being at their house when Track was sixteen. Whatever it was that had happened, Todd said, 'No, you're not going out. You're grounded. Go to your room.' And Track said, 'Fuck you,' and walked out the door."

Like Jeremy, Track apparently had problems with alcohol and drugs during his high school years. "At least monthly," a parent of one of Track's classmates tells me, "Todd and Sarah would be called to the school because of disciplinary problems with Track." The *National Enquirer* reported in 2008 that in high school Track was addicted to Oxycontin, quoting a friend of his as saying, "I've partied with him for years. I've seen him snort cocaine, snort and smoke Oxycontin, drink booze and smoke weed."

In late November 2005, four Valley teenagers were arrested by state police and charged with vandalizing forty-four school buses: cutting brake lines, deflating tires, breaking mirrors, and unplugging the buses from their engine block heaters to prevent them from starting in cold weather. Because one of the vandals was only sixteen, troopers did not release his name, but word spread immediately in Wasilla that the sixteen-year-old, who was also charged with stealing a bottle of vodka from a liquor store, was Track Palin. An Anchorage radio station and an Anchorage television station identified Track by name in 2008, even before the *National Enquirer* published a story that claimed he was one of the vandals. On September 10, 2008, however, the New York *Daily News* quoted one of those charged, Deryck Harris, as saying that Track did not participate.

Whether or not Track was involved in the school bus vandalism, his problems were apparently so serious that in November of 2006, his senior year at Wasilla High, Sarah and Todd withdrew him from school and sent him to live with friends in Portage, Michigan. He returned to Wasilla in the spring of 2007, but did not graduate from high school. He enlisted in the army on September 11, 2007.

"Track was in pretty big trouble," a friend of his tells me. "The school bus thing, theft issues, drugs, multiple stuff. Sarah was governor by then, and Track posed too much risk in terms of PR. So she and Todd sat him down and told him he was going to enlist. They said, 'You're gonna do this. You're gonna do this because you owe us. This is gonna look good for us and you're gonna do it.'"

Sarah made it look even better by arranging the enlistment for September 11, the seventh anniversary of the terrorist attacks on the World Trade Center and Pentagon. On September 11, 2008, Track was deployed to Iraq, allowing Sarah to proclaim forever after that she was the proud mother of a combat vet. Some might see this as a classic example of taking the lemon that life gives you and using it to make lemonade.

I talk to the state trooper who drove Sarah and Track to the enlistment office in Anchorage on September 11, 2007. "There was quite a bit of emotion in the back seat of that car," he tells me, "but patriotism was not one of the emotions."

There is no evidence that Track actually saw combat during his year-long deployment to Iraq, but his presence in a war zone made him a political asset to his mother. Unlike his friend Jeremy Morlock, Track completed his military service without incident.

His army outprocessing order, issued on January 6, 2010, said, "You are released from active duty not by reason of physical disability." But reports of Track's drug use persisted even into the summer of 2010.

A family friend says Track, like the other Palin children, has suffered from being made to perform as a member of Sarah's entourage. "Sarah's always used those kids as part of this fake image, this illusion she tries to keep up about actually being a decent mother," the friend tells me. "Those kids never had any parenting, they had to raise each other. And look how it's turned out."

How the Palin children are turning out would be of interest only to the Palin family, except for Sarah's decision to make them an integral part of her public persona. Sarah wraps herself in her children as ostentatiously as she wraps herself in the arms of Jesus and in the

American flag. She uses them shamelessly, from Track in his uniform to Trig in his diapers. But it's all just part of the show.

DILLINGHAM, WHERE Todd grew up, is more than three hundred miles from Anchorage, has a year-round population of scarcely three thousand, and can be reached only by air or sea. As in so many small, isolated Alaskan towns, drug use and alcohol abuse are epidemic, and when an attractive white woman moves in, she is noticed.

I talked to an attractive white woman who lived in Dillingham in the mid-1990s and who found herself an auxiliary member of "the crew": a group of young Native men that included Todd's younger brother, J.D. Because he returned to Dillingham each summer to direct his family's commercial fishing operation, Todd remained an active member of "the crew." It did not take long for the attractive white woman to catch his eye.

"Todd hit on me," she told me in the summer of 2010.

"During summer, the fishing season, Todd was out there, and they'd all flirt with me. I'd probably flirt back. I remember coming out of a restaurant one day and Todd was in his old Ford truck with a boat hooked up to the back, and he was like, 'Come here.' I had on these overalls with a bikini top, and he said, 'I hear lots about you.' Then he said, 'Turn around,' and I said, 'What?' and he said, 'I hear you got a great heart-shaped ass' and 'Aren't you just adorable?' Todd was hot back in the day, and I remember thinking, 'Hmmm.' Then I found out he was married. I was like, 'Well, I don't roll that way.'

"J.D. had one of those big Native steams behind his house and he always invited the white girls. A bunch of us would go over. One day Todd made a comment about my nipples being pink. I said, 'You've never seen me naked,' and he said, 'Well, maybe there's a peephole.' Todd and his friends had been peepin' on us for months. And he wasn't some horny teenager; he was a grown and married man."

• • •

IT'S TIME for Nancy to leave. She's had a pleasant stay on Lake Lucille. She reconnected with old friends from the 1970s and connected with many of the new ones I've made since I first returned in November 2008. We visit Tom Kluberton and his companion, Hobbs, at Fireweed Station in Talkeetna, and have dinner at the home of Dewey and Gini King-Taylor. Dewey's truck has not been vandalized again.

We have coffee with Verne Rupright in his mayor's office. Catherine Taylor stops by to visit. One night the McCavits, and Shannyn Moore and her partner, Kelly Walters; and Jeanne Devon, who writes The Mudflats, a blog about Alaskan politics, and her husband, Ron, come for dinner.

The lunacy that erupted when I moved in has diminished to the level of nuisance. Some meathead puts up a fake Twitter page with my name on it. My lawyer acts promptly to have it removed. A *Los Angeles Times* blogger repeats the canard that "From his deck, McGinniss . . . can peer into the bedroom of Palin's 9-year-old daughter, Piper." After how many lazy repetitions does a false statement cease to be false? On this one point I agree with Sarah: you can't trust what you read in the mainstream media.

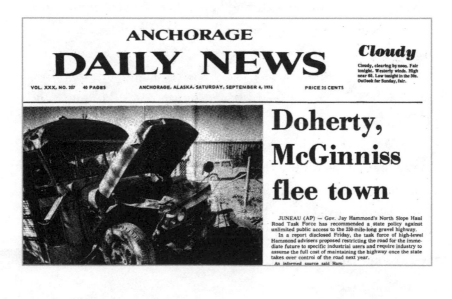

Nancy has joined me in not peering over the fence.

After a farewell dinner with Tom and Marnie Brennan, Nancy flies out of Anchorage airport on the evening of Saturday, June 12. Her departure is lower key than the one we made jointly in September of 1976.

EIGHT

S ARAH LEARNED a lesson from her near recall so soon after her
election as mayor in 1996: there were limits to the power even of
one who believed herself to be on a mission from God. She could get
away with firing a popular police chief, but firing the librarian had
been a step too far. She could clear the way for more big-box stores to
move into Wasilla, but she could not move the museum, which had
been deemed a National Historic Landmark. She could keep the bars
open until 5:00 AM, but she couldn't keep books she disliked out of
the library.

On March 27, 1997, Sarah hired a new chief of police: Duwayne
"Charlie" Fannon, who had been chief in the southeast Alaska town
of Haines for the past eleven years. Before that, Fannon worked for
the sheriff's department in Canyon County, Idaho. He said that as far
as he was concerned, the 5:00 AM closing hour for bars was sacrosanct.
In Haines, the bars closed at 5:00 AM and opened again three hours
later. "I have a philosophy that every time there's a new law or new
ordinance we lose a little more of our freedom," he told the city council. "I don't think the answer to crime is restricting people's freedom
more and more." He was confirmed by a 5–0 vote, with Nick Carney
abstaining.

Spring arrived. As daylight increases and the cold and snow diminish, people throughout Alaska tend to mellow. Although Sarah maintained her stranglehold on city hall, passions faded, and the move to recall her died a quiet death. In June the forced resignations of city planner Duane Dvorak and public works director Jack Felton caused little stir.

Also in June, Sarah gave a commencement talk to a group of homeschooled children at the Assembly of God. Although her own children attended Wasilla public schools, she strongly supported both homeschooling and Christian private schools in which students were taught that the creationist theory about the origins of mankind was God-given truth. The Mat-Su College Community Band played music at the event. Afterward, the band's leader, Phil Munger, spoke to Sarah. Munger, who would later become known for his Progressive Alaska blog, had come to Alaska in 1973 and taught music at the University of Alaska Anchorage. Through his wife's friendship with John Stein's wife, Munger was aware that Sarah's religious views were unorthodox. He asked her about them.

She said she was a "young earth creationist," convinced that the earth was no more than six thousand years old and that humans and dinosaurs had once walked it together. She knew this was true, she said, because she'd once seen pictures that showed human footprints inside dinosaur tracks.

Sarah also told Munger that civilization had reached the "end-times" and that Jesus would return to earth "during my lifetime." She said the signs of his imminent return were obvious. "Maybe you can't see that," she said, "but I can, and it guides me every day."

She celebrated Fourth of July 1997 by signing an administrative order that allowed the open carrying of weapons in the library. Cynics said this was an attempt to put Mary Ellen Emmons in the crosshairs, so to speak, but Sarah noted that the order also permitted guns to be carried or worn in city hall.

There was a slight kerfuffle in August when Sarah told the three women who had been left to run Wasilla's museum after the termination of John Cooper that one of them would have to go and that it would be up to them to decide which one. In response, all three, ages seventy-seven, seventy-four, and sixty-five, quit their jobs. They'd worked at the museum for fifteen years, but decided to resign together in protest against "a city that doesn't want to preserve its history," as they put it in a letter to Sarah.

"We hate to leave," one of them said. "We've been together a long time. But this is enough. If the city were broke, it would be different. If they were even close to being broke." Far from it, Wasilla's cash reserves had grown to more than $4 million. Even so, Sarah had found it necessary to force a senior citizen making $32,000 a year from a long-held job. The women's joint resignation left the museum with no staff, a circumstance that Sarah was in no hurry to change.

In September she ridded herself of city attorney Richard Deuser, replacing him with a friend who also was serving as general counsel to the state Republican Party. "Professionals were either forced out or fired," Deuser said. By midwinter she had replaced all but one of the department heads who had helped to administer the city under Stein, hiring in their places either high school friends or evangelical Christians, none of whom had any experience in public administration.

The one man who stayed on, budget director Erling Nelson, told acquaintances he did so despite, not because of, Sarah, and only because he cared about the city's well-being.

Emmons lasted until 1999, when Sarah's relentless cutting of the library budget finally forced her to take a job in Fairbanks. Even in 2010 she remained so scarred by Sarah's treatment of her that she could not bring herself to discuss it.

Sarah might not have been able to inspire people, but she never had trouble inspiring fear.

. . .

AS FOR her own job, she was known for coming in late and leaving early. "It's not rocket science," she once said about being mayor. The job was particularly untaxing for her because, unlike her predecessors, she had someone, John Cramer, to do the day-to-day work of running the city.

"She didn't really give a shit about her job," says someone who knew her well at the time. "I remember she'd say, 'I have to go to a fuckin' meeting tonight.' And she'd be like, 'I got on my biggest push-up bra. I'm gonna get what I want tonight.' Like she had some motion before the city council and she was gonna use her titties to get their votes."

It was not as if Sarah found it hard to make time for city business because she was immersed in her duties as housewife and mother. Her distaste for domestic chores was well known within her circle. One friend from the time recalls visiting the Palin home only to have Todd ask her to vacuum and clean the toilets and then go out and buy groceries.

Another frequent visitor recalls, "Sarah would just be a bitch. She'd literally come home, scream at everyone, yell at Todd for a while until he'd walk away, and then she'd go to bed. She'd go to bed. Literally. I can remember times she'd come in the door at four o'clock and go to bed. Todd would sleep on the couch. He always slept on the couch; it was an old cream-colored leather thing. Oh, it was filthy from the kids—so nasty—but that's where he slept. Just like Levi told that magazine *Vanity Fair*. Everything that boy said in that story was true."

A friend of Todd's says, "Sarah would get up early and she'd go work out and then she'd come home with her drive-thru mocha. The children would have no breakfast, they'd live off of whatever, and she'd spend an hour getting fourteen pounds of makeup on. She liked that brand called MAC. We'd say, 'She's got her MAC Force Field on, look out!'"

Catherine Mormile, the physical therapist and dog musher whom

Sarah befriended in 1996, called Sarah several times during her first term as mayor, hoping to arrange a hiking date or other type of get-together. But the Sarah at the other end of the phone sounded very different from the woman who'd reached out to her at Carrs.

"There was always screaming and hollering in the background, like I'd just interrupted a terrible fight. When she'd come to the phone, it was hard to talk to her because she'd be yelling at her kids. 'Shut the fuck up! I'm on the phone!' and 'You little fuckers! Shut up!'"

A Palin family friend and occasional houseguest tells me that Mormile's phone calls, more likely than not, did interrupt a fight. "First thing in the morning, Todd and Sarah are screaming at each other, 'Fuck you. I want a fuckin' divorce!' 'Fuck you. I'm gettin' divorce papers!' I probably have heard that five hundred times. It was a daily conversation. Every morning. No 'Hey, baby, here's a cup of coffee.' Always doors slamming. And in front of the kids. 'Fuck you. I'm divorcin'!' 'I'm gonna divorce you. I don't have to take your shit!' Always, always, it was always like that.

"Todd and Sarah have never been happy. It didn't matter which lake they were living on. That home? It was an unhappy place."

Acquaintances were struck by Sarah's frequent and extreme mood swings. "You never knew what Sarah you were going to meet," one told me in 2010. "You never knew if it was going to be happy Sarah. It could even be super, super manic-happy Sarah, like if it was a day that she hadn't eaten in two days and her boobs were sticking out good and her pants were good and tight and she was feeling good and slim and her hair was good. Or you could go all the way to the level of, walk in, look at you, and walk into a room and slam the door. You never knew who you were gonna meet. You never knew. She was a different person every ten minutes."

In public, however, Sarah continued to appear cheerful and energetic. She could be charming in superficial social situations. She had the knack of making people feel they knew her, even if all they ever glimpsed was the façade. This was no small talent. "She was a rock star, no doubt about it," John Stein said.

Having slain all the obvious dragons, Sarah was free to enjoy the fruits of victory, not the least of which was a city council—now minus Nick Carney, who had retired—that gave her unanimous support. With her close friend Judy Patrick producing ideas for which Sarah could take credit, and with John Cramer doing all the scut work that had previously been the mayor's responsibility, Sarah's duties were largely ceremonial. One highlight was performing a wedding at Wal-Mart for two store employees. "It was so sweet," Sarah said in a newspaper interview afterward. "It was so Wasilla."

Sarah almost literally paved the way for the Fred Meyer department store on the shore of Wasilla Lake. Despite concerns from the state's Department of Fish and Game that runoff from the twenty-two-acre site would pollute the lake, Sarah hailed the arrival of Wasilla's newest box store as an unmistakable sign of the city's progress. "I live on this lake and I would not support a development that wasn't environmentally friendly," she said. Shortly afterward, she moved to Lake Lucille.

By the end of her first term she was riding so high that the only candidate willing to challenge her was Stein, and he did so with great reluctance, and with no illusions about what the outcome would be.

Whatever your view of Sarah, you have to give her credit for what she learned on the job during her first term, not about issues—she was still not going to read *The Worldly Philosophers* instead of *People* or *Runner's World*—but about the one skill most invaluable to an upwardly mobile politician: public relations. To go from the brink of a recall petition to being an odds-on favorite for reelection was no small feat. Sarah managed it primarily by curbing her tendency to lash out and pick needless fights. She also benefited from Wasilla's robust financial health—a condition attributable chiefly to the 2 percent sales tax John Stein had put in place.

"Stay the course" was her reelection slogan. "We've continued to take care of the needs," she said. "Roads, water, and sewer are the foundation upon which Wasilla will continue to grow."

The 1999 mayoral race was part of a "broader struggle," the *Anchorage Daily News* reported. "That struggle—part politics, part ideology, and part personality—has to do with competing visions for the Valley. One side advocates minimal government and holds the more conservative view on social issues, while the other pushes for more planning and land-use regulation and believes that social issues like abortion and gun rights are irrelevant to local elections. Stein and Palin have represented opposing sides in this political schism."

During her reelection campaign, Sarah no longer hid either the intensity of her religious convictions or her close ties to the Valley's right-wing evangelicals. Internally, she'd purged city hall of those who she felt were insufficiently Christian and had begun to use her office time to lead staff prayer meetings. A former director of development recalls driving to work one day and seeing a dozen people standing outside the city hall building leaning forward and pressing their hands against the wall. When he asked a receptionist inside what was happening, he was told, "Oh, those are people from Sarah's church. When they know she's in the office, they come over to communicate the word of God to her through their hands."

Outside her office, Sarah became an ever-more-visible cheerleader for God and country. A former resident recalls that before Wasilla High football games, "She'd walk out in front of the stands and lead the crowd in prayer, then in the Pledge of Allegiance."

By Election Day of 1999, Stein felt he was up against not only a popular incumbent, but also God. Although voter turnout was only 17 percent, God won 909–292.

GIVEN SUCH a mandate, Sarah wasted no time accelerating the conversion of Wasilla from rough-and-ready Alaskan frontier town to a city that Jesus might be happy to call home when he returned.

In April 2000, at city expense, she traveled to Indianapolis to attend a conference at the International Training Center of the evangelical Institute in Basic Life Principles (IBLP). The conference had been organized by the International Association of Character Cities (IACC), an affiliate of the Character Training Institute (CTI), an organization that sought to end the separation of church and state.

Among the speakers she heard was seventy-year-old evangelist Bill Gothard, who had founded IBLP, according to the organization's website, "for the purpose of giving individuals, families, churches, schools, communities, governments, and businesses clear instruction and training on how to find success by following God's principles found in Scripture."

Gothard's goal, as described by Silja J. A. Talvi in *In These Times* magazine, was "to rebuild American society according to biblical mandates." He believed that America's failures stemmed from a lack of personal character, which led to acts of disobedience against "God-ordained jurisdiction" represented by four types of authority: "parents, government, church leaders and employers."

IBLP literature distributed at the conference said, "God gives direction, protection, and provision through human authorities. If we rebel against them, we expose ourselves to destruction by evil principalities . . . This is why 'rebellion is the sin of witchcraft.'"

That was a concept in which Sarah must have taken particular delight: in the eyes of God, Mary Ellen Emmons and Irl Stambaugh were witches!

The Character Training Institute sought to instill civil institutions with forty-nine biblically based "character qualities," which it conveniently listed and defined on laminated, pocket-size cards that also used pictures of the animal that represented each trait. For example, "Obedience: Quickly and cheerfully carrying out the direction of those who are responsible for me," was accompanied by an illustration of a mother duck and her ducklings.

Sarah also watched a video presentation by David Barton, an evangelical minister who served as cochair of the Texas Republican Party and who had founded WallBuilders, an organization that emphasized "the moral, religious and constitutional foundation on which America was built." In his talk, Barton proclaimed that the United States had been founded as an explicitly Christian nation and that continued separation of church and state in America was an affront to the Lord.

At the conference, Sarah learned that Wasilla could become a designated "City of Character" if the city council passed a resolution pledging to uphold each of the forty-nine "character qualities" specified by the IBLP.

She returned home enthused, and in short order a pliant city council approved her plan to declare Wasilla a City of Character. It became the only such city in Alaska. The five states with the most Cities of Character are South Carolina (thirty-four), Oklahoma and Texas (twenty-one each), Arkansas (eighteen), and Florida (fifteen). By contrast, there are none in the New England states.

In the real world, the impact of Wasilla's new designation was minimal. A couple of posters went up for a while, and city utility bills and employee paychecks carried the slogan "Wasilla: A City of Character!" but otherwise, life continued as before. Nonetheless, an IACC official praised Sarah's "boldness" in having Wasilla declared a City of Character.

Oddly, for all her public manifestations of religious zeal, there was little evidence of Christian faith inside Sarah's home. "There was no religion in that house," a longtime friend told me. "There was nothing about God. There was no Christ. Nobody prayed. There were no Bibles, there were no Christ Is in This Home signs. There were no crosses. None of that was ever there. Never."

The abortion issue that had propelled Sarah into politics had been resolved a year into her first term when the Alaska supreme court ruled unanimously that Valley Hospital could not ban the procedure.

The hospital was also required to pay more than $100,000 in legal fees incurred by the pro-choice group that had filed the original suit. The court's ruling heightened Sarah's awareness of the need for state and federal officials to appoint Christians to fill judicial vacancies.

New term limits prevented a Wasilla mayor from serving for more than six consecutive years, so Sarah felt free to be bold in her second term. Not long after she pushed the City of Character resolution through the council, she had police chief Fannon boldly criticize a new state law that ensured that rape victims would not have to pay for the kits needed for forensic medical exams. The chief said the new law would "further burden taxpayers."

Sarah continued to expand her horizons. She traveled to Washington several times to lobby for increased federal aid to Wasilla in the form of earmarks. She even hired a congressional lobbyist, Steve Silver, former chief of staff for Alaska's U.S. senator Ted Stevens. Very much the Washington insider—with close ties to both Stevens, who was chairman of the Senate Appropriations Committee, and to Alaska's lone congressman, Don Young, a senior member of the House Transportation Committee—Silver soon got the federal tap flowing.

During Sarah's last four years as mayor, Wasilla received $26.9 million in federal earmarks, or more than $4,000 per resident, based on Wasilla's 2002 population of 6,700. It was an impressive haul for someone who later would complain loudly and frequently about big government, and who would speak so stirringly about the need for self-reliance.

Knowing that her second term would be her last, Sarah wanted to do something big to be remembered by. She decided on a multi-million-dollar sports arena. Despite her supposed aversion to big government, big spending, and taxation, she pushed through a half-cent increase in the city sales tax to finance the project.

First estimates were that the 102,900-square-foot sports complex would cost $14.7 million. It would contain a 17,000-square-foot artificial turf field, an 835-foot rubber jogging and walking track, and the centerpiece: a National Hockey League regulation-size indoor ice rink, surrounded by bleachers with seating for more than 1,500. Spending $15 million to build a sports arena when the entire Wasilla city budget was only $20 million? The hockey mom was thinking big.

Too big, thought some Wasilla residents. In March 2002, Sarah's plan squeaked through by only twenty votes in a citywide referendum. In April the city council had to approve a $14.7 million bond issue to pay for it. Unfortunately, in her eagerness, Sarah authorized construction of the facility on land the city did not own. "Sarah was very focused on the sports complex," a Wasilla council member says, "but the city forgot to buy the land before they started building."

Her handpicked city attorney, Ken Jacobus, advised the council to approve construction despite an ongoing court fight over title to the land. Sarah wanted a monument to her tenure as mayor, but building the sports complex on land to which the city did not have clear title turned out to be a monumental blunder. A parcel of land Wasilla could have bought for $125,000 eventually cost the city more than $1.5 million in judgments and legal fees.

"It's unbelievable that they built a $17 million stadium on land they don't even own," said Gary Lundgren, the developer who did own the land. "The whole thing has been a comedy of errors." In the end, said the *Frontiersman,* "The moral of the story, if there can be anything moral about a story like this, is that competence can be an elusive thing."

Competence? Sarah took a city that had no debt and $4 million in cash reserves and in six years turned it into one that had piled up almost $20 million in long-term debt. During her tenure, the cost of debt service increased by 69 percent. She increased the sales tax from 2 to 2.5 percent to pay for the sports arena. While Wasilla's population grew by 37 percent during her tenure, total government expenditures rose by 63 percent, spending on salaries for city employees by 67 percent, money spent on office furniture and equipment by 117 percent, and administration spending on outside professional services by 932 percent.

On August 9, 2002, with only seven weeks of her mayoral tenure remaining and with the Republican primary for lieutenant governor looming at the end of the month, Sarah suddenly fired the first person she'd hired—and the one who'd done the most to help her during her six years as mayor: John Cramer. "This isn't a controversial thing," she said. "We're just wrapping things up and moving forward."

Cramer was stunned by his dismissal. Asked if there was a specific reason for it, he said, "Not that I'm aware of, no. Not that I can put my finger on. I honestly can't say what it would be."

He couldn't say because even after having worked for her for six years, Cramer couldn't see the obvious. She fired him because she didn't need him anymore.

Also, because she could. It was as if Sarah didn't feel her tenure would be complete without one last gratuitous exercise of her power, without hurting just one more person who had helped her.

NINE

I'M INVITED to a home in Palmer to meet a group of professionals who've had dealings with Sarah over the years. Half a dozen show up, but three or four who were expected do not. Their friends make various excuses for them, but what it comes down to is that they are afraid to meet me—or, rather, they are afraid to have it known that they met me—because Todd and Sarah might find out.

"And what do they think would happen then?" I ask one of those who did show up.

There's no way to know, I'm told, but Sarah is vicious and vengeful. "Don't think for a minute that just because she's no longer governor she doesn't still have dictatorial power in this state." Someone's husband could lose his state job, I'm told. Someone's nephew might not get that university scholarship. Someone's incipient political career could be nipped before it buds. The message: Sarah is omniscient and omnipotent, and Todd has eyes and ears, too, as well as a propensity for hiring private detectives. Sure, I can be brave by moving next door to them, but I don't have to earn a living in this state.

More and more I discover that fear of the Palins is endemic throughout the Valley. I hear repeatedly that they've always been bullies.

"But we're not in tenth grade anymore," I say.

"Maybe we're not," is the response, "but they are."

The atmosphere of anxiety and trepidation is palpable. And these are Alaskans, traditionally known for their backbone. They don't choose not to speak to me out of loyalty to Sarah and Todd, as Todd's father, Jim Palin does. These are people who despise Sarah, who laugh at her and patronize her among themselves, but who then won't risk even being seen in my company.

Fortunately, the fearful comprise only a small minority of the people I want to talk to. But even some who do answer my questions insist on anonymity. I don't like it—Sarah is quick to denounce any comments made about her by unnamed sources—but it's the reality I'm faced with in the Valley in the summer of 2010; it's the legacy Sarah has left behind.

A HANDYMAN comes to the house to replace some defective smoke alarms. He calls me from the Best Western parking lot. "You can take that chain down," he says. "I'll be there as soon as I get my car ready."

I take down the chain and wait for him at the end of the driveway. His battered sedan lurches slowly down the potholed road. I see that he's duct-taped pieces of cardboard over both his front and rear license plates.

"That's what I meant about gettin' my car ready," he says. He points toward the Palin house. "I don't need any bullshit from those paranoid fuckers next door."

NEWSWEEK PUTS Sarah on the cover with a halo around her head and calls her "Saint Sarah."

She tweets: "Gulf disaster needs divine intervention as man's efforts have been futile." I wonder how much a Palin administration would budget for "divine intervention." Undoubtedly, more than for science and the arts.

• • •

IRL STAMBAUGH pays me a visit on June 17. It's another chilly, drizzly day. After a glorious spring, the weather began to turn sour while
Nancy was here and has worsened since her departure. Whole Alaskan summers can pass this way. It's not a day for the deck, so Stambaugh and I sit in the armchairs that Dewey Taylor delivered.

Unlike handymen and locksmiths and certain people I've invited
for lunch and dinner, Stambaugh is not afraid to come to my house.
"She's already done all she can do to me," he says with a shrug. He's
sixty-two, a burly, balding man, just retired from a private security
job on the North Slope. He has no interest in peering over the fence.

In late February 1997, Stambaugh filed suit against Sarah and the
city of Wasilla on grounds of contract violation, wrongful termination, and gender discrimination. His complaint alleged that Sarah
had fired him because of his support for John Stein, and his opposition to the 5:00 AM closing hour for Wasilla bars and proposed expan-
sion of concealed weapon privileges.

It also stated, "Plaintiff Stambaugh is a male, standing well over
6 feet tall and weighing more than 200 pounds . . . Stambaugh had
been informed that Mayor Palin felt intimidated because of his size.
Stambaugh, being sensitive to the Mayor's concern regarding his sex,
size and height, made particular efforts to sit in a chair whenever
discussing matters with Mayor Palin and talk in a quiet soothing
voice . . . Stambaugh's size is a result of his sex. Stambaugh was ter-
minated because of his sex . . . an unlawful employment practice."

Sarah's interpretation of Stambaugh's demeanor, expressed in
writing, was that, "When I met with you in private, instead of engaging in interactive conversation with me, you gave me short, uncom-
municative answers and then you would sit there and stare at me in
silence with a very stern look, like you were trying to intimidate me."

During the course of the litigation, Sarah showed how dirty she
could fight. When Stambaugh was deposed, according to court doc-

uments, Sarah's lawyer asked him about possible extramarital relationships. The judge who presided over the case noted, "Defendants essentially seek to establish that Stambaugh engaged in numerous extramarital relationships during the course of his marriage to Cindy Stambaugh . . . Defendants have filed a motion for an order compelling Stambaugh to testify as to why he was considering separating from his wife . . . and a motion seeking an order compelling Cindy to provide similar testimony regarding her knowledge of Stambaugh's extramarital affairs."

Sarah's message was clear: If you try to stand up to me, I will drag you and your family through the gutter.

The deposition she gave in that lawsuit, on the morning of August 27, 1998, was the first time she'd ever answered questions under oath. The 291-page transcript makes for enjoyable reading.

Asked about her education, Sarah says, "I graduated from the University of Idaho with a degree in journalism."

"Did you seek any further education?"

"Yes, seeking a—working—hopefully will be able to someday work further for a master's degree."

I've been deposed. It's no fun. A good lawyer will instruct you to keep your answers brief and not to volunteer information. But Sarah took this to an extreme. Pages eight and nine of the transcript show that six times she answered questions by saying, "Um-hum." Finally, her own lawyer interrupted: "Excuse me, Sarah, you may want to say 'yes' rather than 'um-hum' so he'll know when you say it."

Sarah was asked about her duties as mayor. "Is there a city manager?"

"In Wasilla? No."

"So the mayor is the administrator?"

"Right."

This would have come as news to John Cramer.

"Do you read the newspapers a lot?"

"Yes, sir."

But the lawyer didn't follow up by asking which newspapers she read, thereby missing the chance to scoop Katie Couric by ten years.

There are other highlights. Sarah was asked if she understood what the word *notwithstanding* meant.

"*Notwithstanding* means unless there is something that says otherwise," she said.

She described her first one-to-one meeting with Stambaugh. "It wasn't a friendly meeting. I felt that Mr. Stambaugh was pretty disappointed that I was going to be his boss."

"How did he manifest this disappointment?"

"Just very unfriendly and unenthused about the questions I was asking . . . not very cordial. Very short with answers."

"Did you find that offensive?"

"Not offensive, but a little bit like pulling teeth to get any kind of answer . . . It wasn't any kind of personal communication between the two of us. It was me asking a few questions and he responded."

"Did Mr. Stambaugh not respond to any question you asked?"

"I don't recall."

She did recall another meeting with Stambaugh a few days later at which he again failed to display the level of enthusiasm for her leadership that she expected. Asked to characterize his demeanor, she said, "Just, I guess, very benign." Apparently, she considered *benign* to be a synonym for *unenthusiastic*.

As to wanting Wasilla bars to remain open until 5:00 AM, Sarah said, "I don't think it's government's role to tell private enterprise when they can open and close their doors."

"Do you feel there's a correlation between bar hours and drunk driving?"

"No."

"Do you feel there's any correlation between bar hours and domestic violence?"

"No."

Nor did Sarah feel there was any correlation between the $1,000 campaign contribution she received from Bernice and Mike Lohman, owners of the Wasilla Bar, and her support for allowing bars to remain open until 5:00 AM.

"Prior to the election [did] either Bernice Lohman or Mike Lohman come to you and ask that if you became elected you would fire Irl Stambaugh?"

"No."

"After the election did either of them ask you to fire Chief Stambaugh?"

"No."

Stambaugh does not believe that Sarah's answers to those questions were truthful.

Sarah had lunch with Bernice Lohman after her election, but all she could recall of that meeting was that Bernice "was happy to see development happen in Wasilla."

"Anything else that you recall?

"I can't recall right now."

She was asked if she'd ever discussed Stambaugh with either of the Lohmans.

"I don't recall that."

In regard to discussing Stambaugh with Marilyn Anderson, owner of the Mug-Shot and also a campaign contributor, Sarah said, "I don't recall." And she said the same concerning discussions with Steve Stoll: "I don't recall . . . I don't recall."

Reading the transcript, I can't help but think of the March 21, 1973, White House tape on which President Richard Nixon, discussing upcoming testimony in the Watergate hearings, said to his aide H. R. Haldeman, "Just be damned sure you say, 'I don't remember, I can't recall.'"

What the deposition in its entirety makes clear is that Sarah's main reason for firing Stambaugh was that he had not been sufficiently deferential. In her termination letter she told him, "Your level of participation in staff meetings was disappointing and when you did speak you often did so in a disrespectful or condescending tone."

"When you say disrespectful," Stambaugh's lawyer asked, "what do you mean by that."

"I felt that he was disrespectful in his tone."

"Can you tell me what leads you to that conclusion?"

"It was sometimes difficult to get any information out of Mr. Stambaugh . . . Instead of being given the courtesy of him offering the information, I had to continually ask . . . That to me is disrespectful."

Later, she said, "He sat and stared at me in silence the vast majority of the time in our meetings." When Sarah said she wanted more "community-based policing," Stambaugh "expressed nonchalance."

Stambaugh's suit was eventually dismissed on grounds that Sarah was within her rights to fire him no matter how well he was performing his job because he served as an "at will" employee. Neither he nor Cindy, to whom he was married at the time, was required to testify about the extramarital affairs that Sarah accused him of having conducted.

In talking to me about his interactions with Sarah, Stambaugh is never disrespectful, but there are one or two occasions when I suspect him of expressing nonchalance. On the other hand, maybe he's just being benign.

A COUPLE of days later, I drive to Eagle River, which is about two thirds of the way to Anchorage, to talk to another ex-cop. This one is Gary Wheeler, recently retired from the state police, where he served as head of Governor Sarah Palin's personal security detail.

The sky remains gray: a week without sunshine since Nancy left. The mother grebe is still on her nest. I don't know the incubation period for grebes, but I can tell from the increased volume and frequency of their squawks that both mama and papa grebe are getting impatient.

Gary Wheeler and his ebullient wife, Corky, are the kind of Alaskans who have you feeling like an old friend five minutes after you meet them. Gary, who was born in Anchorage, spent his whole career in the state police, directing the intelligence unit in Anchorage from 1989 to 1999. In 2000 he was transferred to the security detail for Governor Tony Knowles. Four years later he was named head of security for Governor Frank Murkowski. Sarah inherited him when she became governor in 2006.

"After eight years of dealing with politicians," he says, "I can tell you one thing: they all love themselves and they all think that everybody else loves them, too." Working for Murkowski, he saw quite a bit of Sarah during the gubernatorial campaign. "She comes across as very personable," he tells me. "Give her a group of people and she'll walk up and start shaking hands. In a campaign setting, she makes you feel like you're somebody special, as if she'd like to know you personally, if only she had the time. It's a neat trick, and not everybody can learn it."

Offstage, as Wheeler quickly learned, she was considerably less engaging. "For the first couple of weeks, I picked her up at her house at six AM and drove her to her office in Anchorage. When she was done for the day, somebody else in the detail would drive her home. She'd ride in the back seat and spend a lot of time with her BlackBerrys or on the cell phone, so I didn't try to make small talk. I'd say, 'Good morning, Governor, how are you today?' and she'd nod. When we got to the office I'd say, 'Just call when you're ready to go home.' That's all I said to her for two weeks."

Nonetheless, Wheeler soon got a call from deputy chief of staff Mike Nizich informing him that "The governor does not want anyone speaking to her in the car." Not even good morning? Wheeler asked. "Nothing," Nizich said. "Do not speak. Period."

We talk about Mike Wooten, the state trooper whom Sarah and Todd tried desperately to have fired after he and Sarah's sister Molly divorced. "I didn't know about Wooten at that time," Wheeler tells me. "I didn't know how much she disliked the troopers."

He learned soon afterward when both Todd and Sarah came to his Anchorage office to tell him that they wanted Wooten fired. "I didn't even know the guy," Wheeler says, "but the way they talked about him, he was a menace to society and they couldn't understand why he still had his job, and they wanted me to do something about it."

Personnel issues, of course, were not within his purview, but given Todd and Sarah's insistence that he act, Wheeler called deputy state police commissioner Ted Bachman. He was told that there had been questions about Wooten's performance, that there had been a departmental hearing, that Wooten had been briefly suspended, but that now he was back on the job in good standing and that the matter was resolved.

Wheeler shared this information with Todd. "That's not what he wanted to hear," Wheeler says. "He told me, 'You don't understand: I want him fired.' I told him there was nothing I could do. The case was closed." It was not closed, Todd said. It wouldn't be closed until Wooten was gone. "'I want you to be on the lookout for anything you can find out about the guy,' Todd said, 'and to report to me personally as soon as you hear anything I can use.'"

Wheeler is still unsettled by the memory. "They had it in for this guy. Todd would not accept that nothing could be done. They wanted something and Sarah was governor, so they felt they should be able to have it. For the next few months, every time I saw Todd he'd tell me something else Wooten had done. 'He shot a moose without a license.' 'He had beer in his patrol car.' 'He tasered his stepson.' I couldn't understand why he was so obsessed. Then somebody told me: Wooten had been married to Sarah's sister and it went bad. They were going to spend the rest of their lives trying to get back at him for that."

A few months into her term, Sarah dispensed with Wheeler's driving services. "She and Todd picked out a fifty-thousand-dollar Suburban just so she could drive herself. What it came down to was she didn't want us around. She didn't want anybody to follow her to Nordstrom's when she went shopping every day. Her first year in office, she must have bought a hundred pairs of sunglasses. Every day she'd have a new pair. Overall, she didn't want anybody to know that she wasn't coming in until ten AM and then leaving by three to go home."

Wheeler could not help but compare Sarah's work habits with those of her predecessors. "For six years I was with Murkowski and Knowles," he says. "For them, the job wasn't forty hours a week, it was eighty. Whatever you thought about what they accomplished, those two guys—one a Democrat, one a Republican—worked like hell, up to sixteen hours a day. For her, it was a part-time job."

One of the problems with Sarah's insistence on driving herself everywhere was that she was always getting lost. "There'd be a function in Anchorage," Wheeler recalls, "and we'd be there waiting for her and—zoom!—her Suburban would go flying past. 'There she goes,' we'd say. 'Let's try to talk her back to earth.'"

But they couldn't talk to her because she didn't want to be talked to. So they'd text her, telling her she'd overshot her destination once again. "Her BlackBerrys, they were the closest thing to family to her, maybe closer," Wheeler says. "Texting was how she related to the world."

He takes a sip of the sweet tea Corky has served. "You know what she was? A housewife who happened to be governor. I'd fly cross-country with her many times and she'd spend the whole trip looking at *People* magazine, or one of the others like that. Knowles and Murkowski, they used those hours to work. For her it was like she was waiting for her appointment at the hair salon. She was really into celebrities. She could spend hours looking at pictures of them."

In Juneau, Wheeler soon learned that he was as likely to find Todd in the governor's office as Sarah. "He'd go up to the slope once in a while, but mostly he'd be in her office. He had his own desk in there and he'd do a lot of her stuff."

"Would he sit in on meetings she had with her staff?" I ask.

"She didn't have meetings. If she was meeting with anybody it was with *Vogue* magazine or *Vanity Fair*. We were supposed to get her schedule a day in advance so we could plan who would cover what, but most days there was nothing on her schedule. It was blank. We never knew what she was planning to do or what she did. Her staff would fill it in as best they could later, because they knew it wouldn't look good to have day after day with nothing there."

One day Mike Nizich told Wheeler that he wanted a trooper who'd been on the governor's security detail for sixteen years returned to patrol immediately. Why? "Bristol and Willow don't like him."

Wheeler recalls accompanying Sarah to a National Governors' Association meeting in Washington February 22–25, 2008. One morning he got a call from Sarah's Juneau office telling him to bring her to a meeting at the Willard Hotel at 3:00 PM.

"Who's the meeting with?" he asked.

"John McCain."

Wheeler was stunned. McCain was front-runner for the Republican presidential nomination. "No," he said to himself. "No way. He's got to be smarter than that."

The meeting lasted forty-five minutes. Wheeler stood outside the door. "She never said a word about what happened."

By late February of 2008, Sarah presumably would have been seven months pregnant with Trig.

"She didn't show," Wheeler says. "I can't say she wasn't pregnant, but there was certainly no indication that she was. I remember at National Airport she went into the rest room to change from her nice clothes into jeans so she could wear jeans on the flight home. Did you ever see a woman six or seven months pregnant decide to wear tight-fitting jeans because they're comfortable?"

Wheeler did not accompany Sarah on her trip to Texas when she said her water broke, precipitating the thirteen-hour "wild ride" back to Wasilla, where Trig was supposedly born.

"It was her first trip Outside when she didn't want security. I had to call Texas so they could have their car and their troopers meet her at the airport. I have no idea why she didn't want me along on that trip, but I can tell you this: if I'd been with her and if I'd known her water broke in Texas she would never have got on that plane to come back."

I ask Wheeler what churches Sarah attended when she traveled. Were they always evangelical?

"She never went to church when I was with her. There were a number of times when we'd be out of state on a weekend. She never asked me to check on any services and she never attended any."

I ask if he'd formed any impression about the degree of closeness between Sarah and Todd.

"Well, you can't help but notice things like this: she and Todd never showed any affection for each other. I'd travel with Knowles and Murkowski and their wives, and you could tell that these were happily married couples. Sarah and Todd were like business partners. She could never even hold hands with him because she always had a BlackBerry in her hand."

Of greater concern to Wheeler was Sarah's propensity for putting old friends from Wasilla into jobs that were beyond their capabilities. "The people closest to her were all idiots, little guys in big guys' shoes. They had no qualifications. They were a bunch of loyal little puppies. Kris Perry, Frank Bailey, Ivy Frye? These people had positions in state government? It was a joke. Listen, I know Sarah. She doesn't belong leading people; she's just not smart enough. She has no intellect and no interest in learning, because she thinks she already knows it all."

Sarah's paranoia made the deepest impression. "She was just so defensive all the time. Everybody was out to get her. This ran deep and it made her mean. Maybe she'd be mean anyway. But I'll tell you one thing: she's no mama grizzly; she's a rabid wolf. Take a look at the snow: wherever she's been, there's a trail of blood in her wake."

TEN

EVEN IF she'd been permitted to do so, it's unlikely that Sarah would have run for a third term as mayor. No matter how crazily Wasilla continued to grow, she felt she'd outgrown it. She wanted to perform on a larger stage, and she believed that God would put her there.

She also seemed to need new foes to vanquish. She would ask herself, says John Bitney, "Where's the fight? That's what she's looking for. It gets her juices flowing. If there's no win, she's not interested. She's a terrible manager, finds policy details too boring, but if you put the goalposts in front of her, you'd better get out of the way. She'll chew your ass up."

By November 2001 she was letting it be known that she planned to run for lieutenant governor the following year. It had been more than two years since her last electoral fight, and that one had never been a contest. Like her father before a hunting trip, she was hungry for fresh blood.

According to a number of people in Wasilla, Sarah's domestic life was in tatters at the time. Time with friends—not that there were many friends—would degenerate into marital squabbles, raised voices, and frequent mutual threats of divorce. A recurring cause of conflict was Sarah's inability or refusal to act as a mother to her children. She did so little that Todd had to rely on Debbie Richter, the wife of his close friend Scott Richter, to help raise them. "Take care of the kids?" says John Bitney, who is now married to the former Debbie Richter. "She can't, she won't—whatever it may be—but she doesn't. She just doesn't. Todd has to take care of everything. And that's the way it's always been."

Bitney says, "Todd was both the matriarch and patriarch in that family. That can be a compliment or not, depending on how you want to look at it, but it's the truth. He did the diapers when the kids were young. He was the disciplinarian. Sarah was all about the photo op."

Friends recall that when Todd was working on the North Slope, the children literally would have a hard time finding enough to eat. "Those kids had to fend for themselves," one says. "I'd walk into that kitchen and Bristol and Willow would be sitting there with a burnt pot of Kraft mac and cheese on the stove and they'd be trying to open one of those Ramen noodle packs, and Sarah would be up in her bedroom with the door closed saying she didn't want to be disturbed.

"Todd may have his faults, but when he was off work for two weeks he took care of those kids. He'd come off hitch and land in Anchorage and he knew he'd come home to a house with no food. Sarah would never go to Anchorage to pick him up, so he'd find a ride with someone. First stop would always be Costco, and he'd get a case of peaches, a case of applesauce, like that, hoping there'd be enough to last through his next hitch.

"But when Todd was up north working, those kids were a bunch of wild maniacs, running around Wasilla with no dinner cooked, no breakfast cooked, no homework done, and Sarah lying in bed. If she wasn't working, that's all she did.

"It made her crazy to have to take care of the kids. I remember one time her coming in with Piper in a carrier and sliding it across the foyer and sayin', 'Take this fuckin' baby!' Then she walked out the door.

"She never took care of those kids. They would be dirty, filthy.

Bristol and Willow had a shared bathroom between their two bed-rooms in the Lake Lucille house and it would be—oh, my God!—a poop ring in the toilet. And the girls themselves, they'd be . . . dirty. You know, they were getting to the age where they could take baths by themselves, but you still had to clean their ears, make sure they brushed their teeth, help them fold their clothes—and nobody did. They didn't even have dressers in their rooms. The laundry got done and it was just 'throw it on the floor.'

"When Piper was a baby and Willow wasn't old enough to be on her own, Sarah dumped those kids off on a woman who cleaned houses, a nasty woman. She would take them to wherever she was cleaning and just tell them to sit down and shut up. Todd used to be *liv-id*. Livid. Those kids never had any parenting, they had to raise each other."

Part of the problem Sarah had with feeding her children may have been connected to the fact that she herself ate only sporadically. "I never saw diet pills," Bitney says, "but it's amazing how far she's gotten on Red Bulls and white mochas. She'd start off with a white chocolate mocha, maybe two, then a Red Bull, then switch to Diet Pepsi in the afternoon. It was Diet Pepsi, not Diet Dr Pepper—she just made that up later because she thought it fit better with her image—and she'd go through a lot of Diet Pepsi."

Bitney recalls that Sarah never wanted to eat breakfast, "but if I got a double order of bacon on the side, she'd eat most of it. And any time of day, if it was chocolate, it was gone. I never once saw her eat greens. It was just meat and chocolate and the drinks with caffeine."

Another friend tells me: "She'd never eat. She'd never eat." There were, however, exceptions. "One day she came in with Oreos, bread, bags of fast food, and she ate everything and then disappeared and came out of the bathroom later with blurry eyes, her hair up, and her knuckles red. I said, 'What you up to, girl?' She gave me a look like, 'Don't you even fuckin' go there.'"

There was also the matter of cocaine. "I remember, back before she was governor, one time snow-machining at Crosswinds Lake, way up above Glenallen," a friend tells me. "It was me, Todd, Sarah, five or six other people, and Todd and Sarah had a fight, so Sarah was riding with somebody else. The cocaine was free flowing. Somebody found a fifty-five-gallon oil drum and turned it upside down and we were all doing cocaine lines off the top of the drum."

In 2007, someone mentioned the incident on a blog, writing, "How's that cocaine out at Crosswinds Lake, Sarah?" I spoke to the author of the blog post, who said, "Todd saw it and got a message to me: 'Keep off the fuckin' blog, Sarah's fuckin' pissed.'"

Neither did Sarah find nourishment in the joy of sexual intimacy with her husband. "Todd complained a lot about never having sex with Sarah," a friend of his tells me. "He'd say, 'I must have gotten laid at least four times, 'cause I got four kids.' This was way before Trig." The friend adds, "I can honestly say that in a decade plus of interacting with them I never saw them even show affection."

One former houseguest says Sarah's aversion to intimacy was so extreme that she didn't even like to think about other people having sex. "I get real dry in the winter," the houseguest tells me, "so I keep a bottle of baby oil by the bed. I'll come out of the shower, put it on, and go to bed. One day, when we're staying at the Wasilla Lake house, Todd says, 'I gotta talk to you guys. Sarah's pissed. She found that big bottle of baby oil in your bedroom and she knows you guys are rubbin' it on yourselves and havin' sex.' My husband was like, 'She uses it on her skin, dude.' But Todd says, 'Sarah wants you out. She's really upset thinkin' you're in there havin' sex with baby oil.' We left. We went to a motel. Sarah dresses hot and acts hot in public, so you'd think she'd probably be pretty hot in bed, but that's all just part of the show."

THE LIEUTENANT GOVERNOR of Alaska is paid $100,000 a year to supervise the Division of Elections, to maintain oversight of the state's notaries public, to regulate commercial use of the state seal, and to authenticate the signatures of state officials for foreign countries. In terms of labor intensiveness, it's not exactly piano moving. The job, in fact, is so undemanding that had she been elected to the office, Sarah probably wouldn't even have had to hire someone to do it for her.

In 2002, with Republican U.S. senator Frank Murkowski heavily favored to become governor, it seemed likely that winning the Republican primary for lieutenant governor in August would be tantamount to winning the general election in November.

Sarah entered an already crowded field, which included two state senators, Loren Leman of Anchorage and Robin Taylor of Wrangell, and former speaker of the house Gail Phillips of Homer.

In theory, ethics required that Sarah not campaign for lieutenant governor from her mayor's office. In practice, she effectively turned the office into an unofficial campaign headquarters. She wrote and received campaign-related e-mails on the computer in the mayor's office; she had her administrative assistant use city hall facilities to print thank-you notes to campaign donors; she had her secretary make campaign-related travel arrangements from city hall while being paid by the city. On June 12, 2002, Sarah met with representatives from a campaign advertising agency at city hall. Following the meeting, the agency faxed proposed campaign logos to deputy administrator Cramer at city hall. Paul Jenkins, editor of the conservative *Voice of the Times,* would later write that Sarah's city hall office became "little more than a command center for her lieutenant governor campaign."

While there were obvious differences between a statewide race and a municipal mayoral election—especially in a state the size of Alaska—in some respects Sarah's campaign for lieutenant governor resembled her first race against John Stein: she was the new face; her opponents were the business-as-usual old guard, offering stale ideas that had already proven ineffective. While they touted their legislative experience, Sarah derided it. They were tired old hacks; she was a vibrant young mother who would bring a fresh perspective to Juneau. In the absence of any significant issues, the message played well.

Leman was the favorite in the race, with most observers expecting Phillips and Taylor to provide his strongest opposition. It was Sarah, however, who emerged as the surprise. With voter turnout of only 22 percent, the second lowest in state history, Sarah finished a close second to Leman, losing by less than two thousand votes out of more than seventy thousand cast. "She's a sharp, attractive candidate," Leman said. "I think she had a lot to offer."

As expected, Frank Murkowski easily won the gubernatorial primary, but his daughter, state representative Lisa Murkowski, wasn't assured of victory over her more conservative opponent until the count of absentee and questioned ballots in her Eagle River district was completed in early September.

The Wasilla mayoral election was held in October. Sarah's stepmother-in-law Faye Palin was one of three candidates. Even though Faye had donated $1,000 behind Sarah's first mayoral campaign, Sarah threw her support to Dianne Keller, a right-wing Christian member of the city council. For Sarah, conservatism and evangelical Christianity trumped even family ties. Keller wound up winning the October election with 402 votes to Faye Palin's second-place total of 256.

Sarah campaigned so vigorously for the Murkowski ticket throughout the fall that the *Frontiersman* described her as "a spokesperson for the Republican party through television, radio and newspaper ads," observing that "at times it seemed Palin was more visible than Murkowski's running mate, Loren Leman."

This was not entirely altruistic. If Murkowski were elected in November, he would name a successor to serve the remaining two years of his term in the U.S. Senate. In fact, he not only won but also received the highest percentage of votes in the history of Alaskan gubernatorial elections. Immediately, attention focused on whom he would name to fill Alaska's first open U.S. Senate seat in twenty-two years. Sarah's name was among those most frequently mentioned.

"Everything is up in the air still," she said. "I don't necessarily want to retire, and with Todd's flexible schedule it allows me to serve in a couple of different capacities."

Sarah was one of eight possible successors whom Murkowski interviewed in person. Sarah's interview, apparently, did not go well. "She came off as vapid and uninformed," says Anchorage lawyer C. Donald Mitchell, who spoke to some of those who were advising Murkowski during the selection process.

Within days of the interview, Sarah received a call from Murkowski telling her she would not be his choice. "I knew all along it was a long shot," she told the *Frontiersman*. "Maybe I'm someone who is perceived as being too conservative." Murkowski named his daughter, Lisa, to the seat, a choice that outraged many Alaskans, none more than Sarah.

As Mitchell wrote in the *Alaska Dispatch*, "Sarah, a 38-year old former small town mayor who had never won a statewide election, reportedly was livid and reportedly never fully forgave Frank, because in her self-absorption she was certain that she should have been the obvious choice."

As a consolation prize, Murkowski appointed Sarah to one of the two open seats on the three-member Alaska Oil and Gas Conservation Commission.

When the Alaska legislature created the commission in 1978, it specified that one seat had to be occupied by a petroleum engineer and another by a petroleum geologist. Duties of the commissioners included fixing the liquid-to-gas ratios that well operators must maintain, monitoring oil and gas pool pressures, and regulating the drilling, plugging, and spacing of wells, the disposal of saltwater and oil field wastes, and the quantity and rate of production of oil and gas from particular wells. Despite the highly technical nature of the work, the commission's third seat was open to any member of the public, no matter how unqualified (an oversight the legislature later corrected).

It was this seat to which Governor Murkowski appointed Sarah in February 2003. At the same time, in a display of the deep reverence for patronage that would soon have Alaska voters ruing the day they elected him, Murkowski tapped state Republican Party chairman Randy Ruedrich to fill the slot reserved for a petroleum engineer.

Sarah would be working in the commission's Anchorage offices. It would be a full-time job, paying a salary of $118,000 a year, which, in those days was not an insignificant amount of money to Sarah and Todd.

The two appointments raised eyebrows. Anchorage assemblyman Eric Croft, a Democrat, said, "Anytime you appoint the head of your party . . . and the lieutenant governor runner-up, it looks a little questionable."

Ruedrich, at least, could claim experience. He'd worked in the oil and gas industry for more than thirty years, including stints in Yemen and the United Kingdom. Sarah, on the other hand, said, "There is so much information and it's all very technical. But maybe by the time this is finished I can have an intelligent conversation with my husband."

The appointments required legislative approval. At Sarah's confirmation hearing, one skeptical legislator wanted to know "what you bring to the mix." Cheerfully ignoring the question, Sarah replied, "I'm absolutely motivated, excited and challenged to be able to serve in this capacity."

Another said, "You're going to be asked to make rulings on things of a very technical nature. I don't see where you've had any background in oil and gas development . . . How are you going to keep people from blowing smoke up your skirts?"

"You're right, I don't have all the technical background," Sarah replied. "But thankfully we have a technical staff here at the commission and I have confidence that they do with their technical knowledge give objective and fair advice to the commissioners."

Despite her lack of qualifications, Sarah's appointment proved the less controversial of the two. Both she and Ruedrich were confirmed by the state legislature in early March, but while eighteen legislators—all Democrats—voted against Ruedrich, believing that it would be a conflict of interest for him to serve on the commission while retaining his position as state Republican Party chairman, only three voted against Sarah, citing her lack of qualifications.

She'd been on the job for only four months when rumors began to circulate that she might challenge Governor Murkowski's daughter, Lisa, in the 2004 Republican primary for the full-term U.S. Senate seat. In early August, Sarah said she was considering a run. In September, she said, "It's not out of the question."

But she had more pressing concerns. She was both chairwoman and ethics supervisor of the three-member commission. As Mitchell wrote in the *Dispatch,* "Within weeks of her arrival at the Oil and Gas Conservation Commission Sarah knew she was drowning . . . She had no understanding of, and no interest in, the commission's highly technical work . . . Sarah began searching for a face-saving excuse to quit a job she never should have been given."

By September, the search for a way out had become her highest priority. Winter would soon be coming on. She'd found the commute from Wasilla tedious even during Alaska's long summer hours of daylight, but Sarah had even less desire to make the drive, as Mitchell wrote, "in the pitch dark down an icy, moose-strewn highway."

For months, she'd known that Ruedrich was conducting Republican Party business from his commission office. She'd seemed unfazed by the blatant impropriety. After all, she'd done the same during the final months of her tenure as Wasilla mayor.

But Ruedrich now became her exit strategy. She reported his transgressions to Governor Murkowski's chief of staff in early September. The administration took no action. In October, Ruedrich sent an e-mail promoting a Republican fund-raiser at the Petroleum Club in Anchorage. His attempt to solicit donations from the very energy companies he was supposed to be regulating showed that his conflict of interest was more than theoretical.

Publicly, Sarah came to Ruedrich's defense on November 3, saying the Petroleum Club event would raise money only for national, not state, candidates. "Randy has told me that he is not soliciting funds or raising funds on a state level," she said.

Privately, she was compiling evidence against him. The attorney general's office had begun a clandestine investigation of Ruedrich and had asked Sarah, in her role as the commission's ethics supervisor, for assistance. She later said she was told to "get on his computer and send us anything that you believe to be partisan." But she was instructed to keep her activities secret from Ruedrich, the third commissioner, and the commission's staff. "I printed off things that were obvious Republican Party documents," she told the *Daily News*.

Pressure for Ruedrich to resign from one of his two positions was mounting. Wev Shea, a former U.S. attorney for Alaska and a prominent Republican, said, "I think the conflict of interest is atrocious." Even Wasilla Republican strategist Tuckerman Babcock, who had served three years on the commission, said Ruedrich should quit one job or the other.

On November 7, Sarah said, "It's not fair to Alaskans to have these questions about a possible conflict of interest hanging over the head of this agency." Going further, she said that if Ruedrich didn't soon quit, she would. This, of course, was exactly what she wanted to do. Ruedrich beat her to the resignation punch, however, announcing on November 8 that he was giving up his commission job. "I think the ethics issue was way overblown," he said, "but I felt the right thing to do is to end this." Sarah, in her capacity as chairwoman, announced herself pleased. "The right thing has been done here," she echoed.

Had the matter ended there, it's likely that no one outside Alaska ever would have heard of Sarah Palin.

But Sarah wasn't going to let it end. She'd recognized for months that she could turn Ruedrich's misconduct to her own political advantage. Now, with him gone—and with the assistance of a computer expert—she hacked even more deeply into his electronic files. She found that in the haste of his departure he'd failed to wipe his hard drive clean. Sarah downloaded and printed dozens of e-mails and other documents that proved that Ruedrich had not only been conducting party business, but also leaking commission files to companies the commission was supposed to be regulating.

Under state law, the attorney general's office wasn't allowed to say that Ruedrich was under investigation, much less why, and Sarah wasn't allowed to say anything. While not yet a pit bull, Sarah didn't like being muzzled.

She called Murkowski's attorney general, Gregg Renkes, in mid-November to ask if there actually was an ongoing investigation. He said he was not in a position to answer yes or no. In notes she made at the time, she wrote that Renkes "couldn't advise me on whether an investigation was needed, but agreed RR's departure should be the conclusion to the problem."

In December the assistant attorney general who had first contacted her told Sarah that the investigation was continuing and asked her to send all the materials she'd acquired by delving into Ruedrich's computer. She sent a package on December 11, but heard nothing, not even whether the items had been received.

At about the same time, Anchorage legislators Eric Croft and Ethan Berkowitz sent Renkes a letter asking him to appoint an independent investigator to "look into the ethical and criminal consequences" of Ruedrich's misuse of his commission office.

In addition, the *Anchorage Daily News* made a public records request for the e-mails Ruedrich had sent from his office computer. Acting as commission chairwoman, Sarah denied the request. She wrote, "The records you seek are required to be kept confidential by state law."

Perception grew that both Sarah and attorney general Renkes were involved in a cover-up. A letter writer to the *Daily News* said on December 29, "I used to have an enormous amount of respect for Sarah Palin. She used to have strength, independence and guts . . . No more. She's begun toeing the party line and stonewalling the (non)investigation of her former boss."

Sarah's frustration grew. On January 2, 2004, she sent Governor Murkowski a certified letter in which she wrote, "Since Dec. 11, I have not received any further instructions except to be told to keep things 'confidential,' to deny media requests for information, and I have been threatened that I would face penalties if I were to divulge even whether or not there may be an ongoing investigation into the Ruedrich matter." She demanded that the state either announce that she had been ordered not to speak about the investigation or that they let her "handle this issue the way I deem is most appropriate." She closed with a threat: if she did not receive a satisfactory response to her letter, "I will take such further action as I deem appropriate to protect my reputation."

Whatever else one might say about Sarah, there can be no doubting her sense of timing and the acuteness of her political instincts. Even before she'd become mayor of Wasilla—the only job in her life, incidentally, that she did not quit—she'd said that one day she hoped to be president of the United States. Even with God opening doors for her, she'd never make it if she got dragged into the muck of statewide political corruption.

There was only one way out, and she took it, announcing her own resignation from the commission on January 17, 2004. "I'm forced to withhold information from Alaskans, and that goes against what I believe in," she said, adding that the "oomph" had gone out of her passion for public service.

The state filed a civil complaint against Ruedrich on February 27, but kept the action confidential, which meant Sarah was still not free to discuss her role. On April 6 her lawyer, Wayne Anthony Ross, informed Governor Murkowski that if details of the Ruedrich case were not disclosed within ten days, Sarah would speak publicly about "what she knows about this entire matter and why she chose to resign from the Commission."

On April 12, Ruedrich himself, while again proclaiming he'd done nothing wrong, announced the existence of the investigation. Sarah's muzzle came off. As she told her story of forcing Ruedrich out of his job, the press hailed her for her highly principled resignation and cast her rooting about in Ruedrich's computer as the courageous act of a crusading ethical reformer. The *Daily News* called her a "Republican rising star," and speculation increased that she would challenge Governor Murkowski's daughter, Lisa, in the upcoming Republican primary.

On April 23, Sarah announced that she would not run for the U.S. Senate because her fourteen-year-old son, Track, had asked her not to. She said her three daughters, aged thirteen, nine, and three, were all for her candidacy, but Track was not. "How could I be the [hockey] team mom if I was a U.S. senator?" she said. Instead, she announced her support of Lisa Murkowski's more conservative opponent, former state senate president Mike Miller of Fairbanks (no relation to Joe Miller, whom Sarah would support against Murkowski in 2010).

In June, Ruedrich admitted his violations of state ethics law and agreed to pay a $12,000 fine. But Alaskan ethical standards were so low that he was allowed to continue as state Republican Party chairman.

In August, Lisa Murkowski trounced Miller in the primary. In September, Sarah went public with the inside story of how she herself instigated the Ruedrich investigation, telling all—or at least her version of all—to *Daily News* reporter Richard Mauer, who published a 5,695-word story on September 19.

Public acclaim was deafening. A *Daily News* column in October said Alaska Republicans should adopt as a motto: "What Would Sarah Do?" She was described as "part Nathan Hale, part Sherlock Holmes" and "that rarest of all creatures, a politician with a conscience—and the guts to follow it."

The *Daily News* hadn't yet called her "the Joan of Arc of Alaskan politics," but that would come.

ELEVEN

THE GREBE CHICKS have hatched!

I've seen only two, but there may be more. I find myself wanting a cigar. That grebe couple and I have been through a lot this spring and I'm delighted to welcome their babies to the neighborhood. I'd like to go down to the lake and take a picture, but I don't want to risk being seen with a camera in my hands.

On the downside, T. C. Mitchell, who wrote the "deadly force" editorial in the *Frontiersman,* has been fired. This disturbs me. Yes, it was careless and even dumb for him to write what he did. But I feel bad for Mitchell. This is Alaska, where there's a tradition of people saying what they think. And I don't like to see a publisher fire someone for something he wrote.

I get Mitchell's e-mail address and write him to say that if he thinks it will help, I'll contact the publisher and ask her to reconsider. He says not to bother, that there were other issues besides the editorial. We agree to meet for lunch sometime soon.

ON YET ANOTHER gray, drizzly morning in late June—if this weather continues, I'm going to combine "gray" and "drizzly" and just call it "grizzly"—I'm heading for Jitters coffee shop in Eagle River for an early-morning meeting with Walt Monegan, the man Sarah fired as director of public safety because he wouldn't knuckle under to her and Todd's demands to fire her ex-brother-in-law from the state police.

The Monegan-Wooten saga wound up as the subject of two separate state investigations that came to different conclusions. One, commissioned by the bipartisan state legislature, said Sarah had abused the power of her office in her effort to have Wooten's head served to her and Todd on a silver platter; the other, commissioned more or less by Sarah, absolved her of any blame, although it left open the possibility that she had perjured herself during her sworn testimony to an investigator.

The one point both investigations agreed on was that Walt Monegan sacrificed his job for the sake of his principles. He wouldn't do what Todd and Sarah wanted him to do, so she canned him. Cut through all the Sturm und Drang and that's the core of the story.

"Sarah only talked to me about Wooten twice," Monegan says once we're seated. I've ordered a latte. Monegan, in character, drinks regular and drinks it black. "Of course, in eighteen months of working for her, I only talked to her four times in all. I thought at the time she must have been preoccupied with oil and gas issues. Now I realize she was only preoccupied with herself."

Terry and Walt Monegan

Monegan is relaxed and affable, although he'll have to leave in half an hour for his job with the Anchorage Board of Education. No chips are visible on his shoulders. He's moved on. He ran for mayor of Anchorage in the spring of 2009, but finished a distant fourth. "After thirty years of not being allowed to accept a free cup of coffee," he says, "my biggest problem was asking people for money. I knew I had to do it, but I hated it, and I didn't do it either well enough or often enough. That's okay. I got a taste of campaigning and found out for sure it's not for me."

One of the things I didn't know about Walt Monegan—and I didn't learn it this first morning, either—is that he's the only man in Alaska who ever peed on Harry Truman's leg.

Monegan's father, also named Walt but later nicknamed Tank Killer, was a U.S. Marine from Melrose, Massachusetts, who received a posthumous Medal of Honor for heroism in the face of an enemy tank and infantry attack near Sosa-ri, Korea, in 1950.

Walt was born in spring of 1951. He was nine months old when his mother brought him from Seattle to Washington, D.C., for the Medal of Honor ceremony. After the award was presented, President Truman invited the young widow into his office. He told her he loved babies and asked if he could hold Walt. And he did, on his lap, behind his desk in the Oval Office—for about sixty seconds. Then the president said, "Mrs. Monegan, I think your son needs some attention." Walt's mother looked in horror at the urine stain on the president's trouser leg. Walt was already showing he was not afraid to express himself to a higher authority.

He did it again in 2008 when the Palins made it clear that if Wooten didn't go, Monegan would. Monegan was chief of police in Anchorage in 2005 when Todd and Sarah launched their campaign against Wooten, and didn't learn how obsessed they were until Sarah appointed him director of public safety in 2006.

"The fact is, from having reviewed the files, I didn't think Wooten was a very good cop," he says. "The department probably made a mistake by hiring him. But that wasn't the issue. Every charge against him had been investigated and considered, and after he'd come back from his suspension he'd been as pure as Snow White. There was no decision for me to make: unless he screwed up again, he couldn't be fired. Todd just couldn't swallow that."

The Troopergate imbroglio is worth examining in detail because Sarah's actions, and those of her husband on her behalf, expose so clearly the vengeful, obsessive nature of the person who lurks behind the mask of sexiness and chirpy insouciance.

Mike Wooten married Molly Heath McCann in 2001. She was his third wife. He was her second husband. Molly and Mike had two children: McKinley and Heath. Also, each had a child from a previous marriage.

Molly filed for divorce in April 2005. At the same time, Sarah and Todd filed a complaint against Wooten for professional misconduct. In response, state police sergeant Ron Wall interviewed Sarah at her Lake Lucille home on May 5, 2005.

Sarah told Sergeant Wall that Molly had called her on February 17 to say that Mike "was on his way home and was in a rage." According to a state police transcript, Sarah said, "Molly called me. I was here at home with my kids and Molly was on her cell phone driving home from work and she said, 'Uh-oh, Mike's really mad, he's in a rage. I don't know what he wants, but he just told me to get my F'n ass home and don't tell him F'n no, and you guys better not be F'n with me.'"

Sarah said that when Molly arrived home, she "put the speaker phone on so I could listen. I was on my regular phone here. I could hear Mike come whammin' through the door, screaming F'n this, F'n that, tellin' Molly, 'If your dad helps you through this divorce, if he gets an attorney he's gonna, he's gonna eat an F'n lead bullet. I'm gonna shoot him.' He was in such a rage. I knew that if he had just walked in the door he probably did have his gun on, 'cause he wore it all the time. I was fearful of that. He just kept screaming, 'I'm gonna

F'n kill your dad if he gets an attorney to help you.' My fear was that he was gonna kill my dad.

"I drove over to Molly's house . . . It was dark but the lights were on in the house, so I could see right into the living room. Payton, the twelve-year old, was standing there with one of the babies on his hip. Mike, Molly was standing in the living room. I could see all this so clearly on a dark night. He's got his gun. He was flying his arms all over, obviously in a rage, waving his arms around, pacing. I could tell he was screaming. I could see this clearly through the window and I thought, 'He is gonna blow.' There's no other step for him to take next except from [sic] physical violence."

Sarah said she watched through the window "for probably fifteen minutes." Then, she said, "I had to leave. I had to head on into Chugiak. I had a meeting that I couldn't miss."

Sergeant Wall found this hard to understand. She was in mortal fear that at any moment Wooten might "blow" and possibly kill both her sister and her father, but she left to go to a meeting?

Did she at least warn her father to lock and load because his crazed son-in-law might show up at any moment at his place with gun in hand?

No, Sarah told Sergeant Wall, not "till weeks later."

Why not?

"Well, maybe Mike won't."

"Why didn't you guys call the police?" Wall asked.

"We knew Mike's job was probably on the line."

Wall struggled to make sense of this. At one point, he said, "We don't mean to frustrate you with facts, but our life is fact-driven, okay?"

Sigh. "I know," Sarah replied.

With the assistance of Chuck Heath, Bristol, Track, and, of course, Molly, Todd and Sarah spent months searching for "facts" that could cost Wooten his job. They even hired a private detective to keep Wooten under off-hours surveillance.

Wooten had tasered his stepson. Wooten had had affairs. Wooten drove while drunk. Wooten had been required to take an anger-management class. Wooten had illegally killed a wolf. Wooten had illegally killed a moose.

Between the spring of 2005 and spring of 2006, Palin and Heath family members filed twenty-five complaints against Wooten. All the charges were investigated. Only one was found to have merit. To that one—shooting a moose without a permit—Wooten fessed up.

In 2003, on a hunting trip, Wooten and Molly spotted a moose. Wooten told her to shoot, because she was the one with the permit. She told him she just couldn't do it and handed the rifle to him. Standing next to his wife, close enough to touch her permit, Wooten shot the moose. Chuck Heath butchered it in his garage. He and Sally and Todd and Sarah and Mike and Molly dined off it all winter.

SARAH WAS at loose ends professionally, having resigned from the oil and gas commission, and she pursued her vendetta against Wooten obsessively. On August 10, 2005, angered because Wooten had not yet been fired, Sarah sent a three-page e-mail to state trooper director Colonel Julia Grimes. The letter was filled with distortion and exaggeration.

She began by saying that Wooten was "described by many" as "a ticking timebomb and a loose cannon." However, only Sarah herself had used those terms to describe him. She added that although she had a family connection to Wooten (he was divorcing her sister), she was forwarding information about him "objectively."

She then ran through a laundry list of all the allegations Sergeant Wall had already investigated, and she repeated that Wooten was "a loose cannon" and "a ticking timebomb," and said, "I am afraid his actions . . . may cause someone terrible harm."

As she concluded her letter to Colonel Grimes, Sarah resorted to using boldface for emphasis:

Wooten does not tell the truth. He intimidates people and abuses his position. I don't know what more can be said, except that considering just a few examples from those I've shared with you (namely, **the death threat** against my father, who is merely trying to help his daughter escape a horribly abusive relationship, **the illegal hunting** and the **drunk driving!**) all would lead a rational person to believe there is a problem inside the organization.

She tacked on a P.S.:

Again, Wooten happens to be my brother-in-law, and after his infidelity and physical abuse of his wife (my sister) surfaced, Mike chose to leave his family and has continued to threaten to "bring down" anyone who supports her. I would ask that you objectively consider this information, disregarding my sister's pending divorce from Wooten, as I have objectively separated the divorce and Wooten's threats against me and my family with the fact that the Troopers have a loose cannon on their hands.

As Wall later observed in his report, "many of the issues that were noted in Palin's email had previously been investigated." Nonetheless, in a doomed attempt to pacify her, he conducted a new round of interviews.

He traveled to the Palin home on the afternoon of August 18, 2005, to reinterview Sarah. Time and again, under Wall's questioning, she was forced to concede that she had no personal knowledge of any of the "incidences" she described in her e-mail to Grimes.

Wall's report of the interview is littered with phrases such as "based on information she received from her sister Molly . . . ," "She again related that she had no personal knowledge . . . ," "Palin stated that Molly told her," "the story was told to her by Molly," "Palin again had no personal knowledge," "She didn't have personal knowledge," and so on.

An administrative investigator later stated that he'd never seen such a concerted effort against an individual officer. The judge handling the divorce case told the Heath/Palins that if their actions cost Wooten his job they would be financially liable. He also warned them to curtail their attacks. "Disparaging will not be tolerated—it is a form of child abuse," he said. The judge added that "the parent [Molly] needs to set boundaries for her relatives."

The judge granted the divorce decree in January 2006, but added a further warning to Molly, saying he'd be paying close attention to any problems in the custody arrangement, specifically "the disparagement of the father by the mother and her family members. It is the mother's responsibility to set boundaries for her relatives and ensure they respect them, and the disparagement by either parent or their surrogates is emotional child abuse."

Extraordinarily, the judge went further, writing that "If the court finds it is necessary due to disparagement in the Mat-Su Valley, for the children's best interests, it will not hesitate to order custody to the father and a move into Anchorage."

Sarah, by then a candidate for governor, finally received her pound of flesh on March 1, 2006, when Grimes suspended Wooten for ten days, later reduced to five after the state police union objected. Grimes cited a number of Sarah's complaints and warned Wooten that "any further occurrences of these types of behaviors or incidents will not be tolerated and will result in your termination."

But Sarah and Todd wanted Wooten fired. And they would not be satisfied until he was. Almost a year later, on February 7, 2007, after she'd been governor for two months, Sarah sent Monegan an e-mail in which she complained, "It was a joke, the whole year long 'investigation' of him."

Monegan knew how improper it was for Sarah, as governor, even to discuss the Wooten situation with him, much less ask him to fire the trooper without cause. He told her, "Ma'am, I need to keep you at arm's length with this."

As he finishes his coffee at Jitters and looks at his watch, Monegan tells me, "She didn't seem to understand that if Wooten were fired and filed a wrongful dismissal suit, any conversations she had with me would be subpoenable and I might have to testify under oath. She didn't seem to think in those terms. She just thought she should be able to do anything she wanted to, and that anybody working for her had an obligation to help."

Monegan did speak to Todd. "I tried to explain to him, 'You can't headhunt like this,'" he told the *Washington Post* in 2008. "'What you need to do is back off.'" Monegan also told the *Post* that he'd called Sarah to explain, "there was no new evidence, the issue was closed. She also was unhappy with that."

Nonetheless, Sarah praised Monegan's performance publicly almost until the day she sent a deputy chief of staff to tell him he was fired because he had, as she later said, a "rogue mentality." This was back when *rogue* was a bad word in her vocabulary.

"When Sarah was mayor of Wasilla, she had the power to fire the police chief, which she did," Monegan tells me as we walk toward our respective cars outside Jitters. "As governor, she had the power to fire me, which she did. But neither she nor Todd nor any of her staff nor any member of her family had the power to fire a state trooper. Maybe she hadn't realized there were limits on her power. Maybe she thought being governor meant she could do anything she wanted to anyone. I loved my job and I'm sorry she took it from me, but I've never had a moment's doubt about what I did. It wasn't an act of courage. My father was the one with the courage. All I did was what's right."

TWELVE

A S WITH EVERYTHING in regard to Sarah, two schools of thought about her actions in the Ruedrich case would emerge: her critics would say that everything she did was the result of political calculation and that her pursuit of Ruedrich was akin to her Wooten obsession; her supporters would see it as evidence that she was a beacon of integrity shining through the murk of Alaskan political corruption.

In 2004, however, the critics were not yet on the horizon. As the year ended, Sarah found herself at the high point of her political career, without even holding an office.

She claimed a new triumph when Governor Murkowski's attorney general, Gregg Renkes, resigned in February 2005, at least in part because of an ethics complaint that Sarah had filed against him in December. By April—notwithstanding her frustration about Wooten—she was the happiest camper in the Valley. She even wrote a column for the *Anchorage Daily News* just to say how wonderful the Valley was.

"Plato said you can learn more about a person in an hour of play than in a year of conversation," she wrote. "Same goes for cheering next to someone caught up in the insane intensity our Valley teams bring out in their fans. That's because diverse demographics coalesce with the elation and heartbreak shared on the roller coaster ride called 'Competition.'"

But the Valley was more than just an amusement park. "For instance, thankfully, we don't have cumbersome land use regulations that rid us of our beloved duct-taped blue tarps. Nor have we too many intrusive zoning laws that bid adieu to big stores with four walls, thus creating that boxy look that some curiously find so offensive . . ."

In June, as she first mentioned that she was considering a run for governor, the *Daily News* profiled her more extensively. "Sarah Palin arrives at a coffee shop for an interview looking like any other soccer mom running late for her next rendezvous with an offspring," the piece began. "She's dressed down in a pantsuit, her youngest, daughter Piper Indy, tugging at a pants leg. Her son Track will arrive later with a friend, and mother will dutifully hand over a few dollars. She needs a job, and soon, she quipped, just to keep her brood in gas money."

The story continued in Q-and-A form:

Q: I noticed there was a new business license acquired in the Mat-Su under your name.

A: Rouge Cou, it's a classy way of saying redneck. It's a French word, rouge is red, cou is neck. It's for marketing and consulting, in case I wanted to go that route, I'd have my ducks all lined up and have a business license . . .

Q: I see that you have a penchant for quoting people like John Wooden and Plato, do you consider yourself well-read?

A: (Laughs.) I'll let other people judge that. I'm glad you mentioned John Wooden. Most of my inspiration has come from being involved in sports . . .

Q: Do you have your sights set on any particular office that you'd like to serve in?

A: The list is long and I think the most, maybe the most fruitful office would be in the executive branch . . . I wouldn't hesitate if at some point in the future a door opened for me to be able to serve Alaskans in the executive branch . . .

For Todd, June meant his annual escape to Dillingham to supervise the family's fishing business. And to enjoy himself in other ways.

"Todd's a player, especially when he's out there at fishing camp," a friend of his from Dillingham told me in 2010. "I could probably fill up most of my fingers with the names of women Todd has screwed in Dillingham. That man has sowed his oats. The ones in Dillingham, he knew them from growing up. Today, they're in their forties, still caught up in drugs. In the summertime, when Todd came into town without Sarah, it was a fun time. Todd was partyin', we all had a good time, daylight twenty-four hours a day."

Sarah visited only infrequently. "Those people out there hate her," a former Dillingham resident says. "All of Todd's family hated her. She never interacted with any of them. J.D.'s wife, Wendy, cannot stand Sarah. Sarah has always treated Wendy like she was a piece of trash. And she hated J.D., was always mean to J.D., was always basically like, 'J.D.'s not comin' over here with his trashy friends,' and Todd used to always be like, 'I can't even have my own brother around.'"

Sarah wanted no part of commercial fishing. "She's never fished," a longtime acquaintance says. "I was out there for years. She was never on the boat. She never was up at the fish camp. J.D., and I think Todd was part of it, they bought into a fish camp at the mouth of the Nushagak River. It was called Fishing Adventures or something like that. You'd bring the people in, you have a cook on site, you have tents, and basically you make big bucks.

"Sarah was never there. Sarah was never part of that. What she would do, maybe every two years she would show up and dump the kids and stay hidden. She'd never even come out to eat.

"When she was in town—for maybe three days, or two days, if she even came—oh, Todd was a completely different guy. We were all warned. When Sarah was around we were always pre-warned. 'Don't tell her I did this, don't say anything about that, don't say nothin'.'

"If she didn't win the governorship, they were going to divorce," this acquaintance says. "Of course, back then they were divorcing every other month."

IN 2005, Alaskans outside a closed circle of Wasillans were hearing none of these stories. Sarah was portrayed as the blessed mother of the Valley, a God-fearing Christian hockey mom wielding the big stick of true reform.

On October 18 she became the first Republican officially to enter the race for governor. "Keeping it simple is my philosophy," she said. The *Daily News* reported on December 11 that she had "promising early poll numbers," but said, "the former Wasilla mayor needs to work on name recognition."

IT WAS NOT until late May that Frank Murkowski announced his intention to seek reelection. Having been elected in a landslide, Murkowski had used cronyism and imperiousness and an abject devotion to the interests of Big Oil to turn himself into the most unpopular governor in the country, with a June 15 disapproval rating of 78 percent.

A poll in late July, one month before the primary, showed Sarah leading with 36 percent, former state senator John Binkley of Fairbanks coming in second with 23 percent, and Murkowski last with 20. Twenty-one percent were undecided. Sarah's one negative seemed to be her lack of experience. An August 4 letter to the *Daily News* called attention to this:

Sarah Palin has no business running for governor. Where is her experience? What should concern people is she will have to come into this office at full gallop and won't have a clue about leading the state. Ms. Palin, why don't you run for state representative and work your way up? . . .

I'm sure Sarah Palin is a nice person and deeply regarded by the Christian community. But Christian doesn't cut it if you don't have what it takes. Stay home, be a wife and mother, isn't that fulfilling enough?

But that was a minority view. A week before the primary, a poll showed her leading Binkley 40 to 29 percent, with Murkowski trailing at 17. In the campaign's final days, Murkowski tried to turn the ethical tables on Sarah, charging that, Ruedrich-like, she had used her mayor's office to conduct political business. She responded by charging Murkowski with running a "smear campaign."

On August 22, Sarah won the primary with 51 percent of the vote to Binkley's 30 and Murkowski's 19. In November she would face former two-term Democratic governor Tony Knowles and conservative independent Andrew Halcro, a former state legislator whose family operated the Avis franchise in Anchorage.

There was to be no stopping her. She was a fresh face—and a very pretty one—at a time when the Alaska media were starved for fresh faces. Where once she'd sought "glamour and culture" by driving to Anchorage to watch Ivana Trump sell perfume, now she personified at least the first of the two. The *Daily News* said she emerged from the primary "with a Joan of Arc glow," and soon thereafter the paper christened her "the Joan of Arc of Alaska politics." She was uncorrupted and incorruptible. She had fought her own party's decadent power structure and had won. How could she not be heaven sent?

As the general election campaign began in September, Anchorage *Voice of the Times* columnist Paul Jenkins, as diehard a conservative as could be found in the Alaskan press, described the media's embrace of Sarah as "nympholepsy," a frenzy induced by nymphs.

He wrote about the "breathless, incredibly embarrassing fawning" over her, pointing out that her most prominent supporters, former governor Walter Hickel; former state senator Rick Halford; and her personal attorney, Wayne Anthony Ross, an avid gun collector who drove a Hummer with a license plate that read WAR, were members of the very faction Sarah had sworn to overthrow.

"The pseudo-coverage has gotten so bad that we are treated to stories about her winning smile," he wrote. "And women, the talking heads now tell us, nowadays are dressing just as she does. The entire state, they blubber, is all atwitter over the lovely Ms. Palin. Oh, my."

Any prospect that the media might recover its wits vanished with the explosive news, made public in early September, that the FBI had raided the offices of seven Alaskan legislators, all but one Republicans, seeking evidence that they'd accepted bribes from Veco, the oil services company founded by former welder and now multimillionaire Bill Allen.

That there was a corrupt coterie of Republicans in Juneau had been an open secret in Alaska for years, although no one in the timid media had ever revealed it. They even had a name for themselves, The Corrupt Bastards Club, and printed T-shirts and baseball caps with the slogan.

The FBI investigation eventually led to guilty pleas from or convictions of eleven Republicans, including the later overturned conviction of Alaska's greatest living icon, U.S. senator Ted Stevens. The scandal colored the entire gubernatorial campaign. The Democratic candidate, Tony Knowles, was not implicated in the Veco scandal, but he had served eight years as governor, which was enough to make him a charter member of the privileged "good old boys" structure that Sarah was vowing to dismantle.

Given that climate, scant attention was paid to the fact that Sarah herself, while running for lieutenant governor, had accepted contributions from Veco. It was only $5,000, but that represented 10 percent of the money she raised for her lieutenant governor campaign.

Tony Hopfinger would later write in the *Dispatch* that she'd personally solicited a contribution from Allen in 2001, driving to his Anchorage home and sharing a bottle of wine with him. Following her charm offensive, Sarah received a total of ten five-hundred-dollar contributions from Veco executives and their wives.

As with her improper use of her Wasilla mayor's office for political purposes, this blemish was ignored by media outlets more eager to sanctify her than report on her. Knowles, sixty-three, who'd run for the U.S. Senate and lost to Lisa Murkowski only two years earlier, was not a fresh face. In fact, in the aftermath of the FBI raids, the accomplished and affable Knowles was a dead candidate walking.

EVEN THOSE at the highest levels of Sarah's campaign knew that she was not qualified to be governor. But they rationalized, and they hoped. As John Bitney told me in the summer of 2010, "We had a corruption issue. That's one of the main reasons I worked on her campaign. I was pissed off. Watching Bill Allen float around the halls of my state capitol: it was disgusting. What I thought was, okay, we had this woman who couldn't stick to a schedule and couldn't make a decision about anything, and we had this cadre of crazies that were her circle, but if we get her into the governor's office we can scissor off all the nut jobs, get a professional staff, and she will grow into the job and it will mold her."

Sarah herself never slowed down long enough to let doubts about her abilities catch up to her. Other than scheduling—"a nightmare that not even Kafka could envision," Bitney says—the hardest job her staff had was to keep her quiet about her religious beliefs. This wasn't Wasilla, this was all of Alaska, and not everyone had a taste for her evangelical Kool-Aid.

Knowles sent a letter to voters who'd expressed support for abortion rights, pointing out Sarah's opposition. As John Stein choked on his oatmeal, Sarah said with a straight face, "I think it's a shame that anyone would try to make this a banner issue in the campaign when it's not."

A month before the election, Sarah had an eleven-point lead over Knowles, with Halcro trailing in single digits. But she didn't hide. She enjoyed taking on Knowles and Halcro in televised debates. Using index cards, a dazzling smile, and short, snappy answers, and—having studied video of Ronald Reagan—often responding to Knowles by saying, "There you go again," in what the *Daily News* called "the sing-songy voice she uses when trying to score a zinger," Sarah won the hearts, if not minds, of most viewers. The *Daily News* credited her with "classic schoolyard one-upmanship." Her gift for it was not surprising, given that in so many ways she remained a tenth-grade Mean Girl.

Toward the end of the campaign, a despairing Halcro said, "We're going to elect a candidate who never truly answered any questions." Alaskans, as it turned out, didn't want answers: they wanted Sarah, however imperfect she might have been. "The voters aren't looking for perfection," she said. "If they are looking for perfection, they should vote for God." Clearly she was the next best thing.

She slipped up once, when she said that public schools should make creationism part of their curriculum as a valid alternative to evolution. Toward the end of a televised debate on October 25 she said, "Teach both. You know, don't be afraid of information . . . I am a proponent of teaching both."

Bitney pulled her aside immediately.

"You just fucked up, girl."

"I was just saying there needs to be both."

"No, that's wack! People think that's wack."

"I don't see the problem," she said.

"Trust us on this one," Bitney said. "You're way out there, too fucking far, you're going to freak people out, Sarah. Don't do that."

After a heated backroom discussion, "We got her to backpedal and we couched it down as best we could," Bitney told me. In an interview the next day, Sarah said that all she'd meant to say was, "I don't think there should be a prohibition against debate if it comes up in class. It doesn't have to be part of the curriculum."

"Even so," Bitney recalled, "we still barely skated. Mostly she did a good job in the campaign of not letting that stuff seep out, but that's who she is. She believes that stuff."

It didn't matter. In the climate of the time, nothing mattered except the image that Sarah presented to the voters. As the *Daily News* said in late October, "Her campaign has sometimes struggled this fall to put ideas and positions into clear focus. But they seem almost secondary. The main product Palin is selling this year, as in Wasilla ten years ago, is Palin herself."

As Election Day neared, Bitney—like Sarah herself—was already looking beyond Juneau. "I was telling her in October, 'You'd better be thinking of running for vice president,'" he said. "Here was a gorgeous young reformer, a woman, a fresh face with an intriguing story that could be developed. I thought, we can have this woman in the limelight going into the 2008 convention. So we need to be mindful of framing the story."

She beat Knowles 48–41, with Halcro receiving 9 percent of the vote. But even before she moved in, Sarah saw the Governor's Mansion as only a way station en route to her true destination, the one that God had always envisioned for her: 1600 Pennsylvania Avenue, Washington, D.C.

THIRTEEN

ON THURSDAY, June 24, I drive to Fairbanks. From Wasilla, on a fine summer's day, it should take less than six hours to get there.

For me, Fairbanks evokes. In 1975 it gave me my first exposure to serious subzero cold. Forty below was normal, with ice fog, a phenomenon you don't want to know about unless you're considering moving to Fairbanks. But I was also there in July 1976, when the temperature was uncomfortable in a different way.

I drove to Fairbanks with my older three children, then aged nine, eight, and five. I was divorced from their mother, with whom they lived in Swarthmore, Pennsylvania. They'd been out for a two-week summer visit. In those days, there was a direct flight to Philadelphia from Fairbanks, but not Anchorage. Undoubtedly, it had to do with Fairbanks's brief and not-so-shining status as the epicenter of oil pipeline development.

I decided to drive the kids to Fairbanks so they could have a non-stop flight home. They'd get to see a bit more of Alaska, at least from a car window, and we could stop overnight at a roadside cabin halfway.

My first mistake was buying a used car in Anchorage for the trip. I thought I'd be okay because, I told myself, the dealer was a friend of a friend. It turned out that the dealer was a friend, or maybe acquaintance, of someone who turned out to be my acquaintance, not my friend. It was a battered blue station wagon of indeterminate vintage, which would have been fine, except the radiator leaked.

I mean *leaked*. I had to stop every fifty miles and refill it from a five-gallon water jug. It was like a trip through Death Valley. My kids never saw the scenery: they were on the lookout for sources of water.

It was still light out when we pulled into a roadside cabin at about 10:00 PM. This was my children's first experience with the concept of no running water, which meant no indoor toilet, which meant an outhouse. Because it was only for one night, they decided to treat it as an exotic adventure.

I unloaded the car and cooked dinner. As I recall, we ate bacon and eggs and grilled cheese sandwiches. After they went to bed, I put what I hadn't cooked in a cooler on the porch.

It was dark out—and it wasn't dark for long, so this must have been about 2:00 or 3:00 AM—when my eight-year-old, Suzy, woke me up to tell me she'd seen a bear.

"I was coming back from the bathroom by the woods," she said, "and I saw him. He was eating all the stuff you left on the porch. Can you get my camera out of my backpack? I want to go back and take his picture. He's so cute."

Thus was I almost responsible for the mauling or premature death of sweet Suzy, now the mother of three of my grandchildren. It was Suzy, in fact, who'd been thinking of bringing her husband and children to Wasilla to stay with me on Lake Lucille for a couple of weeks this summer, until the Andrew Breitbart commenter wrote, "can't wait for your grandkids to show up and play in the woods and water." After that I told her to forget it.

In the morning, we drove on to Fairbanks. Even with the water stops we got to the airport in plenty of time. I spotted a bank thermometer registering ninety-two degrees. My nine-year-old, Chrissy, said, "I can't wait to get out of Alaska: it's too hot."

Now I'm heading north again, in a Toyota Rav4, rented from

Andrew Halcro's Avis franchise in Anchorage. The radiator works. Even in summer, in daylight, it is still one hell of a drive. I encounter a half-hour delay due to road construction between Willow and Talkeetna. Just outside the entrance to Denali National Park, I come upon the astonishing apparition of "Glitter Gulch," an explosion of private-enterprise resorts. There's even a traffic light!

Cruise ship passengers who have arrived by bus wander from hotels on one side of the highway to restaurants and souvenir shops on the other. I sit at the red light, stunned at all this construction thrown up in the middle of what had been nowhere. Glitter Gulch is a good name for it, however unofficial. It's like the sudden, shocking sight of Las Vegas in the middle of the desert, and it's every bit as artificial.

I reach Fairbanks at 4:00 PM. My first appointment is at 5:00. I need a place to stay and I head for the most obvious, Pike's Waterfront Lodge, on the Chena River, near the airport. Holland America and Princess cruise line tour buses are parked in front. As unlikely as it seems, even Fairbanks has become a summer tourist destination. I get one of the worst rooms in the joint, and it costs nearly $200. The hotel is owned by a Republican state legislator, Jay Ramras, who's currently running for lieutenant governor. Ramras used to be known as Chicken Man because he'd stand in front of his chicken wing restaurant dressed up like Big Bird from *Sesame Street,* hoping to entice customers.

The people I've come to see tell me they can't make it at five, but they'll call back by six thirty. They don't call. I call at seven and seven thirty and eight and get only voice mail. I don't know what's going on, but it's too magnificent a night to waste worrying about it. (It turns out to be a medical emergency, and I see them in August.)

It's only three nights after the longest day of the year and in Fairbanks there's literally midnight sun. Even with the smell of smoke from forest fires in the air, how sweet it is to sit at Pike's Landing with a glass of white wine and feel the warmth of the sun and enjoy the sights on the river.

I'm reminded of what my old Alaskan friend Ray Bane said during our Brooks Range hike in August 1976: "All this is a lie. A beautiful lie. Winter is the truth about Alaska." Ray and his wife, Barbara, I should note—after many winters of running dog teams in Bettles, where the average lows from November through March are below zero—now live in Hawaii.

I have breakfast with Jim Whitaker, former mayor of Fairbanks. Whitaker, fifty-nine, is a Republican who served as mayor from 2003 until 2009. In his final run for reelection, in 2006, he received more than 75 percent of the vote. He endorsed Barack Obama in 2008 and spoke at the Democratic National Convention.

"It was an easy choice," he tells me over buffet-line scrambled eggs at Pike's Lodge, "and it had nothing to do with Sarah. I simply felt Obama was better suited to lead the country than John McCain. I spoke at the convention before the choice of Sarah was even announced. But I must say I was surprised by the choice, and also disappointed."

"Why?"

"Surprised because I had spoken to her in March, right here at Pike's Landing, at the finish of the Iron Dog. I'd heard that she'd been trying to promote herself as a vice-presidential candidate and I asked her if it was true. 'Absolutely not,' she told me. 'I have a job and I intend to see it through.' I was disappointed because I realized she'd lied to me, and also because I'd persuaded myself that she'd meant all the other things she said: about caring for the state and about the need to rise above political considerations. She fooled me like she fooled a lot of others."

Whitaker had been impressed by Palin's exposure of Ruedrich's improper conduct at the oil and gas commission. "I knew Ruedrich from when I was first elected to the statehouse in 1999," he tells me. "I was one of four newly elected Republicans. As soon as we got to Juneau, Ruedrich brought us into a room with two guys from Bill Allen's company, Veco, and told us, 'These are the guys who put you in office. I wanted you to listen to what they say.'"

Whitaker shakes his head, as if still in disbelief more than ten years later. "This shit really does happen," he says.

He was convinced Sarah would be different. "The real rub," he says, "relates to her failure to uphold the public trust. I really believed that she would subordinate her personal interests. In the end, she didn't. But I was also surprised and disappointed when she resigned. It was a cut-and-run to take the big money she knew was out there. Profiteering, pure and simple. I never thought she would do that."

Nonetheless, Whitaker is quick to praise her political abilities. "She really understands the phrase 'the theater of politics.' I've never seen a person who could connect with thousands of people the way she can. It's just too bad she's unwilling and unable to understand issues. She can't seem to grasp that there are situations out there that are bigger than her."

He recalls a visit he made to her Anchorage office soon after she'd been elected governor. "I thought we'd have a discussion about substantive matters. Instead, I had to listen to a forty-five-minute diatribe about what was being said about her on talk radio."

Some months later, after Track had enlisted in the army, Whitaker was with Sarah in the lobby of the Princess Hotel in Fairbanks. "There were about half a dozen of us, just having an informal chat about policy, when someone came in and told her that Track was outside. He'd just finished basic training and was on his way back to Fort Wainwright and she hadn't seen him for several months. I said, 'Well, I guess that's our cue to wrap things up.' But she said, 'No, no, he can wait. Let's keep going.'

"I said, 'Governor, you need to go see your son.' She wouldn't do it. For at least another half hour we kept going, really just talking about silly stuff."

The strongest and most disturbing recollection Whitaker has about Sarah comes from her appearance at the Fort Wainwright deployment ceremony on September 11, 2008, while she was campaigning for vice president. Track was among those being deployed.

"I said to her, 'Look, I've spoken at these events and they're very emotional, so know that it's okay to show your feelings. You're talking to 4,500 soldiers going off to war, and some of them will not be coming back. We know that and they do, too. And your son is one of them. So don't be embarrassed if you cry.'"

He pauses, then resumes, speaking slowly and deliberately for emphasis. "I have never," he says, "seen such a detached and self-absorbed speech to deploying soldiers. Her lack of emotional involvement was scary. Her speech was all about her. Then, at the end, it was suddenly, 'Go! Fight! Win!' That was the moment I lost the last of my faith in Sarah Palin."

JOHN STEIN didn't want to talk to me. He said that recalling his last years in Wasilla and Sarah's campaign against him made his heart sink. I kept trying to persuade him. Eventually he stopped answering my e-mails.

In mid-June, at a social gathering in Wasilla, I met Clyde and Vivian Boyer. Clyde was Catherine Taylor's ex-husband. He and Vivian, who were just returning from a trip to Russia, now lived in Homer, the town 222 miles south of Anchorage that lies at the very end of the North American road system. Because there are not six degrees of separation among Alaskans, but fewer than one, they also knew John Stein. They said they'd contact him about talking to me. A week later, they wrote back: "John responded that he doesn't have the emotional energy at this time to talk to you."

I kept trying. I e-mailed Stein the story about T. C. Mitchell getting fired by the *Frontiersman.* He wrote back, "And you wonder why I don't want to go there. Makes me want to puke." But at least he wrote back. That gave me the chance to guilt-trip him.

I wrote, "To the extent that those who can keep the record straight decline to do so—and emotional exhaustion with Palin is certainly understandable—it becomes easier for her people to repaint the past and thus more effectively position her to run for president in less than two years. It will be a lesser book without my having access to your recollections. You were there, in the cross-hairs, during her first step up the ladder. I'd be sorry to have to publish without your input."

His sense of civic virtue finally outweighed his entirely understandable desire to refrain from dredging up such a harrowing chapter from his past. He wrote back, "You SOB, and I mean that in the most friendly and collegial way. Reliving that period will be both painful and engaging. My heart is not in it. You had better come here. I can pick you up at the airport. Let me know your itinerary. I have a bedroom and bath for your use. We can cook king salmon I caught yesterday. There is a cat in the house."

I stayed overnight in Anchorage on June 28 and caught the early flight to Sitka in the morning.

As promised, he's waiting for me. Stein is sixty-five years old and about to retire as executive director of the Sitka Sound Science Center, a nonprofit "dedicated to increasing understanding and awareness

John Stein

of terrestrial and aquatic ecosystems of the Gulf of Alaska through education and research."

We have a quick lunch, then he's off to a meeting at the science center, which gives me a chance to stroll through picturesque Sitka on a rare sunny day. I'm not a photographer, but I snap a picture of a small piece of the Sitka Harbor.

Stein drives a battered blue pickup. He lives with his cat, three miles east of town. His oldest son, Reber, thirty-two, who is running for a seat in the Alaska statehouse, and his youngest son, Jackson, twenty, live in Sitka. Two other sons live out of state. His second wife, to whom he was married while mayor of Wasilla, died of breast cancer in 2005.

He shows me to comfortable private quarters downstairs. When I come back up, I'm faced with an awkward moment: after putting all this effort into persuading Stein to see me, I have to request a slight delay. In the chaos of my departure from Lake Lucille—my attention deficit disorder tends to make all my departures chaotic—I neglected to record the Spain-Portugal World Cup match, being played this afternoon, Alaska time.

"I don't suppose you've been following the World Cup," I say.

"Of course I have. Day before yesterday I saw Argentina run all over Mexico."

"Don't they look great? I think they're going to win it. Messi is definitely the best player in the world."

"So there's a match this afternoon?"

"Spain-Portugal."

"That's a big one. Let's watch it. We'll have plenty of time to talk later."

Spain wins 1–0 on David Villa's goal in the sixty-third minute, his fourth of the tournament.

IT'S DINNERTIME and clouding over. The sun is an infrequent visitor to Sitka skies. Stein carries his freshly caught salmon out to the deck and turns on his gas grill. His cat follows, lost in an impossible dream.

The salmon, predictably, is delicious. Not quite as good as it would have been on my Traeger, but memorable. You'd have to stomp on a fresh-caught king in a manure pit and then boil it in yak piss for a week to render it anything less than sublime.

After dinner we sit down with coffee and start to talk. We talk for hours, as he shares his recollections of Wasilla and Sarah. Much of the information in earlier chapters about Sarah's years in Wasilla politics comes from our conversation that night. At bedtime, he summarizes: "If Sarah had a political philosophy, it would be 'You don't have to know anything about anything: just pray, and the answer will come out of thin air.'"

It's pouring in the morning, but my flight doesn't leave until 6:00 PM, so Stein decides to give me an all-weather tour of the island, which will culminate at the Fortress of the Bear, a facility at which brown bear cubs orphaned in the wild are taken for protection and training until they can be shipped on to zoos. We start with a visit to his son Reber, who is just gearing up for his state House of Representatives run against the Republican incumbent.

Sitka, which occupies the western side of Baranof Island (the eastern side is virtually uninhabited), is as different from Wasilla as two Alaskan cities of approximately the same size could be. Many non-Alaskans probably know the fictitious Sitka of Michael Chabon's novel *The Yiddish Policemen's Union* better than the real thing.

The actual Sitka is, by area, the second largest incorporated city in the United States, exceeded only by Yakutat, on the south coast of Alaska's mainland. Sitka covers more than six times the square mileage of Jacksonville, Florida, the largest city by area in the Lower Forty-eight. By Alaskan standards, the climate is balmy, with the average low in January scarcely below freezing (though the average high in August is only sixty-three). On the other hand, rain or snow falls more than 250 days a year. Sitka gets so much rain that they sell freshwater to India for distribution in the Middle East.

The way it's raining this morning, they could fill a whole tanker before noon. We pull into Reber's driveway and trot to his front door, where we remove our shoes before entering (standard etiquette throughout Alaska). He's affable, but busy, as befits an underdog political candidate. He's also got a long memory, as befits a man whose father lost his job to Sarah Palin.

"One of her problems," John Stein says, over excellent espresso that Reber has made on his home machine, "is that, in her mind, if you can't write it on a bumper sticker it's too complicated to try to understand. That's why she always speaks in jingles."

"What I remember," Reber says, "is how angry Sarah and Chuck and Sally always were. Todd wasn't around much then, but every time there would be an event for the two candidates, Sarah and her parents would be there and they'd be so hostile. It was really off the scale, like they felt we were about to disclose something awful and they were reacting in advance."

After lunch we drive to the Fortress of the Bear. The "fortress" consists of two three-quarter-acre clarifier tanks left over from an abandoned pulp mill, each with walls fifteen feet high. Inside each, a natural bear habitat has been created. There are only two bears in residence at the moment, a few having just been shipped to the Bronx Zoo, but they are clearly enjoying their stay.

The caretaker calls them, and they come to a steel-barred window at the edge of one tank. The caretaker raises a metal door just high enough for one of the bears to put his snout through, but not high enough so he can open his mouth.

"Get as affectionate as you want to," the caretaker says. "This might be your only chance to kiss a brown bear."

The rain subsides as Stein drives me to Sitka's tiny airport. "My question about Sarah," he says, "is if God wants her to be president, why didn't God equip her with education enough to have at least basic knowledge of geography, science, and social systems?"

"You mean so she wouldn't say she could see Russia from her house?"

"She never said that," he says, smiling. "She said she could see rush hour."

I'M BACK at my house half an hour before the end of June. Sarah has just made a speech at California State University Stanislaus, for which she received a $75,000 fee. She told her audience it was no wonder Ronald Reagan had always had such a sunny disposition: after all, he'd grown up in the "Golden State" of California and had received his education at "California's Eureka College."

Even though he's her greatest political hero, she didn't know that he grew up in Illinois, where Eureka College is located, about halfway between Normal and Peoria.

• • •

I START JULY by making sure there's enough seed on the deck railing for my resident squirrel.

He comes around every day, usually in late afternoon. Often I'm not there, but when I am I feed him. He's grown incredibly tame. I think we've developed an understanding. There are those who consider both of us pests, and for the moment each of us is pretty much alone in the world, so we might as well be friends—at least until I run out of birdseed. Between the grebes and kissing a brown bear in Sitka and now this little fellow, who one evening actually eats out of my hand, I'm starting to feel like Joseph of Assisi.

The recently fired *Frontiersman* editor, T. C. Mitchell, comes over for lunch. We have hamburgers and beers on my deck. He says there's nothing I can do to help him. We don't talk much about his editorial and not at all about Sarah. Instead, we talk about our earlier days in Alaska and we decide to try to get together to see a Mat-Su Miners Alaska League baseball game before too long.

Months later, after the shooting of Representative Gabrielle Giffords in Arizona, the *Frontiersman* would issue a further apology for Mitchell's editorial.

We know first-hand the weight of words. As a commenter on our Facebook page was quick to point out . . . we made national news last year with our own careless use of inflammatory words. Words we used in an editorial invoking Alaska's self-defense laws were meant in jest, but readers didn't see it that way. Your reaction to our blunder was swift, loud and lasting. The editorial went viral and we could only watch in dismay as commentators on radio, television and the Internet threw our words back at us in condemnation. Red-faced, we apologized repeatedly for our carelessness. And we repeat our previous apology.

I don't need an apology from Mitchell. We've all made careless mistakes. It's not like he drew a bull's-eye around my head and left it up on his Facebook page for months.

I DRIVE TO Palmer, back to Vagabond Blues, to meet with Reverend Howard Bess, who at least won't try to loan me a gun.

I met Bess for the first time in the fall of 2009, as I began my Alaskan research on Sarah. With the possible exception of Daniel

Howard Bess

Berrigan, he's probably the most engaging man of the cloth to whom I've ever spoken at length. At eighty-two, he could walk me into the ground. With wit, reason, knowledge, and passion he also can talk pretty much anyone into submission.

Bess is less than thrilled by Sarah's continuing presence on the national political scene. Her religious extremism is what most alarms him. "Hers is a dualistic Christianity," he says, "in which everything and everyone is either good or evil. If you disagree with her you're not just a bad guy, you're evil and you must be defeated."

Bess points out that Sarah could exist only in America. "This is the only country on earth that has this freewheeling evangelicism, not responsible to any hierarchy. There's no vertical structure, but there's a vast horizontal reach, through networking. What that can lead to at worst—and it doesn't always, and I mean no disrespect to evangelicals, many of whom are friends of mine—is not just disrespect for other points of view, but a warrior mentality, where your life becomes all about stamping out anything you construe as evil."

Bess doesn't question Sarah's sincerity. "I'd be a lot happier if I thought she were cynical and doing things for selfish reasons, but she's not. She absolutely believes these are what the evangelicals call the Last Days. She absolutely believes, as she's told Phil Munger, that the earth is six thousand years old and that dinosaurs and man once lived together. And she absolutely believes that Jesus will return to earth during the course of her life. These beliefs are at the core of everything she says and does. She is locked into that worldview. If you don't appreciate how totally she is governed by these beliefs, you'll never understand Sarah Palin."

There is no doubt, Bess tells me, that "Sarah feels chosen. She feels called. It's a common theme in the Bible that God calls certain people to do certain things. And I have felt this in my own life. Why am I a minister? Not because I went through some rational process, but because I felt God calling me. Everything I've done in my life since has been in response to that calling. So when I say she feels chosen, or called, or annointed, I'm not being patronizing: I respect that. I honor that."

"Why her?" I ask.

"She doesn't know. But she knows in her heart that it's true."

"Really?"

"All religion is nonrational. God calls Moses and says, can you lead a bunch of slaves out of Egypt? Now, I don't mean that literally— I take it mythologically—but the point is that God calls people to do things that appear to be impossible. And Sarah has that sense of calling. She knows herself to be on a mission from God."

"But let's say she lies and she hurts people and she's a hypocrite. How can that be part of God's calling?"

Bess laughs in delight. "Because," he says, the teacher concluding his lesson in triumph, "if you're on a mission from God to destroy evil, there are going to be all kinds of expendables along the way. Collateral damage. It's irrelevant when you look at the stakes involved."

I start to close my notebook, but he stops me. He's enjoying himself.

"Our little children's summer theater group just put on a play that I went to before coming over here. It was called *The Amazing Mr. Fox.* It starts off with the fox killing lots of chickens. All the kids, naturally, feel sorry for the chickens and hate the fox. But then it comes out that the fox needs to feed his family: Aha, we never thought of it that way. There are little foxes to worry about, too. And to the amazing Mr. Fox, the chickens are expendable."

"And the moral?"

"If anybody gets in her way, Sarah says, 'Tough luck, you're a chicken.'"

FOURTEEN

O N MONDAY, October 10, 2005, Sarah filed a letter of intent with the Alaska Public Offices Commission, saying she intended to seek public office the following year. She didn't specify the office, nor did she say whether she planned to run as a Republican or an independent.

"I don't know yet if my run is for governor or lieutenant governor. I haven't ruled out any of the scenarios that people have been rumoring about," she told the *Frontiersman*. "I just want to do what is right for Alaska. If that means running as an independent for lieutenant governor, then I'll do it."

The following Sunday, October 16, she attended services at the Wasilla Assembly of God. During her campaign for lieutenant governor, Sarah had switched her allegiance to the Wasilla Bible Church, which was marginally less extreme in its views and had a significantly larger congregation.

But now she went back to her roots, having arranged for a special blessing from a guest preacher, Reverend Thomas Muthee, of Kiambu, Kenya. Muthee had given nine sermons at the Assembly of God church during the previous five days. He'd first gained fame in Pentecostal circles in the late 1980s by claiming to have used prayer to drive a witch called Mama Jane out of the city of Kiambu, just as Sarah's longtime spiritual mentor Mary Glazier had driven a witch out of Alaska.

The tale Muthee told to Pentecostal congregations around the world was that Mama Jane had been amusing herself by arranging fatal traffic accidents in front of her house. He proclaimed, "Mama Jane either gets saved and serves the Lord, or she leaves town. There is no longer room in Kiambu for both of us!" Her response was to cause a triple fatality.

Muthee's followers swarmed all over her house, wanting to stone her. In the ensuing melee, police encountered her pet python. One of the officers, recognizing that the snake was a "demon," shot and killed it. With the snake's death, according to Muthee, "the demonic influence was broken," Mama Jane left town, and the streets of Kiambu were again safe for driving.

Muthee's claim to have recaptured Kiambu for Christ by breaking Mama Jane's demonic hold on the city coincided with the 1989 publication of a book called *Taking Our Cities for God*, by a Pentecostal preacher from Los Angeles named John Dawson. The book resonated throughout the Pentecostal universe as a spiritual call to arms. Dawson believed that "satanic forces manifest themselves in the culture of the city," and that only "strategic-level spiritual warfare" (SLSW) could defeat them.

The following year, George Otis, Jr., who later founded and became CEO and president of The Sentinel Group, a Seattle-based "Christian research and information agency," coined the term *spiritual mapping*. He wrote that Satan had sent powerful demonic forces to particular countries, regions, and cities in order to thwart Christian teaching. These "territorial spirits" destroyed the moral fabric of the societies in which they operated. He wrote that "spiritual darkness is palpable and geographically concentrated."

In his 1991 book, *The Last of the Giants: Lifting the Veil on Islam and the End Time,* he posited the notion that "territorial demonic strongholds" literally existed in various locations, and that SLSW, if concentrated in the proper areas, could free whole societies from demonic control.

This notion gained traction among Pentecostals throughout the 1990s, aided considerably by the 1997 publication of *Breaking Strongholds in Your City: How to Use Spiritual Mapping to Make Your Prayers More Strategic, Effective, and Targeted* by C. Peter Wagner, cofounder (with the later disgraced Ted Haggard) of the World Prayer Center in Colorado Springs, Colorado. Described in *Charisma* magazine as "a spiritual version of the Pentagon," the World Prayer Center is the command post for Wagner's worldwide campaign against demons.

Writing in The Plumbline, Orrel Steinkamp describes the role of spiritual mapping in strategic-level spiritual warfare: "Spiritual mapping is the process of gathering information regarding a region or a people in order to determine the identity and function of the territorial ruler . . . 'Team Orange' are a specially trained cadre of spiritual mappers. They gather information regarding any area to which they are sent . . . They call spiritual mapping 'Night Vision Goggles' which enable them to see, purportedly, into the darkness of a city."

Wagner believed that the "Third Wave of the Holy Spirit" broke upon the beaches of America in the 1980s and that it represented the last chance for Christians to position themselves before the end-times, which would lead to the Rapture, but only for those who'd earlier dedicated their lives to fulfilling the wishes of Jesus Christ.

He literally believed that Satan sent "senior demons from the hierarchy of evil spirits" to control everything from individual neighborhoods to whole countries. But all was not lost. Spiritual mapping, a sort of divine GPS, could identify their whereabouts, and strategic-level spiritual warfare could destroy them.

In 1998 the World Prayer Center created a "spiritual mapping repository." Otis said, "Spiritual mapping is especially needed now because Satan will increase his resistance to the church as it moves toward fulfillment of the Great Commission."

In 1999, Otis not only published a book called *Informed Intercession,* a guide to how to "transform" a city or region, but also produced a video called *Transformations,* which purported to show how spiritual mapping and spiritual warfare had improved the quality of life in four different cities, including Hemet, California, and Kiambu, Kenya.

In Hemet, Otis said, "The Transcendental Meditation center was literally burned out. Shortly after the intercessors prayed for its removal, a brush fire started on the mountain on the west side of the valley. It burned only the Transcendental Meditation facility and didn't touch any of the buildings on either side."

In 2000, Wagner wrote a new book called *Praying Through the 100 Gateway Cities of the 10/40 Window,* the premise of which was that locations between ten and forty degrees north latitude (i.e., "the 10/40 window") should be the primary targets of spiritual warfare.

At sixty-one degrees north, Wasilla was not in the danger zone. Nonetheless, as mayor, Sarah had taken the precaution of having it declared a City of Character, trusting that the designation would strengthen its defenses against demonic onslaught. Now she was concerned with Satanic control of a larger realm: the state of Alaska.

In 2001, Otis released a sequel video called *Transformations II,* which exponentially increased the reach and strength of the message he and Wagner were trying to bring to the world. Among those caught up in this Third Wave, or New Apostolic Reformation, was Ed Kalnins, pastor of Wasilla's Assembly of God church.

Although the general council of the Assemblies of God had again denounced the New Apostolic Reformation as heretical the year before, Kalnins retained his allegiance to it. Thus the church in which Sarah had been baptized and to which she'd belonged for more than twenty-five years, until she abandoned it in an election year for one with a larger congregation, was so extremist that even the radically right-wing Pentecostal Assemblies of God had declared it beyond their pale.

In 2005, Muthee, the star of the *Transformations* videos, had been on a lucrative worldwide lecture tour for five years. Kalnins had booked him for a week's worth of sermons in Wasilla in October. Having borrowed the first *Transformations* video from a previous Assembly of God pastor in 2000, Sarah knew well who Muthee was and considered the chance to receive his personal blessing as a sign from God that she was on the right path, both spiritually and politically.

And so it was to her original church that she returned on Sunday, October 16, 2005, to hear Thomas Muthee preach the last of the ten sermons Kalnins had hired him to deliver. She knew she'd play a starring role.

The video of Muthee's sermon, including the laying of hands on Sarah as he prayed to Jesus to make her governor, became an Internet sensation during the 2008 campaign. In it, Muthee says:

> In a moment, I'll be asking you that we pray for Sarah, and I'll tell you the reason why . . . God wants to take the political dimension of our societies. That's why I was so glad to see Sarah here. We should pray for her, we should back her up. And, you know, come the day of voting, we should be there, not just praying, we should be there . . .
>
> We need God taking over our education system. If we have God in our schools, we will not have kids being taught, you know, how to worship Buddha, how to worship Mohammed, we will not have in the curriculum witchcraft and sorcery . . .
>
> We need God taking over the media in our lands . . . and government . . . We need believers there. We need people that are born again, spirit filled, people who know God, and people who are serious with God. So I'll ask Sarah, would you mind to come, please? Would you mind? Come, please. Let's all stand up and let's hold hands all over this house. Come, Pastor, come.

At this point, Sarah steps to the altar, turns, bows her head, and extends her arms in front of her, palms upraised. Muthee lays a hand on her head as Kalnins and Phil Markwardt of Wasilla's Crossroads Community Church lay hands on her shoulders. Muthee accelerates into exhortation mode:

Thank you, Jesus. Let's all pray. Let's pray for Sarah. Hallelujah! Come on, hold your hands up and raise them. Hold them and raise them up here! Come on, talk to God about this woman! Come on, talk to God about this woman we declare favor from today. We say favor, favor, favor! We say praise my God! We say grace to be rained upon her in the name of Jesus. My God, you make your judgment, you make room. You make ways in the desert, and I'm asking you today, we are asking you as the body of Christ in this valley, make a way for Sarah . . . Make her way, my God. Bring finances her way, even in the campaign, in the name of Jesus, and above all give her the personnel, give her men and women that will back her up in the name of Jesus . . .

Our Father, use her to turn this nation the other way around . . . so that the curse that has been there long can be broken . . . In the name of Jesus, in the name of Jesus! Every form of witchcraft, it will be rebuked in the name of Jesus. Father, make her way now! In Jesus' name. Amen.

Members of Wagner's Third Wave/New Apostolic Reformation are convinced that their prayers can literally destroy individuals whom they've identified as demonic. Among those for whose deaths they claim credit are Mother Teresa and Princess Diana.

Wagner taught his followers that a female mega-demon whom he called the Queen of Heaven (aka "the Great Harlot of Mystery Babylon") lurked near the summit of Mount Everest, "in a huge castle made of ice." He also taught that "each of the surrounding mountain peaks housed high-ranking demonic spirits."

It was imperative, in Wagner's view, that the Queen of Heaven be toppled before the millennium. He did not underestimate the difficulty of the task. "This is not Spiritual Warfare 101," he wrote. "The notion of confronting the Queen of Heaven is not fun and games. It is an advanced, high-risk assault . . ."

One of Wagner's leading apostles in Mexico was a woman named Ana Mendez, a former witch in a Haitian voodoo cult. She established a 10/40 window prayer tower in Mexico City, which, Wagner wrote, was "continually occupied by fervent intercessors." While Mendez herself was praying there one day, God told her it was high time to launch an assault on the Queen of Heaven in her Himalayan stronghold. In September 1997 she did, leading a team of twenty-six "intercessors" to Mount Everest in an assault she called Operation Ice Castle.

Some of the group chose to provide long-range support from the Everest View Hotel at an altitude of thirteen thousand feet. Others pushed on to a base camp at eighteen thousand feet. Mendez and a small cadre "scaled the ice cliffs and crossed bottomless crevasses," Wagner wrote, eventually climbing to twenty thousand feet.

There, Mendez later said, God revealed to her "a large, brown stone formation, completely surrounded by walls of ice resembling a castle, and shaped exactly like an idol of the Queen of Heaven."

Either that, or cerebral edema was causing her to hallucinate.

She and her elite force launched highly targeted intercessory prayers directly at the Queen inside her palace. Apparently the prayers found their mark, killing the Harlot Queen. Wagner wrote, "It had been a successful venture and . . . had deeply affected the invisible world. If not the strongest, it would be seen as one of the strongest assaults on the Queen of Heaven ever undertaken."

The effects, according to Mendez, were almost immediate. "Within two weeks," she wrote, "there was a huge fire in Indonesia, the largest Muslim nation; an earthquake destroyed the basilica of Assisi, a hurricane destroyed the infamous temple 'Baal-Christ' in Acapulco;

Princess Diana died, a representative of the British throne, to which Sir Edmund Hillary dedicated Mount Everest, and Mother Teresa died in India, one of the most famous advocates of Mary as Co-Redeemer."

This was the kind of power with which Muthee and Kalnins sought to equip Sarah as she prepared for her next step up the political ladder. "The more violent you become," Muthee says, "the quicker you will see things happen."

Sarah retained enough contact with the real world to understand that the depth of her commitment to Third Wave ideology could prove awkward politically. Therefore, while continuing to proclaim herself a born-again Christian, she carefully shielded the extreme nature of her beliefs from public view.

But the very day after Muthee blessed her and sent her forth to do battle, she announced she was running not for lieutenant governor, but for governor, and not as an independent, but as a Republican.

God took it from there, keeping both Thomas Muthee and Sarah's original spiritual mentor, Mary Glazier, well hidden.

FIFTEEN

I SPEND A QUIET Fourth of July with the grebes and the birds and my squirrel. Retired judge Beverly Cutler sends me a column written in November 2008 by a sixteen-year-old Palmer High School student named Waverli Rainey and published in the *Frontiersman*. Its description of Valley mores is dismaying, especially when read on this, the day set aside to celebrate the birth of our nation.

On Nov. 4, 2008, Sen. Barack Obama was elected the first African-American president of the United States of America. I went to the Wasilla Sports Complex for what was called a community event. We were told it was non-partisan . . . However, once inside, it seemed as if it was a Republican-only event . . . I felt joy as I saw Sen. Barack Obama's electoral points grow and grow . . .

I anxiously awaited what Present-elect Obama would say. Between speeches, a live band played music. However, when President-elect Obama began to speak, those running the event had to be asked to have the band stop so we could hear him speak. Eventually, they stopped playing, but we missed the beginning of the speech. Then half way through this historic speech, former Mayor Keller turned down the audio of President-elect Obama and put on a call from Governor Palin . . .

No one paid respect to President-elect Obama's historic moment. So the next day I borrowed my mother's Obama shirt and walked into school . . . I expected complaints and qualms about the new president, but I was not prepared for the flat-out racist remarks said openly in the halls and classrooms. I was appalled. While I sat at my desk trying to do my work I could hear my fellow classmates:

"I think we should kill Obama," one said.

"I hope someone comes up and shoots him in the head," another would say.

"I hate Obama . . . he's black."

On went the racist words for the full 80 minutes of that class. I began to think of the ignorance of the students I was surrounded by. I wondered where they learned to be so hateful, and I wondered why the teacher never stepped in—why no adult . . . had the guts to cut in and say it was not OK.

Sarah's Fourth of July message "www.troopathon.org or call 866-866-6372 to support greatest military in the world; show our troops we care, we've got their back, bless them" comes via Twitter.

Back at Soap Opera Central, *People* reports that Levi Johnston has apologized to Sarah and Todd. When last I read about him he was spilling his guts to *Vanity Fair* for money, telling tales out of school about what went on behind the Palins' closed doors. It wasn't pretty. Now that he's realized that his own "career" can go nowhere without Bristol, he's busy patching things up.

"Last year, after Bristol and I broke up, I was unhappy and a little angry," his prepared statement says. "Unfortunately, against my better judgment, I publicly said things about the Palins that were not completely true . . . I owe it to the Palins to publicly apologize."

Bristol's PR people add a statement of their own, in her name. It says, "Part of co-parenting is creating healthy and honest relationships between the parents. Tripp one day needs to know the truth and needs to know that even if a mistake is made the honorable thing to do is to own up to it."

So all is well again. For the moment.

I MEET WITH Sherry and Mercede Johnston again, this time—because Sherry has been granted a rare afternoon out—at the Kaladi Brothers coffee shop in the Carrs mall, probably second only to the Mat-Su Family Restaurant as a gathering place for Wasillans, and even more of a magnet for Wasilla youth during the day.

Sherry is pleased because she's just seen Levi, not a common occurrence. "He came up for a haircut," Sherry tells me. "He said he had a big photo shoot coming up. He wouldn't tell me with whom and he wouldn't tell me what it was about. It was strange: I felt like there was something important he wanted to say."

Levi went to his mother's bathroom, looking for Percocet. "He said Bristol had just had another plastic surgery and she was hurting." He wouldn't speak to Mercede because he's been on the outs with Mercede since getting back with Bristol because Bristol is on the outs with Mercede because Mercede posted a blog that Bristol didn't like and Bristol told Levi to tell Sherry to tell Mercede that if she didn't take the blog down she'd never see Levi or Tripp again.

Instead of removing the offensive post, Mercede blogged anew: "Why would he let this happen all over again? . . . I wish Levi could be the man I know he is and have a mind of his own and finally stand his ground, but I guess he is blinded by love. How is it fair that I can't speak my mind on a blog without Levi threatening to never speak to me again, but Bristol can go on Facebook daily and call me nasty names with no repercussions at all?"

At Kaladi Brothers, she's unrepentant. She tells me she was recently subpoenaed for a deposition in Bristol's custody fight with

Levi, a fracas that may be paused for a while as the couple struggles to reunite. "Bristol's lawyer, Van Flein, he just sneered at me. He also told me I wasn't allowed to talk to you. I said, 'Who are you to tell me who I can talk to?' He said, 'That's if you ever want to see your nephew again.' Bristol was sitting there smirking."

The next day, *US Weekly* has Bristol and Levi on the cover holding Tripp. "We're Getting Married! The reunited couple reveals their sudden, secret engagement—and why they hid it from Sarah. 'I Hope My Mom Will Accept Us.'" They were reportedly paid a hundred thousand dollars for the exclusive.

This was the photo shoot for which Levi wanted his mother to cut his hair. This was the "something important" he seemed to want to tell her but did not.

Rumors immediately run rampant that Bristol is pregnant again—and not by Levi, because she was living with Ben Barber at what would have been the time of conception. Barber, who was offered an electrician's job in Delta Junction, 450 miles to the northeast, as an inducement to leave without making a fuss, speaks to The Daily Beast.

"I helped her out with Tripp more than Levi ever did," he says. "What does Levi have going for him? Nothing. I don't understand how Bristol can go and spend her life with someone who can't get his GED." He says Bristol never had a good relationship with either of her parents and that both Todd and Track are incensed at the news of the engagement.

Truly, the Palins are a circus of many rings.

THE FUSS OVER my moving in here has finally wound up where it belonged all along: in a comic strip. I'm in *Doonesbury* this week.

• • •

I TOLD TODD back in May that not only was I not going to be paying attention to anything that happened on his side of the fence, but that even if I inadvertently saw or heard any activity I would refrain from writing about it. I keep my promises—most of them, anyway. In any event, I'm keeping this one. Thus, Roland Hedley would have had a fruitless trip.

As for my side of the fence, almost anytime I glance out my kitchen window, I see a car parked by the chain. Not the same car—dozens of different cars and trucks and campers. Often, people will be standing outside the vehicles taking pictures of the fence.

It reminds me of the looky-loos who throughout the O. J. Simpson trial flocked to the condo on South Bundy Drive in Brentwood to see where O.J. killed his wife and Ron Goldman. The difference was that something had actually happened there.

Here, there is nothing going on. There is only a fence: two fences, actually, the original and Todd's addition. Pictures have appeared all over the Internet for six weeks, but still the curious drive down the rutted dirt lane until they reach the chain that lets them go no farther, except on foot.

Despite the POSTED and DO NOT ENTER and NO TRESPASSING signs, some do walk around or duck under the chain, wanting to get closer to the fence. If I'm there, I tell them that they are trespassing on private property and they have to leave. "But we just want a picture." I tell them they can take all they want from outside the chain. And they do, morning, noon, and night, as if the fence itself has become some sort of quasi-religious shrine, protecting Queen Esther of the North from prying, agnostic eyes.

FINALLY, I FIND a friend of Sarah's who will talk to me. I've put a lot of time into trying, but, forget fences, Sarah has dropped an iron curtain of silence around herself. Not only will she not talk to anyone who isn't paying her, but she's made family and friends take an oath of omertà, at least in regard to me.

By insisting that those close to her rebuff my requests for interviews, she is ensuring that I'll wind up speaking mostly to those who do not feel bound by her wishes. Then she and her acolytes can complain that my book is not "fair and balanced" like Fox News.

Even this friend of hers, who at first tells me I can use her name, then changes her mind, is trepidatious about talking to me, to put it mildly. She insists on meeting where we will not be seen, eventually agreeing to The Digital Cup, on Knik-Goose Bay Road, which is almost deserted on the afternoon we meet.

Despite all the precautions, she's so jittery it's hard for me to concentrate on what she's saying.

"Tell me about Sarah."

"The first time I saw her was at aerobics. She had no makeup on and her hair was in a ponytail. Then I saw her at a PTA function, wearing makeup, and I said, 'Oh my God, she's beautiful!'"

"But beyond her looks, what drew you to her?"

"She was exciting. Even at city council meetings. She's much more exciting in person than she looks like on TV. And then, when she ran for mayor, they ran such a dirty campaign against her. They misused a state law just to find out that Todd had a DUI charge against him in Dillingham. She got so afraid they were after her that she had to paint her car a different color. And then, of course, they slashed her tires."

"By 'they,' whom do you mean?"

"Stein's people, of course. Who else would do it? They were sexually harassing her, pretending to be in her aerobics class just so they could make her feel uncomfortable by looking at her. And then, after the council meetings, they'd all get together at Nobody's Inn and do their real business, and Sarah knew that was unethical and she had the courage to stand up and stop them."

"How well did you know her socially?"

"For fifteen years my friends and I had a Christmas ornament exchange, and until she got too busy Sarah always came. She'd come late and leave early."

"Did you ever have any serious talks with her, one-on-one?"

"She's not that kind of person. She's too busy for talk because she's always doing something to try to make things better for everyone else."

"Really?"

"I remember when she quit the oil and gas commission after she forced Ruedrich to resign. She was with a bunch of us, I think it was at an ornament exchange, and she said, 'Well, the Democrats have always hated me, and now the Republicans hate me, too. I've ruined myself politically, but I just had to do what I knew was right.'"

"But it turned out that the publicity she got because of Ruedrich was what made her viable as a statewide candidate."

"Yes, but she didn't want that. Sarah never thinks of herself. She only thinks about the good she can do for others. Maybe people in Alaska have gotten cynical, but just go Outside and take a look. I've been to lots of places in the past couple of years and people just love her. It's oozing out, from all kinds of people."

"Then why have people here lost their enthusiasm for her?"

"Because of the press and the bloggers. All that negativity. Nobody ever writes about the good that she does. There was a boy a couple of years ago, when she was governor, who was in a bicycle accident. She actually went to his house and brought him a gift. The *Frontiersman* wrote it up, of course, but the rest of the press just ignored it."

"So you're still friends with her?"

"She's too busy now to have time for that. But last year a vehicle I didn't recognize came up to my house and Piper jumped out of it and gave me a present. It was a wind-chime bell from Arizona. I called out, 'Sarah!' She slid down her window for a sec and said, 'Love you, bye—gotta take my kids to the library.' That's how she is: always a mother first."

"Were you surprised when she quit as governor?" I ask.

"At first, yes, but then I realized, just like she said, it was because of all the attacks. Attack, attack, attack, that's all people wanted to do. My daughter in Colorado sent me an e-mail after Sarah resigned, and I'm just so proud of her because, even living so far away, she understood. 'People are so cruel,' she wrote. I don't think Sarah wanted to resign, but so much cruelty didn't give her any choice."

This goes on for another hour. Dutifully, I take notes. This woman's eyes are like laser beams on my notebook. She seems able to read my handwriting upside down better than I can read it as I write.

"I said she deals with stress with grace and dignity. Why didn't you write that down?"

"It's one of those phrases I won't forget."

"Well, write this: her only problem is Todd. He's a lot more controlling than we realize. When my dad died, I never got a card from Sarah, and by the way, she never supported me through my divorce, even though I had told her that for twenty-two years I'd been in an abusive relationship and she'd cried when I told her that. I think it's all because of Todd. The last time I called her, Todd answered and he wouldn't even let me talk to her. I don't know how she puts up with that. I think she's actually a saint."

I'm reminded of this conversation months later, when I talk to Catherine Mormile. Although her friendship with Palin never deepened, Mormile and her husband continued to support Sarah politically. When she ran for governor in 2006, her Anchorage campaign office was near Mormile's office and she'd frequently stop by there in late afternoon. "She'd storm in the door in her red outfit, all aglow," Mormile told me. "She'd have Bristol with her. She always has one of her kids with her in public, like a human shield. She'd say, 'There you are! You're my hero! You're my role model!' And she'd give everyone in my waiting room a big smile. By then I was starting to wonder, what's with all the hyperbole?"

Having contributed a thousand dollars to Sarah's gubernatorial campaign, Mormile and her husband were invited to the inaugural ball in Wasilla. Long recovered from the effects of carbon monoxide poisoning, Mormile had earned a doctorate in physical therapy, was a board-certified orthopedic specialist in physical therapy, and was writing a textbook, *Temporomandibular Joint Disorders: One Name for Two Diagnoses,* which would be published in 2008. She was no longer the wounded creature to whom Sarah had reached out eleven years earlier.

"I congratulated her on her election," Mormile told me, "and said I'd be happy to offer her any help I could, especially with health care issues. She said, 'My, aren't you stuck on yourself.'

"I was dumbfounded. I said, 'All I'm doing is offering my help, if you think you could use it.' She said, 'No, you just keep on doing your little health care things and leave it to me to do the heavy lifting. I'm the governor.'

"I backed away. I didn't know what to say. Then she said, 'Oh, here, at least let me give you a hug.' That's a trait of hers: when she doesn't know what to say to someone, she hugs them. She's never spoken to me again."

Mormile now feels that Sarah's attitude toward her changed once she recognized that Mormile was not simply a victimized dog musher, but rather, an educated, accomplished professional.

"She recruits those who feel worthless and powerless and uses them as tools," Mormile told me. "Lyda Green and I call them zombie rats: people who feel their lives are so meaningless that only commitment to Sarah can give them purpose. She takes the transactional analysis concept of 'I'm okay, You're okay' and twists it into, 'I'm okay, you're not.' Somebody who worked for her once actually said to me, 'I'd gladly drown facedown in a puddle if Sarah could keep her feet dry by walking across my back.' That's a zombie rat.

"I almost became one myself. Sarah approached me when my life was at its lowest ebb. I felt she wanted to help me climb out of a hole, and I was so grateful that I would have done anything for her. The people who stay with her—Ivy Frye, Frank Bailey, Linda Menard— are the ones who never get beyond that. Wasilla is the perfect place to find them because there are so many victims in Wasilla. It's the kingdom of the addictive personality, and Sarah has made a career of seeking out people she senses will grow addicted to her."

BACK AT MY house, the beat goes on. I'm locking the chain one afternoon when a car with Texas license plates comes down the dirt road. Two middle-aged women get out.

"Excuse me," one of them says. She points at the fence. "I know that one on the other side of the fence is Sarah's house and that little one up there on this side must be where that writer is living, but which one is Roland Hedley's house?"

"There's no one named Roland Hedley living around here," I say.

"Oh, yes there is! He's up here for Fox News. We read it in the paper."

They leave grouchily, convinced that I knew where he was but wouldn't tell them.

ON ANOTHER ESPECIALLY vile day in late July, a flotilla of floatplanes lands on the lake and, single file, taxis to Sarah's dock. I'm heading out to buy groceries, but I get no farther than the chain when an SUV comes splashing down the dirt road at high speed. It stops and a highly agitated man in a poncho jumps out into the downpour.

"Have they left yet?" he asks me.

"Has who left? Left where?"

"Kate Gosselin and her kids. I followed them up from Anchorage. I know they're at Palin's house. They're going camping with Sarah."

"You know more than I do."

"Are you the writer? The guy living next door?"

"I am, but you still know more than I do."

"Listen, I'm a photographer. If I can get the right shot, I'll make the cover."

"I'm afraid I can't help you."

"But you can. Listen, I'll give you five hundred dollars cash, right now, if you'll let me onto your deck so I can take pictures."

Five hundred dollars? If I'd been a corrupt Republican in Juneau, I would have hit Bill Allen up for more than that.

"Sorry, but I can't let you do that," I told him.

"But Sarah and Kate Gosselin together! Do you know what a great picture that would be?"

The photographer leaves, disappointed. I decide to delay my shopping trip until all the planes have left the dock, because I don't want anyone sneaking in behind my back.

What a very strange society we've become.

I THINK it's time to take a break. I'm heading home for ten days to see Nancy and my children and grandchildren. My tire tracks are still fresh in the mud of my driveway—in fact, I haven't even boarded my flight from Anchorage to Philadelphia—when Sarah goes on the Chris Wallace show on Fox News to complain that I've ruined her summer.

After talking to her about Obama, taxes, immigration, Afghanistan, and her plans for 2012, Wallace closes his interview by asking if I'm still living next door. What a perfect chance for Sarah to take the high road, to say, "Yes, he is, but it hasn't been the problem I was afraid it might be. He's respected our privacy and we've respected his and everything's fine."

In response to Wallace's question, she says, "He is. And we just avoid certain angles in the house. And we avoid the front yard . . . We've changed our behavior as a result of our new neighbor."

It's true that since late spring Sarah has spent the vast majority of her time away from her house, but I'm hardly the reason why. She's been flying all over the South, Southwest, and Midwest endorsing Tea Party candidates. When in Alaska, she's been everywhere but Wasilla, filming *Sarah Palin's Alaska* for The Learning Channel and flying around with Greta Van Susteren and her Fox News crew in an orgy of self-promotion. The notion that my presence next door has forced her and her children to skulk around behind their curtains is as nonsensical as her next comment.

"Only dead fish go with the flow," she says. "We won't ever just go with the flow and accept that somebody has infringed upon our privacy to try to kind of hamper some of our freedom and hamper our fun. So, no, not just going with the flow. Changing our behavior. But in October the guy finally moves back to the East Coast and goes and does his thing with somebody else. You know, like Todd says, some people just need to get a life. Well, bless his heart. He needs to get a life."

SIXTEEN

SARAH'S ELECTION as Alaska's youngest governor and first woman governor was decisive, but the wave of support that carried her to Juneau was hardly a tsunami. Only about two hundred thousand people voted, the smallest turnout in a statewide election since 1990.

Her fresh face and feisty spirit proved appealing, as did the girl-next-door persona she presented, but the two biggest positive factors in her success were voters' distaste for Frank Murkowski—which led to his being so emphatically repudiated in the primary—and fallout from the FBI raids on legislative offices. Sarah had put herself in the right place at the right time and she used serendipity to maximum advantage.

Cunningly, she also turned Knowles's and Andrew Halcro's presumed advantages—intelligence, education, experience—against them. The *Anchorage Daily News* interviewed Tilly Ketchum at Sarah's election night victory celebration at the Captain Cook hotel in Anchorage, and Sarah's former college roommate said, "I can understand what she's saying. She doesn't talk over your head."

The campaign taught Sarah that ignorance, if accompanied by a bright smile and a catchy phrase or two, was not necessarily a drawback. On the contrary, it allowed her to connect with that bloc of churchgoing, gun-toting, God-fearing, government-distrusting voters who, like her, might not grasp the intricacies of public policy, but who knew, doggone it, how they felt. Sarah would encounter these people in far larger numbers on the 2008 national campaign trail and beyond.

But Sarah's most significant accomplishment as a candidate was a negative: she and her advisers did not let voters learn the true extent of her religious views. She kept her opposition to abortion and stem cell research off the table. Except for that one slip late in the campaign, she did not let on that she wanted creationism taught in public schools, nor that she did not believe in the separation of church and state.

Both her opponents and the bedazzled Alaskan press gave her a pass on her radical dominionist theology. Her relationships with Thomas Muthee and Mary Glazier were never mentioned, nor was her belief that the earth had been created only six thousand years ago, that men and dinosaurs had walked it together, and that civilization was so far into the end-times that Jesus would return to earth during her lifetime.

Speaking at a New Apostolic Reformation conference in June 2008, Glazier made it clear that Sarah's election as governor had been divinely ordained.

"We were given an assignment in Alaska," she said. "There was a twenty-four-year-old woman that God began to speak to about entering politics. She became part of our prayer group in Wasilla. Years later, became the mayor of Wasilla. And last year [sic] was elected governor of the state of Alaska. Yes! Hallelujah! At her inauguration she dedicated the state to Jesus Christ. Hallelujah! Hallelujah!"

Within two weeks of her election, Sarah made a decision in accordance with Romans 12:19. "Vengeance is mine; I will repay, saith the Lord." Juneau had given her only 20 percent of its vote, and she wasted no time showing the city what payback looked like: she refused to take her oath of office there, shifting the ceremonies to Fairbanks.

In her inaugural address—in which, despite Glazier's claim, she did not explicitly dedicate Alaska to Jesus—Sarah debuted the imagery she'd later refine into the "mama grizzly" meme, saying, "I will unambiguously, steadfastly and doggedly guard the interests of this great state as a mother naturally guards her own." After a full minute of applause, the crowd began to chant, "Sarah! Sarah! Sarah!"

Alaska's infatuation with its first woman governor reached a fever pitch. The bumper stickers appeared overnight: ALASKA—THE COLDEST STATE WITH THE HOTTEST GOVERNOR. Outsiders took notice. The Wonkette blog posted a photo of a bare-shouldered Sarah taken during her reign as Miss Wasilla. A *Daily News* columnist wrote, "There's something refreshing about Palin. She's like your high school English teacher, quite capable of scolding when necessary." Men with dominatrix fantasies took note.

In such an adulatory atmosphere little attention was paid to the fact that, as she'd done in Wasilla ten years earlier, Sarah was peopling her administration largely with high school friends and/or born-again Christians, whose qualifications in no way matched their job descriptions.

She named born-again Talis Colberg, who ran a one-man law office in Palmer, as state attorney general, and Wasilla High friends Joe Schmidt, Franci Havemeister, and Curtis Menard respectively as director of prisons, director of the division of agriculture, and director of the Alaska Railroad. This took cronyism to a level that not even Frank Murkowski had dared to contemplate.

The first glimpse she gave the public of how her religion spilled into areas of policy came five days before Christmas, when she said that while she had no choice but to comply with a state supreme court ruling that extended health and retirement benefits to same-sex partners of state employees, she would seek an amendment to the state constitution that would overturn the court order. She signed a bill that called for a nonbinding referendum on the issue in April.

As the legislature convened for its annual session in mid-January, Sarah grew nervous about delivering her first State of the State address. "This was the moment," John Bitney said. "This was it. She was going to stand in front of the legislature and give a live, televised, forty-minute 'what the hell is going on' speech to a bunch of political insiders who thought she was a fluke."

Bitney, a friend of Sarah's since their days together in a junior high school band, was perhaps the most politically astute of the campaign operatives who'd taken jobs in the new administration. As Sarah's legislative director, he was particularly eager for her first major address as governor to be a success.

He spoke to her privately only minutes before she appeared. Her nervousness was apparent. "It was time for her to go on, and I remember coming in and saying, 'Sarah, let's say a little prayer together.' The best thing I'd found to calm her down before big moments was prayer. I held her hands and we bowed our heads and she gave a nice little out-loud prayer asking for strength and for the ability to speak from the heart and praying that God would help her deliver a good speech. Then she went out and she hit it out of the park, every bit as much as she did at the Republican National Convention."

The highlight of the speech was her announcement that she would jettison the natural gas pipeline agreement that Frank Murkowski had reached with energy producers and would instead present a bill called the Alaska Gasline Inducement Act (AGIA) during the legislative session.

For a generation, Alaska had been seeking a natural gas pipeline to complement the Trans-Alaska Oil Pipeline that carried North Slope oil from Prudhoe Bay to Valdez. AGIA would be Sarah's attempt finally to turn the dream into reality. "Like a knight slaying a dragon, she used a mighty ax to kill the proposed contract that former governor Frank Murkowski negotiated with the state's major oil producers," the *Daily News* wrote.

Columnist Tim Bradner added, "Gov. Sarah Palin put on a su-
perb performance in her first State of the State address . . . She was
articulate, forceful, cheerful, warm and full of energy as she laid out
her vision for the state and a natural gas pipeline. It was fun to watch
her work the crowd in the legislative chambers, as if she were still on
the campaign trail. Some political leaders sway events by sheer charm
and personality, and Palin may have this gift."

Her charm was less evident offstage. During her early months in
office, another of her long-suppressed attitudes, her distaste for people
of color, became manifest. As governor, Frank Murkowski had given
state jobs to about two dozen members of racial or ethnic minorities.
After he lost the primary, he directed all state workers to help Sarah
get elected. About twenty minority employees formed a coalition
called the Diversity Group. They worked as campaign volunteers for
Sarah when not on the state clock. Almost as soon as she was elected,
she ordered them all fired.

"She didn't keep any of them," John Bitney told me. "I said, 'Wow,
you could at least keep one, for appearance's sake,' but she wanted
every one of them gone: Filipinos, Hispanics, blacks, Samoans, Kore-
ans. Nobody who was dark skinned got a job and a lot who were dark
skinned lost jobs to make space for the white guys. Her chief of staff,
Mike Tibbles, came in one day and said, 'They're all fired. That's what
she wants.' I was like, 'All of them?' He said, yes, all the dark-skinned
people had to go."

The racially motivated firings received no attention in the press.
"None of these were director-level positions. They were like fifth-tier,
so nobody knew. They were fired only because they weren't white. I
remember the NAACP threatening to picket at the Anchorage inaugural ball in March 2007, but they backed off. Sarah just isn't comfortable in the presence of dark-skinned people."

She had pledged to cut state spending, but she did not hesitate
to use government money to finance initiatives that might turn her

personal religious convictions into law. The referendum on same-sex benefits was a case in point. Sarah believed that a strong anti-gay turnout would pressure legislators into placing the constitutional amendment on the 2008 general election ballot. She therefore pushed the referendum bill through the legislature, even setting aside $1.2 million to cover its cost. This was more than four times the amount that had been paid in benefits to the fewer than one hundred same-sex couples who qualified.

Anchorage Democratic state representative Mike Doogan said, "If our purpose is to find out what Alaskans think about same-sex benefits, we should pay twelve thousand bucks and get a scientific opinion poll, not pay $1.2 million for an unscientific poll."

BOTH SARAH and Todd had told people in Wasilla that if Sarah were elected governor, one of her first orders of business would be to have Mike Wooten fired.

In January, Todd went to Walt Monegan's office and recited the laundry list of the trooper's offenses that he and Sarah had compiled. Monegan explained that all those had already been investigated, leading to Wooten's suspension. He also said that if he fired Wooten now, for conduct for which he'd already been disciplined, the trooper would likely sue the state and would no doubt prevail.

Todd said he wanted criminal charges filed against Wooten for shooting the moose—which was quickly becoming the most famous dead moose in Alaskan history—without a permit. Monegan explained that because the incident had occurred more than three years earlier it was unlikely that a prosecutor would pursue the charge. Further, if charges were filed, they might be filed also against the woman who had willingly allowed Wooten to shoot the moose on her permit, and against the man who'd butchered it knowing it had been illegally taken.

As Monegan put it in a later deposition, "Todd Palin reacted very negatively to that assessment and insisted that Trooper Wooten and only Trooper Wooten should be charged."

SARAH INTRODUCED her AGIA bill on March 2. The "inducement" part of the Alaska Gasline Inducement Act obligated the state to pay up to $500 million to offset the costs that a pipeline builder would face. There were some who questioned whether such an expenditure was consistent with Sarah's pledge of fiscal conservatism, but the outright lust that Alaskan legislators felt for a gas pipeline was so intense that it overrode such concerns.

Looking at Sarah's first hundred days in office, the *Daily News* found that, unlike her rocky start as mayor of Wasilla, she was "enjoying an unusually long honeymoon with both lawmakers and the public." The newspaper did its part to keep the honeymoon going, writing that Sarah had "the aura of Joan of Arc" and, later, that "Compared to the legislature, Gov. Palin looks like Joan of Arc, with a better smile and personality."

A poll put her approval rating at 73 percent, with only 7 percent of respondents expressing a negative view. Reports had even surfaced on a few blogs that she could be the vice-presidential nominee on a ticket headed by Rudy Giuliani. "Oh, come on," Sarah said. "I got enough to worry about here in Alaska for the next four years."

As spring 2007 approached, things could scarcely have been better for her. Not only did Todd win the Iron Dog, but Wasilla High won both the boys' and girls' state basketball championships. No longer could Wasilla be called "The Hovel That Hugs the Highway" or "The Mistake by the Lake," as appeared in the *Daily News*.

Moreover, the referendum that Sarah hoped would lead to a constitutional amendment to deny health benefits to gay partners of state employees passed by a six-point margin—hardly a public clamor, but enough to motivate the House Judiciary Committee to approve moving forward with the proposed amendment.

On April 24 she chose a grizzly bear with a salmon in its jaws as the symbol to appear on the Alaska state quarter. "I think nothing could be more Alaskan," she said. "I like to think this is a mama grizzly doing what she does best: taking care of her young."

And Sarah's relentless lobbying for AGIA paid off. Bradner's Legislative Digest website noted that "Lawmakers would like to do real surgery on this plan, but Palin has them cowed with an aggressive public relations campaign that combines weekly radio talks and op-ed articles." The extent of the cowing became clear on May 11, when the legislature passed the AGIA bill with only a single dissenting vote.

In late May, polls showed Sarah's approval rating climbing to an astonishing 90 percent. She had become the most dazzling star ever to shine in the Alaskan political firmament.

Anchorage right-wing radio talk show host Dan Fagan wrote in the *Daily News* in late June that "Tony Soprano has nothing on Sarah Palin. A small town hockey mom with the clout of a mob boss . . . Barracuda Palin can have you swimming with the fishes, never to be heard from again . . . While she's whacking people left and right she also charms the public and the media . . . How does she do it? . . . She has a heart of gold [and] . . . she is obsessed with integrity."

She remained obsessed also with Mike Wooten, complaining to Walt Monegan in a midsummer e-mail, "He's still a trooper and he still carries a gun and he still tells anyone who will listen that he will 'never work for that b————(me)' because he has such anger and distain [*sic*] towards my family."

In mid-July, at Todd's insistence, she fired John Bitney. This was his punishment for having dared to embark on a romantic relationship with the estranged wife of a friend of Todd's. Bitney's abrupt dismissal demonstrated how much power Todd wielded in Sarah's administration. Andrew Halcro wrote on his blog, "In six months, Bitney guided the governor's policies through the legislature, including her hallmark, AGIA. But John Bitney made the fatal employment mistake: he got on the bad side of Todd."

Bitney agrees with Halcro's assessment. Speaking to me at his home in Big Lake in late August 2010, he said, "Todd and I were very close friends. When he was in Juneau, he'd come down to my office every day. I'd boot everybody out and shut the door and it was just the two of us sitting there, a couple of old friends saying, 'Here we are in this position and, wow, what a crazy ride to get here' and 'Hey, did you see so-and-so?' and 'Check out the caboose on that one' . . . just buddies. We could let our hair down."

Or so he thought. "I was in the inner inner circle, and that's what created the dramatic blast," Bitney said. "Debbie was very close to Todd. He'd relied on her to help him raise their kids, and Scott was a friend and business partner. He had woven them into his family, and by being perceived as breaking up the marriage, I was violating his family circle. It was maybe even worse than breaking up his own family, because it was the part of his family he thought was stable. It was the best part of his family from that point of view."

Bitney had no doubt that in firing him Sarah was only obeying Todd's order. "Todd is the one you want to watch out for," he told me, "because he's the most emotionally unstable. Sarah is just flighty in terms of, she goes with the wind, the flavor of the day. She wants to see herself on TV every day, so whatever that takes. She may harbor a grudge—and she does—but she doesn't act upon them unless she finds that it's in her interest, that it can be woven into whatever her script is for the day. She doesn't forget, but she waits for the opportunity to come around to get you.

"Todd—oh, no, he'll go proactive. He'll call in the carpenters to put up the fence; he'll not only get me fired, he'll call my new boss and try to get me fired again. Todd is the one who's really vindictive. He holds grudges and he's obsessive about them and he doesn't let them go."

Afterward, if anyone asked Todd about Bitney, all he would say was "Who?"

Later in July, expanding her horizons, Sarah flew to Kuwait to visit Alaska National Guard troops stationed there. Except for vacations in Hawaii, it was the first time she'd traveled outside North America. She was asked how she felt about Track enlisting. "I would be willing, because I support our troops, and I support my son's independence," she said.

Spurred on by a worshipful press, Alaskans could scarcely contain their midsummer enthusiasm for Sarah. At the annual Governor's Picnic in Anchorage on July 28, she shouted, "I love you!" to the crowd. The *Daily News* reported that the crowd "replied in kind in so many ways, lifting thumbs, smiling big and screaming words of encouragement . . ."

Was physical attractiveness part of her magic? Absolutely, a female singer said from the bandstand. "Is our governor a babe, or what?" she asked rhetorically.

Sarah was so popular that some speculated that in 2008 she might challenge Alaska's congressman Don Young or even U.S. senator Ted Stevens in a Republican primary. Both men were under FBI investigation as the Justice Department extended its corruption probe from Juneau to Washington, D.C. But such a bid, Sarah told the *Daily News,* "isn't real bright on my radar screen. Just being governor is keeping my plate very full."

Having already spurned Juneau for her inauguration, Sarah announced in late August that she planned to be the first Alaskan governor not to live in the state capital year-round. She'd live in Wasilla and work out of her Anchorage office except when the legislature was in session. She did not announce that she'd be billing the state a per diem charge for every night she slept at home.

She kicked off September by giving a lengthy interview to one of Alaska's most able journalists, Tom Kizzia of the *Daily News*. Discussing the cozy relationship Alaska politicians had long enjoyed with the state's business leaders, she said, "I am not from that other world. My dad, as a school teacher, wasn't a mover and shaker developer making big bucks off of property development. My husband isn't that way. I am not raising my kids to be that way . . . If you want to be in public service, it is being willing to serve Alaskans for the right reasons. It is having to have a servant's heart . . . It's not to get rich."

Kizzia mentioned complaints that it was a conflict of interest for Todd to work for BP while she, as governor, was making decisions that affected the oil company's ventures in Alaska. Sarah seemed ruffled. "But what is unethical about Todd working?" she said, neatly dodging the point of the question. "He's created to work. I respect him for wanting to work. I would disrespect him if the father of my children did not want to work. Todd loves his job. He loves his crew. He loves the schedule and I say more power to him."

When Kizzia asked how her children had adapted to her being Alaska's chief executive, Sarah softly began what would grow into a deafening drumbeat: that some people were picking on her kids. "Just a few individual incidents," she said, "Like, you know, 'Your Mom sucks as governor. So here's what I'm going to do to you next time I see you.' Something like that coming around in an e-mail to one of the girls."

She never produced evidence of such an incident. But at that point the Alaskan press and public were believing everything Sarah said.

She added that the burdens of the governorship put no strain on her family because they were used to her working around the clock. "Don't know if people are aware," she said, "but being mayor and manager of the city of Wasilla for those six years was quite taxing also, timewise, and it took a huge commitment to get the job done there also."

Kizzia didn't seem aware that far from handling managerial chores herself, as mayor, Sarah had employed a full-time manager to deal with Wasilla's day-to-day business.

Returning to her comfort level, Kizzia asked, "What does it feel like to be called the most popular politician in America?"

"Well, I haven't heard that one," she said, but then attributed her popularity to "Americans' desire for change." She didn't say "Alas-kans"; she said "Americans."

It would be almost a year before John McCain would wave his wand, but Kizzia mentioned "talk out there" of Sarah being a vice-presidential nominee.

"Um, haven't really contemplated that."

Was she sure she wouldn't be tempted by the prospect of higher office?

"Something very, very, very drastic would have had to have hap-pened to get me to think along those lines," she said, "because, again, I feel that I certainly have a responsibility and an obligation that I will be fulfilling. That is putting my name on the dotted line to serve as governor for four years; that's what I believe I should be doing."

Stephen Haycox, professor of history at the University of Alaska Anchorage, soon chimed in with an op-ed piece for the *Daily News* that ran under the headline "Palin Interview Bolsters Positive Image." He wrote that Sarah's girl-next-door persona was a "refreshing image at a time when the rich and famous and the hobnobbers are in trouble."

Haycox noted that "Some critics, particularly those in her own party, have suggested that the governor is simply a canny politico, capitalizing on the missteps and isolation of her predecessor, cyni-cally cultivating an image of hometown wholesomeness for the sake of ambition."

He said, however, "her interview did not suggest canniness; rather, it sounded thoroughly genuine, as have most of her public statements since she first broke into public consciousness," and he quoted George Burns about the qualities most important to an actor. "Sincerity and honesty," Burns said. "If you can fake those you've got it made."

Haycox's conclusion: "If Gov. Palin is 'puttin' on the style,' she's doing a terrific job."

Which she was. Allowed to cavort across the stage on her own terms, Sarah both dazzled and flourished.

She scored another publicity coup on September 11, 2007, when Track enlisted in the army. The *Daily News* reported that "the reasons why he enlisted and why he signed his military contract on the sixth anniversary of the September 11, 2001, terrorist attacks were unavailable . . . The governor declined to comment. The Palin family wants to keep private some aspects of his decision."

With Track safely off to basic training—no longer a short-term PR risk—Sarah turned her attention back to the circumstance that had helped propel her into the governor's office in the first place: the ever-expanding federal investigation of corruption among Alaskan politicians.

The day after the Associated Press reported that Bill Allen, founder of the oil services company Veco, which had been implicated in the federal investigation of Alaskan political corruption, had secretly recorded phone calls with U.S. senator Ted Stevens, Sarah said she was frustrated that Stevens had not given assurances that he'd done nothing wrong. "Alaskans are getting more anxious to hear any information he can provide regarding his innocence," she said.

On September 25, Pete Kott, a Republican from Eagle River and former speaker of the house, was convicted by an Anchorage jury of conspiring with Veco to work for lowering taxes on Alaskan oil companies. Once again, timing worked in Sarah's favor. She'd already called a special session of the legislature to deal with the oil tax question.

She announced details of her tax proposal, called Alaska's Clear and Equitable Share (ACES), on October 2. The highlight was an increase in the state tax rate on net profits from 22.5 to 25 percent.

Big Oil had been so entrenched in Alaska for so long and the Alaskan economy had grown so dependent on oil company revenues that Sarah's plan to raise taxes actually met with opposition. For the first time, legislators were willing to go on record with critical remarks.

Representative Jay "Chicken Man" Ramras claimed that Sarah

had introduced "a new era of McCarthyism" in Alaska. He accused her of "getting out her red can of paint and playing Joseph McCarthy with the legislative branch" by suggesting that opponents of ACES might be tainted by the same corruption that had already led to the indictment of six legislators for accepting bribes from Bill Allen.

The oil tax structure then in place had been created the previous year with the help of at least four legislators accused of accepting Veco bribes. Thus, an outside expert told a legislative hearing as the special session began on October 18, a "cloud of corruption" hung over existing tax rates.

Debate raged. Exxon said taxes were already too high, but Exxon was the one oil giant unpopular in Alaska since 1989, when the *Exxon Valdez* spilled almost eleven million gallons of oil into Prince William Sound. With the price of oil at ninety-five dollars a barrel and rising, it was hard for even the expert lobbyists and public relations crews hired by Big Oil to cry poverty convincingly.

By the end of October, with her approval rating still at 83 percent ("quite unprecedented in the recent history of Alaska politics—only Ted Stevens in his heyday could really match this kind of public approval," Anchorage pollster Ivan Moore said), Sarah took a break from the debate to cut the ribbon at the grand opening of the new Wal-Mart Supercenter in Wasilla.

"There's something about Wal-Mart in the Valley that is always an event," she said, recalling 2002, when the original Wasilla Wal-Mart sold more duct tape than any other Wal-Mart in the world.

She also took time to oppose the listing of polar bears as an endangered species. "The polar bear has become a metaphor in the highly charged climate debate," she said. Her stance on that issue was clear: only "snake oil science" suggested that man-made carbon emissions were responsible for global warming, not that she believed in global warming. In Sarah's mind, God managed the earth's climate and he'd done a pretty darned good job up to now.

In early November a Johns Hopkins University study classified seven Alaska high schools, including Wasilla High, as "dropout factories": those in which fewer than 60 percent of freshmen advanced to senior year. Without mentioning that Track had failed to graduate, Sarah said she wanted to help. "I'd remind the kids that no matter where they are in life . . . there is no circumstance that would necessitate them just giving up."

On November 16, in a combined senate-house vote of 40–18, the legislature approved an even stronger version of Sarah's ACES proposal. The net effect was to guarantee that oil companies would pay at least $1 billion more in state taxes than they'd paid under the previous "cloud of corruption" law.

Juneau economist Gregg Erickson wrote, "It was as if Gov. Sarah Palin asked the legislature for a nice sensible winter jacket and they sent her a full-length mink parka with a wolverine ruff, seal skin trim, and a catalytic hand warmer in each pocket."

Calling the passage "a major victory" for Sarah, the *Daily News* said, "Palin's high public approval ratings clearly helped get the tax through . . . Many lawmakers are reluctant to pick a fight with such a popular governor."

Sarah's only setback of the fall was a state supreme court decision that said underage teenagers did not need parental consent for abortions. She said she'd seek yet another constitutional amendment to overrule the decision.

For someone who so incessantly preached reverence for the U.S. Constitution, Sarah was awfully quick to advocate changes to Alaska's constitution that would bring it more into line with her religious beliefs.

As Christmas approached, Sarah did a *Vogue* photo shoot at her Lake Lucille house. The AP wrote, "She's well suited for the magazine, attractive as she is accomplished. The forty-three-year-old Palin's high cheekbones could rival any runway model's; she's well dressed, and often wears her brown hair with gold highlights fashionably swept up."

Sarah said, "Yes, it's humbling, but it's also a responsibility we've taken on: changing Alaska's image."

Posing for *Vogue* seemed a fitting climax to her first full year in office, a year in which she'd been interviewed by CNBC, MSNBC, *Newsweek,* and Charlie Rose. A *Daily News* columnist said Sarah deserved "a big smooch under the Christmas mistletoe." The newspaper said she'd "emerged as a national figure and a media darling." This was before the media became "lamestream" for no longer considering her a darling.

An AP story quoted a political scientist from conservative Claremont-McKenna College in California as saying Sarah "could be an ideal presidential running mate next year." Even Rush Limbaugh offered a tentative embrace on his radio show, describing her as "a babe."

Sarah repeated that she had no plans to do anything other than serve out her term, which would extend until 2010. "My role as governor is where I can be most helpful right now unless something drastic happens."

The possibility of something drastic happening was not one that Phil Munger thought likely. "National attention has come Palin's way," he wrote on his Progressive Alaska blog. "Although blogs like Wonkette and magazines such as *Vogue* see Palin as a babe, Palin sees herself more as an athlete or mom. There is too much cognitive dissonance between what outsiders want of her and what she feels is important right now for her popularity to snowball nationally."

What Munger, an unpaid blogger, could not know—and what none of the paid members of the Alaskan media ever discovered—was that what they assumed Sarah felt was "important right now" could not have been further from her real priorities.

As Jane Mayer first disclosed in the *New Yorker* during the 2008 presidential campaign, Sarah learned in the spring of 2007 that two conservative magazines, the *Weekly Standard* and the *National Review,* were planning cruises to Alaska that would stop in Juneau.

Overcoming her distaste for life in the Governor's Mansion, Sarah arranged to be there to meet both. On June 18, as the *Weekly Standard* cruise ship docked, Sarah invited editors William Kristol and Fred Barnes and *Washington Post* columnist Michael Gerson (former chief speechwriter for George W. Bush) to lunch.

She made sure her Christian lieutenant governor, Sean Parnell, and her Christian attorney general, Talis Colberg, were present. Then she simply floored her guests by saying a pre-meal grace. A Palin assistant told Mayer, "There are not many politicians who will say grace with the conviction of faith she has."

She filled in the picture postcard by having seven-year-old Piper perform a cameo role in which she asked people what they wanted for dessert. After the meal, Sarah further dazzled her guests by taking them on a helicopter ride (for which she billed the state $4,000).

The payoff was immediate. Barnes scarcely waited for the cruise to end before writing in the *Weekly Standard* that Sarah was "a Republican star" and "a politician of eye-popping integrity." He quoted Anchorage radio host and occasional *Daily News* columnist Dan Fagan as saying, "She's as Alaskan as you can get. She's a hockey mom, she lives on a lake, she ice fishes, she snowmobiles, she hunts, she's an NRA member, she has a floatplane, and her husband works for BP on the North Slope."

Barnes also quoted Sarah: "In my own personal life, if I dedicate back to my Creator what I'm trying to create for the good . . . everything will turn out fine."

She returned to Juneau on August 1 to host a *National Review* cruise group that included publisher Jack Fowler, editor Rich Lowry, rejected Supreme Court nominee Robert Bork, and political consultant and Fox News pundit Dick Morris.

"This lady is something special," Fowler said later. "She connects. She's genuine." Another guest said, "She has that aura that Clinton, Reagan and Jack Kennedy had." Another *National Review* editor later effused that she was "a former beauty pageant contestant, and a real honey, too." Morris told her that someday she could become a vice-presidential nominee.

Basking in the adulation of these older men and glorying in her ability to seduce them, Sarah asked, "Hey, does anyone want to stay for dinner? We can eat right now." When they declined, she invited them to come back the next day. "All you have to do is knock. Yell upstairs, I'll be right down." She did everything but say, "Or come on up."

As 2008 would demonstrate, it worked.

As for Alaska? Its poor, benighted residents, who continued to give her approval ratings of 85 percent, had no idea that she'd already discarded them, as she'd earlier rid herself of Laura Chase, John Cooper, Irl Stambaugh, John Cramer, John Bitney, Walt Monegan, and everyone else for whom she no longer had any need.

SEVENTEEN

I FLY BACK to Alaska on August 10. I land at Ted Stevens International Airport on the evening of the day when Stevens is killed in the crash of a small plane just outside Todd's home town of Dillingham, in western Alaska.

The pilot of Stevens's plane was an Alaska Airlines veteran with more than thirty thousand hours to his credit, but that didn't stop him from flying into a mountain in the fog. Stevens was on a fishing vacation, paid for by one of the Alaska corporations whose interests he served for so long, even as, with the help of Bill Allen, he served his own.

Stevens survived a 1978 crash in Anchorage that killed his first wife, but he is not among the three survivors of this one. Many Alaskans, including friends of mine, will forever remember him as the saintly "Uncle Ted," because for so many years he went to Washington and scooped up hundreds of millions of federal dollars that he sent back to the state, keeping only a small portion for himself.

Flying in a small plane in Alaska in good weather can be among the most transcendent of experiences available to those of us who don't climb to mountain summits. Flying in a small plane in Alaska in bad weather is a bitch. Also, it can kill you.

When I was here in the 1970s, almost everyone I met who'd lived in Alaska for more than a couple of years knew someone who had been killed in a plane crash. This doesn't seem as true now, but it's been a notably ugly year in Alaska's skies. Since January 1, twenty-three people have died in eleven different crashes. Undoubtedly, the relentlessly pissy weather this summer is a factor. It was chilly and wet when I left, and it's chilly and wet when I return, and I'm told it rained every day I was gone.

The first thing I do is catch up on Sarah's tweets. In one, she stakes out her claim to the job of Cheerleader in Chief: "Watching Blue Angels about to fly at the Alaska Air Show, Elmendorf AF Base. No better place to be! USA! USA!" She did not mention that on July 28 four air force crew members were killed in a crash at Elmendorf as they practiced for the show.

In another tweet, she squeezes all her scientific knowledge into 140 characters: "Earth saw clmate chnge4 ions; will cont 2 c chnges. R duty2responsbly devlop resorse4humandkind/not pollute&destroy; but cant alter naturl chng."

Other than pointing out that "ions" are not "eons," what can you possibly say to that except to bemoan the existence of Twitter?

Sarah's newest campaign is on behalf of Laura Schlessinger, a right-wing radio personality who recently berated an African American woman who'd called in to her program. In the course of her diatribe, Schlessinger used the word *nigger* thirteen times. Afterward, she promptly resigned, a choice that, though voluntary, struck Sarah as a violation of Schlessinger's First Amendment rights:

"Dr.Laura:don't retreat . . . reload! (Steps aside bc her 1st Amend.rights ceased 2exist thx 2activists trying 2silence isn't American,not fair)"

"Dr.Laura=even more powerful & effective w/out the shackles, so watch out Constitutional obstructionists. And b thankful 4 her voice,America!"

Neither at Wasilla High nor at any of her five colleges, apparently, did Sarah learn that the First Amendment protects individuals against government interference with their right to free speech. Schlessinger's vile expression of racist sentiment during a commercial broadcast and her decision to quit before she was fired have nothing to do with any constitutional amendment.

Next, I catch up on the soap opera episodes I've missed. Apparently Bristol and Levi are splitsville again. As soon as the check from *US Weekly* cleared, Bristol bared her heart to *People*, picking up another check in the process. Whatever skills the Palins may lack in other areas, they are grandmasters of the art of gaming the glossy magazines.

Bristol is upset because Levi might be the father of Lanesia's baby. (Lanesia is a new character with only a bit part in the series.) But "the final straw," she says, "was him flying to Hollywood . . . He's just obsessed with the limelight." Bristol doesn't mention that she'll soon be flying to Hollywood herself to appear on *Dancing with the Stars*.

Levi's sister, Mercede, is not surprised by the breakup. "I could not help but have serious doubts that Levi and Bristol would make it to the altar," she blogs. Nonetheless, Mercede is irked. "There is no way Bristol didn't know about the rumors circulating about Lanesia! Especially because of how much attention Bristol still pays to Lanesia out of leftover middle school jealousy."

Levi denies that he's the father of Lanesia's about-to-be-born baby. Lanesia, herself no raw recruit to the tabloid wars—in 2008, she spilled to the UK's *News of the World* that she was "distraught for a year" after Bristol stole Levi from her—tells *US Weekly* "exclusively": "It's not true . . . We haven't hung out since eighth or ninth grade."

But hold the line! *E! News* reports that the real cause of the breakup is not Lanesia, but another of Levi's exes, Briana Plum, who either dissed Bristol in an interview somewhere and/or was seen with Levi in a picture posted on Facebook.

Whatever the truth, Mercede remains displeased. She blogs that Bristol once called her mother, Sherry, and "exploded in anger, screaming and saying, 'How dare you allow Lanesia to stop by your house!' . . . She then claimed that we had a chaotic f**cked up family and then went on to compare Lanesia to the woman my father had cheated on my mother with."

Boldly, Levi tries to reclaim the high ground by announcing that he'll run for mayor of Wasilla in 2011. He'll do it only because a "reality" show will pay him to, but that doesn't mean he won't mount a vigorous campaign against Verne Rupright. To those who doubt Levi's commitment, his spokesman, Tank Jones, points out, "People questioned Jesus Christ."

Rupright is not exactly shaken by the news. Taking note of Levi's lack of education and his posing nude for *Playgirl* in 2009, he says, "I think it would be wise for him to get a high school diploma and keep his clothes on."

God, it's great to be back.

I'M STOPPED at a red light next to a guy in a pickup truck. The bed of the truck has been fitted with a large cage. Inside the cage are at least half a dozen pit bulls. A sign on the cage reads YOUR PICK—$200.

I'm tempted, but I don't want to scare the neighbor's children.

There's a big new sign on the Parks Highway side of Catherine Taylor's property, urging support for Dianne Woodruff in her bid to retain her seat on the Wasilla City Council. Dewey Taylor called Catherine to ask her permission to put up the sign, and Catherine was glad to oblige.

Dewey tells me that a couple of days before I got back he parked his truck on the Nevada right-of-way that cuts across Catherine's property to the Palins' driveway, hauled the sign out of the back, and was in the process of putting it up when three vehicles turned on to the dirt road and surrounded him.

Track jumped out of one. He told Dewey to take down the sign and get out. "You can't put that there," Track said.

As he demonstrated when someone shot out his truck window in retaliation for his bringing me a couple of chairs, Dewey is not a man who responds well to what he perceives as belligerence. He told Track that he was on Catherine Taylor's property and that she'd given permission for the sign to be put there and that he was going to put it there. Period.

"But it's right next to our driveway, so people will think my mother is supporting Woodruff, and she's not."

Dewey explained that he didn't care what people would think. He also told Track that he and his friends had best move their vehicles. He'd be leaving when he finished putting up the sign and it would be a shame if he bumped into any of them on his way out.

At that point, Dewey told me, Track's attention shifted from the sign to Dewey's truck, which boasted a new driver's-side window. Track told Dewey how much he admired the truck. Then he asked, "How much would you sell it for? I'd love to buy it."

Dewey said it wasn't for sale, but everything ended amicably. "I had to give him a lesson in the concept of private property and ownership rights. I think he believed that everything back there belonged to his parents, or even if it didn't, that they controlled it just because they were the Palins. But once we got to be just a couple of good old boys talking trucks, things were fine."

As for Sarah during my absence? She hasn't spent enough time at home even to realize I wasn't there. She's been flying all over the state filming episodes of *Sarah Palin's Alaska.* Apparently, it hasn't all been smooth sledding.

The crew drove down to Homer to do a halibut fishing episode but had a hard time finding someone willing to take Sarah out on his boat. Producers approached one prominent commercial fisherman, Todd Hoppe, and he said, "Not my boat. I'd sucker-punch Todd Palin if I had half a chance."

The Palins are not popular in Homer, which describes itself as "A quaint little drinking village with a fishing problem." In Homer, authenticity and common courtesy are considered to be among the highest of civic virtues.

While in Homer, Sarah posted on Facebook that she was "out on a commercial fishing boat, working my butt off for my own business" and that because "the Left" was getting so "wee-wee'd up" by her criticism she would "go back to setting my hooks and watching the halibut take the bait."

On Jeanne Devon's Mudflats blog, Shannyn Moore, who has actually earned a living fishing commercially out of Homer, points out that "The Palins' fishing business doesn't include IFQ's [individual fishing quotas] necessary for commercially harvesting halibut." So Sarah is breaking the law if she's actually working her butt off for her own business, unless by "my own business" she means appearing on TLC, which is paying her $250,000 per episode. Also, "Her baiting hooks and keeping a manicure is laughable," and, finally, "Halibut are on the bottom of the ocean, hard to watch them 'take the bait.'"

Unsurprisingly, Homer voted for Tony Knowles over Sarah in 2006. Her popularity in the town declined further as she embarrassed herself and Alaska during her run for the vice presidency. But the bottom really fell out when she quit as Alaska governor in July 2009. Homer has no respect for quitters.

A fifty-two-year-old Homer schoolteacher named Kathleen Gustafson, wife of a commercial fisherman, decided to show Sarah how Homer felt. She hung a thirty-by-three-foot banner that read WORST GOVERNOR EVER from a railing outside a fish-processing shack owned by her friend Billy Sullivan, at the top of the boat ramp on the Homer docks. Gustafson was rankled by Sarah's pretending to do, for a television stunt, what Gustafson's husband and many others in Homer did for real: fish for halibut.

Sarah and her entourage were more than fifty yards away, at the other end of the public dock, when Gustafson put up her banner. The TLC crew was setting up for filming while members of Sarah's private security force were spreading across the area patting down citizens who happened to find themselves on the dock.

Coincidentally, Walt Monegan and Gary Wheeler and their wives were in Homer that day and had considered a morning walk along the dock. What would have been a classic moment in Alaskan history came very close to happening: Sarah Palin's private security guards trying to frisk her former chief of security and the man she fired as director of public safety before letting them continue on their walk.

That confrontation did not occur, but Sarah could not resist provoking another. Having spotted Gustafson's banner, she was unable to ignore it. Trailed by Todd and Willow and a couple of her security specialists, she marched straight toward it. Billy Sullivan saw Sarah coming and took a cell-phone video of what happened next.

Palin: What's up?

Gustafson: You swore on your precious Bible that you would uphold the interests of this state, and then when cash was waved in front of your face, you quit.

Palin: Oh, you wanted me to be your governor! I'm honored! Thank you!

Gustafson: I wanted you to honor your responsibilities. That is what I wanted. I wanted you to be part of the political process instead of becoming a celebrity.

Palin: Here's the deal. Here's the deal. That's what I'm out there fightin' for Americans to be able to have a Constitution protected so that we can have free speech.

Gustafson: In what way are you fighting for that?

Palin: Oh my goodness!

Gustafson: In what way?

Palin: To elect candidates who understand the Constitution, to
protect our military interests so that we can keep on fightin'
for our Constitution that will protect some of the freedoms that
evidently are important to you, too.

Gustafson: By using your celebrity status . . .

Willow Palin: How is she a celebrity? That's my question.

Palin: I'm honored! No, she thinks I'm a celebrity!

Willow Palin: That's funny that you think she is.

Gustafson: Well, you're certainly not representing the state of
Alaska any longer . . .

Willow Palin (gesturing with both hands, as if outlining a map of the
United States): She's representing United States!

Gustafson: Yes, I know. You belong to America now, and that suits
me just fine.

Palin: What do you do here?

Gustafson: I'm a teacher.

Palin (rolling her eyes and grimacing): Ooh!

Willow Palin: Ooh!

As Sarah rolls her head, mother and daughter exchange a glance
that seems to say, "That explains it!"

Gustafson: I also have a few other jobs. I'm married to a commercial fisherman. And so I fish.

Palin: Oh, that's cool. So am I!

Palin (waving to Sullivan's camera): Hi! Are we on video?

Once Sarah becomes aware that the encounter is being recorded
she shifts to conciliatory mode and wraps things up within a few sen-
tences, as one of her security people sticks his hand in front of the
camera and then tries to stand in front of it. Later, members of Palin's

entourage come back and tear down the banner, in a display of Sarah's respect for the right of free speech.

Almost everywhere she goes this summer, Sarah is shielded from the once-adoring Alaskan public by either private security or by throngs of cameramen and soundmen and television producers and technicians. The days of her high approval ratings are long gone. A majority of Alaskans now disapprove of her. They don't even like her. They don't like how she walked out on her duties as governor in order to become an instant millionaire and they don't like how she's made the state, in the minds of outsiders, synonymous with herself.

It used to be that when an Alaskan traveled Outside, the questions would be about bears or cold winters or mountains or darkness or fish. Now, invariably, the only questions are about Sarah. I'm meeting many Alaskans who have taken to claiming to be Canadian when traveling Outside, just so they won't have to talk about her.

Nonetheless, despite what Willow said, Sarah is inarguably a celebrity, and therefore the center of attention in public places. She once basked in this, confident of her popularity. Now she can only do that Outside. Within Alaska, she shies away from unguarded public places, aware that glances in her direction are likely to be less adoring than disgusted.

Both she and Todd have become hypersensitive to cameras they can't control being aimed in their direction. An example of this occurs on August 17 at the Valdez Airport.

Sarah and Todd have arrived with Greta Van Susteren and her Fox News production team for a flight to Anchorage. A local small businessman named Hawk Pierce (the very sort of person whose interests Sarah so often claims to have at heart) has brought his wife to the airport for the same flight.

He sees Sarah at the airport entrance talking to the interim mayor of Valdez, Dave Cobb. Keeping his distance, Pierce starts to take a video. As soon as Sarah notices him, she breaks off her conversation and turns to him:

Sarah: Hello there, how are you?

Pierce: Good.

Sarah: What's your name?

Pierce: What's your name? You look familiar.

Sarah approaches him.

Sarah: Hi, I'm Sarah . . . what's your name?

Pierce: Hawk. Nice to meet you, Sarah.

Sarah: Nice to meetcha. This is my husband, Todd Palin. What do you do here?

Pierce: Hi, Todd. I'm a small-business owner.

Sarah (voice getting higher): Okay! What kind of business do you own?

Pierce: I have skateboard shops, espresso shops, things like that.

Sarah: Very good. And you live here in Valdez?

At this point, Todd steps to the side and begins to take pictures of Pierce.

Pierce: I do.

Sarah: Do you mind if I take a picture of ya? Love meetin' the locals.

Pierce: Not at all.

Sarah takes a picture of Pierce.

Sarah: That's wonderful. Todd, ya wanna stand by him and I'll take a picture?

Todd: Hey, I'm good right here.

Pierce pans his camera to show Todd.

Sarah: Good, good. Okay, we're gettin' on the flight.
Todd: What was your name again?
Pierce: Hawk.
Sarah: Hawk. And he's got the local skateboard shop.
Todd: And you're doin' the video for what?
Pierce: Just me.
Sarah: Nice to meet you, Hawk.

At that point, Todd and Sarah walk into the airport. No harm, no foul. It seems slightly odd that both Sarah and Todd would take pictures of the owner of a Valdez skateboard shop, but then, taking pictures of presumed critics and then disseminating them is a tactic commonly employed by Scientologists. It's not unreasonable to assume that Van Susteren, a Scientologist, has suggested that Todd and Sarah try this approach as a way of discouraging unwanted cell-phone videographers. No matter. Pierce takes their picture, they take his, pleasantries are exchanged, they move on.

Then things start to get weird. Inside the airport, Sarah poses for photographs with airline employees. From a distance, Pierce starts taking more video. Suddenly, Todd steps in front of him.

Todd: What do you need a video camera for, man?
Pierce: You got a problem with that?
Todd: I mean, you got a life, or what?
Pierce: I'm here with my wife. She's getting on the plane.

Pierce is clearly unsettled by Todd's aggressiveness.

Todd: Why you shaking so bad?

Moving toward Pierce, Todd takes more photographs of him, as Pierce backs away.

Todd: Why you shaking so bad? Why you shaking so bad?

Todd takes more pictures of Pierce, then turns away and returns to Sarah at the other end of the terminal. Ten minutes later, Pierce is seated, his camera off, when Todd suddenly springs up from behind him.

Todd: Why are you videotaping my wife?
Pierce: Why do you have a problem with it?
Todd: Why are you doing that?
Pierce: I was never—
Todd: Why did you stick the camera in Sarah Palin's face? Why did you do that?
Pierce: I didn't stick it in her face. I wasn't within ten feet of you guys.

Pierce stands and starts to back away. With his camera phone held in front of him and aimed at Pierce, Todd advances. Pierce retreats.

"Do you have a problem with me being here with a camera?" he says.

Todd glares at him. Then one of Van Susteren's production assistants jumps in and says, "No, there's no problem. There's just nothing to see here," and starts hitting Pierce's camera with papers she's holding in her hand.

Then the flight is called and those who are going to Anchorage, including Sarah and Todd and Van Susteren and her crew and Pierce's wife, board the plane. Pierce goes home.

Clearly, being reduced to the role of Chihuahua carried around in a rich lady's purse is proving stressful for Todd.

ALL SUMMER, I'VE been wanting to get to Homer. It was one of my favorite places in Alaska in the seventies and I've wondered how it's fared over the thirty-five intervening years, during which its population has more than doubled. Sarah's tête-à-tête with Kathleen Gustafson gives me all the excuse I need to accompany Shannyn Moore and her partner, Kelly Walters, on a visit to Shannyn's hometown on Saturday, August 21.

The town was named for Homer Pennock, a gold-mining entrepreneur who arrived in 1896 to find lots of fish but no gold. When I first went there in 1975 the mayor put me up in his house. Because other guests were occupying the guest room, he put me in his own bedroom and went to sleep elsewhere that night. Nothing out of the ordinary in Alaska.

On this trip, we're planning to stay with Shannyn's parents. They moved to Alaska from Tennessee in the late 1960s to teach orphaned Native children at Cookson Hills Christian Home, at the head of Kachemak Bay. Like so many from Outside who have made Alaska their home, they planned to stay for only a year. Shannyn's father wound up teaching in a Russian Orthodox settlement featured in a *National Geographic* article in 1972 and later became a commercial fisherman. He and his wife are still here, Alaskan to the core.

Whenever she's in Homer, Shannyn touches base with special friends, one of whom, Clem Tillion, I wrote about in *Going to Extremes*. Clem, a native of Long Island, came to Alaska after World War II, almost straight from Guadalcanal, where he fought as a member of the U.S. Marine Corps. He literally walked into Homer in 1947 "with long hair and a beard and not a penny to my name. I was the first hippie in town."

He and his wife, Diana, an artist known particularly for her work in octopus ink, lived in Halibut Cove, on the south shore of Kachemak Bay, six miles from Homer by water. Clem became one of the most powerful Republican politicians in Alaska, serving many years in the legislature, winding up as state senate president, and becoming one of Alaska's legendary figures.

One of his accomplishments in Juneau was seeing that the four hundred thousand acres that surrounded his home in Halibut Cove became Kachemak Bay State Park, ensuring that the only development the cove would ever see would be whatever Clem himself decided to do. The population of Halibut Cove is now about twenty-five, almost all of them descended from Clem and Diana.

The Tillions had been married for fifty-nine years at the time of Diana's death in February 2010. At a memorial service at her grave site in June, Clem explained the success of the marriage by saying, "You can't talk a woman out of anything, but if you kiss her enough, she'll follow you to the end of the world." A few mourners commented that Clem apparently never figured out that in her own quiet manner it was Diana who'd led every step of the way.

Shannyn calls Clem to tell him that we're coming to Halibut Cove tonight, to have dinner at The Saltry, the cove's one and only restaurant, owned and operated, not surprisingly, by Clem's daughter Marian. He invites us to come to his house afterward and spend the night. Shannyn's father takes us across the bay in his boat.

Marian tells us that Sarah and her crew wanted to book The Saltry for dinner after their day of filming on Kachemak Bay for *Sarah Palin's Alaska*. Marian informed them that the restaurant's ethics committee disapproved. A TLC producer asked if he could speak to a member of the committee. "You are," Marian said. "It's a committee of one. Me. I'm not serving dinner to Sarah Palin."

Clem's house is a ten-minute walk, by boardwalk, from The Saltry. Though still grieving the loss of Diana, he's as gracious a host to us as he was to me thirty-four years earlier. He tells us stories by the fire as we sip a fine brandy from his wine cellar, which is as extensive as any I've ever seen in a private home. Being an Alaska fisherman all his life has done nothing to dull Clem's appreciation of Grand Crus (not to be confused with Sarah's marketing company, Rouge Cou). At the age of eighty-eight, he feels he has the right to tell anyone who asks that he believes Sarah to be a nitwit.

The next morning, after he cooks us pancakes and takes us to Diana's grave, we ride a Tillion-operated ferry back to Homer. We go to Billy Sullivan's halibut shack, where Billy re-creates the Gustafson-Palin confrontation for us, then to meet Kathleen Gustafson herself at the Salty Dawg Saloon.

Inside the Salty Dawg are hundreds, probably thousands of dollar bills tacked to the walls and ceiling. This is a tradition started many years ago by a regular customer who tacked a bill to the wall as he left so the friend who was supposed to meet him there would find his first drink paid for when he arrived.

Billy Sullivan's video has been viewed more than a million times on YouTube. But it captured only about two minutes of the eight- to ten-minute exchange. Gustafson tells us that before Sullivan turned on his camera, Sarah approached her and winked.

"I said, 'Don't flirt with me,'" Gustafson says. "So I think that kind of set the tone. I tried really hard not to be a bitch, but when somebody's throwing that at you, it's hard. When I made that banner I specifically chose a criticism that was true no matter what your politics are. She quit."

At another point, Gustafson says, "She was talking about being a leader and using her influence to help Americans, and I said, 'You're out there for yourself. You're not a leader, you're a climber.'"

"Obviously we're not welcome here," Sarah replied.

"I haven't asked you to leave and I haven't told you you're unwelcome. Have a seat at the picnic table. We'll talk all day."

It wasn't to be. Willow, apparently thinking that the word *governor* should have been spelled with an *-er* not *-or* at the end, interjected one more comment: "You're a teacher; you should learn how to spell." Then the whole TLC crew moved on, ending a wholly unnecessary incident caused by Sarah's inability to ignore a sight that displeased her.

I ask Gustafson if she's received any hostile reactions from Sarah's supporters. "I haven't heard a single thing," she says. "Nothing but love from Alaskans. And I came home one day and my husband had put up a banner that said 'Best Wife Ever.'"

• • •

AUGUST 24 IS primary day. Tea Party candidate Joe Miller, a lawyer from Fairbanks, is challenging incumbent Lisa Murkowski in the
Republican primary for U.S. Senate. Sarah has been seething about
Murkowski ever since her father chose her over Sarah to fill his unex-
pired term in 2002. But Miller is loony enough on his own to appeal
to Sarah and Todd.

Marching alongside children in an Eagle River community parade
on the Fourth of July, Miller supporters carried assault rifles. Later in
the year, members of a private militia force that Miller employed as
security guards handcuffed Tony Hopfinger of the *Alaska Dispatch* as
he attempted to ask Miller a question. Miller himself declared that
the way to stop illegal immigration was to "build a wall. If the East
Germans can do it, so can we."

He is unmistakably Sarah's kind of candidate for a U.S. Senate
seat, and her pro-Miller Twitter barrage has been relentless:

"Please check out this great all-Alaskana video by my friend Joe
Miller who is the commonsense conservative running . . ."

"Vote for our pro-Constitution, pro-life, pro-private sector candidate Joe Miller for U.S. Senate!"

"Wow! What dfference betwn candidates'worldview! I'll post KAKM
Senate debate,you'll see who'll serve AK for right reasons&protect
Constitutn"

But it's a sign of just how unpopular Sarah has become in her home
state that she's kept her enthusiasm for Miller confined to tweets. Despite campaigning for Tea Party candidates in southern and western
states throughout the summer, she's been afraid to present herself at

even a single Miller campaign event in Alaska. What once was nectar now is poison. The less Alaskans see of Sarah, the more they like it.

Miller wins the primary by just over a thousand votes, taking advantage of Murkowski treating the race as a minor nuisance best ignored. Immediately, Outside news outlets misinterpret the significance. The Huffington Post says, "The stunning result was a huge validation of the political power of Palin."

Actually, it was nothing of the sort, as became evident in November, when Murkowski defeated Miller through a write-in campaign. All the August primary showed was that any candidate supported by a vocal and zealous minority can defeat a lethargic incumbent content to rest on her insubstantial laurels.

Riding high because she's given credit for Miller's primary triumph, Sarah jets off to Washington, D.C., where adoring crowds do await. On Saturday, August 28, at Glenn Beck's "Restoring Honor" rally in Washington, she speaks to a crowd variously estimated as being between eighty-five thousand and more than five hundred thousand. In any case, it's the largest live audience she's ever addressed. Her speech comes scarcely more than a year after her ignominious resignation as governor, when her flighty, rambling remarks had listeners wondering if she might be careening toward a full-fledged nervous breakdown.

The day after Sarah's speech at the Beck rally, I drive down to Chugiak for lunch with Walt Monegan and his wife, Terry. Throwing a curve, he cooks chicken, not salmon, on his grill. Terry makes a baked bean dish that's the best bean dish I've ever had. If I were putting recipes in this book, I'd start with hers. These are the kind of people I'm going to miss when I have to head home to start writing.

I mention the most highly publicized line from Sarah's Washington speech: "Say what you want to say about me, but I raised a combat vet, and you can't take that away from me."

"Is that the son that was given the choice by the judge of either joining the military or going to jail after the vandalism of those buses?" Monegan asks.

"I wonder who that judge was."

"I'm sure they've got the case file sealed tight," Monegan says.

"What Todd and Sarah do," adds Terry, herself a former police officer, "is they go over and talk to everybody involved, and the authorities, and then make a deal, like they did for Willow with the vandalism."

It seems to be the Palin way: do whatever you want and don't worry about it because you can always escape the consequences. Sarah stood on the Mall in front of the Lincoln Memorial and talked about "restoring honor" after having fired perhaps the most honorable man in Alaska for not doing her vengeful bidding.

"I've had no contact with either Todd or Sarah since," Monegan says, "but late last winter we went to this event called the Festival of Seafood. We had our youngest and her boyfriend with us and we got seated at a table and I'm going back to get a glass of wine and I hear, 'Walt! Walt!' I turn around and there's Chuck Heath. He was sitting at a table with Sally and he gets up and he walks over and shakes my hand and gives me a hug and says, 'Aah, it's all politics. I still consider you a friend.'"

Driving back to Wasilla in late afternoon, as the day's clouds lift, I'm struck by the incursion that autumn has already made. Leaves that were green are now yellow. The brilliant magenta of roadside fireweed is suddenly part of my peripheral vision. It's been a chilly, wet, and dismal summer, setting a new record for consecutive days of rain in Anchorage: thirty-one.

Not that I've minded. For me, it's been thrilling just to be back in Alaska. Nowhere else do I feel so at home. Were it not for the impossible distance from the ones I love, I could happily live the rest of my life here. Maybe even on Lake Lucille, despite the grouchy neighbors.

EIGHTEEN

S ARAH KICKED OFF her year of destiny on January 4, 2008, by choosing a foreign company, TransCanada, based in Calgary, to partner with the state in building a natural gas pipeline from Prudhoe Bay.

Unfortunately, TransCanada had neither gas to flow through the line nor access to any. AGIA was smoke and mirrors and pipe dreams, except for Alaska's obligation to repay TransCanada for the first $500 million it committed to the project.

During the third week of January, the *Anchorage Daily News* noted that "critics are questioning TransCanada's bid and Palin's optimism." Her persistent nemesis Andrew Halcro, who ran against her for governor in 2006, said, "They've already admitted they can't do the job, so why are we giving them $500 million and a state license?"

But even as ferment at home increased, so did national interest in Alaska's brash young woman governor. She was asked her views on the 2008 presidential election. In early February she said she'd like to support John McCain, but could not because of his opposition to opening the Arctic National Wildlife Refuge (ANWR) to exploitation by oil companies.

After meeting privately with McCain at the Willard Hotel in

Washington in late February, Sarah stopped saying she could not support him. Back in Alaska, perhaps to prepare for making the biggest decision of her life, she called her spiritual mentor Mary Glazier. "She asked me to pray with her for wisdom and direction," Glazier said. "I sensed a real heart of surrender to the will of God in her."

On March 5, Sarah brought all attention back to herself—and ensured that it would be uncritical—by announcing that even though she looked as slim and trim as ever, she was, in fact, seven months pregnant with her fifth child. Yes, it was a surprise, she said, but "I've always been a believer that God's not going to give us anything that we cannot handle." She did not say the baby would be born with Down syndrome.

The *Anchorage Daily News* wrote: "That the pregnancy is so advanced astonished all who heard the news. The governor . . . simply doesn't look pregnant." A few days later one of the newspaper's columnists wrote, "I look more pregnant when I'm constipated than Palin looks two months before delivery."

In mid-March the *Daily News* published a story that said, "With Palin riding extraordinarily high popularity ratings, pundits have mentioned her as a potential vice presidential candidate. But she said she's 'not pursuing or perpetuating it,' adding, 'I have no desire to leave my job at all as governor.'"

Less than a week later the newspaper reiterated that there was "an undeniable national buzz" surrounding Sarah. "The vice presidency may be far-fetched, but the hype has only helped Palin's future political prospects." The story also said, "Palin is quick to note that she has not spoken to McCain . . . about the prospect." The reporter, of course, could not have known that her security chief, Gary Wheeler, had escorted Sarah to a private forty-five-minute meeting with McCain only two weeks earlier.

In addition, her proposed AGIA partnership with TransCanada was losing favor fast. Its fatal flaw—that TransCanada had no gas to put into a pipeline—was reemphasized on April 8 when Conoco-Phillips and BP, two oil companies that did have access to North Slope natural gas, announced their own $600 million pipeline project.

The *Juneau Empire* wrote that this new effort, called Denali—The Alaska Gas Pipeline, "reshaped the gas line debate. There's every reason to think that the announcement will cause legislators to wonder about the wisdom of giving TransCanada the $500 million in state money that would go with the exclusive pipeline license." The newspaper urged Sarah to support the Denali line.

Dan Fagan went further, writing in the *Daily News* that the Denali plan "obviously means the death of AGIA," which was fine, because AGIA "would have never led to a pipeline."

ON SATURDAY, April 19, the *Daily News* reported that Sarah had given birth to her fifth child, Trig Paxson Van Palin, at the Mat-Su Regional Medical Center in Wasilla at 6:30 AM the previous day. "The sequence of events surrounding the labor was unclear," the story said.

Chuck Heath told reporters that Trig had been the name of an ancestor of his, while Paxson was a favored snowmobiling location in central Alaska. Sarah said that Van was in honor of Van Halen, which had been one of her favorite rock bands when she attended Wasilla High. She said she thought having a child named Van Palin would be cool.

Questions about Trig's birth—which occurred a month before Sarah's announced due date—were raised immediately. Her spokespeople responded with a chronology of the events that led up to the birth. It was a simple, straightforward account.

Sarah and Todd had flown to Dallas on April 16. Early the next morning, hours before she was to address the Republican Governors Conference, she noticed amniotic fluid leaking. Nonetheless, she proceeded with her lunchtime speech. After consulting with her Wasilla doctor, Cathy Baldwin-Johnson, she and Todd flew home. She was having only minor contractions and was not showing signs of active labor.

A spokesman for Alaska Airlines said, "Governor Palin was extremely pleasant to flight attendants and her stage of pregnancy was not apparent by observation."

In *Going Rogue,* Sarah writes that she'd told her four children about the new baby by e-mailing them a letter she wrote in the voice of God.

> I heard your heart when you hinted that another boy would fit best in the Palin family, to round it out and complete that starting five lineup . . . Then I put the idea in your hearts that his name should be Trig . . .
>
> Trig will be his dad's little buddy and he'll wear Carhartts while he learns to tinker in the garage . . . He'll want to play goalie and he'll steal his mom's heart . . . I created him a bit different . . . Doctors call it "Down syndrome."
>
> I know it will take time to grasp this . . . Remember though: "My ways are not your ways . . . for as the heavens are higher than the earth, my ways are higher than yours!" . . .
>
> Trig can't wait to meet you. I'm giving you ONLY THE BEST!
> Love,
> Trig's Creator, Your Heavenly Father

Sarah was back in her Anchorage office on Monday, April 21, where she and Todd confirmed that Trig had Down syndrome. She said that she and Todd felt "blessed and chosen by God." She said that after noticing the amniotic fluid and feeling contractions, she called her doctor, Cathy Baldwin-Johnson, at about 4:00 AM. In a telephone interview, the doctor told the *Daily News,* "Things were already settling down. I don't think it was unreasonable for her to continue to travel back." Another doctor, however, said Sarah should have gone to a Dallas hospital as soon as she noticed the leaking fluid, because of the risk of infection. Todd didn't want her to do that. "You can't have a fish picker from Texas," he said.

For the time being, that was that: baby born, story over.

BY MID-MAY, Sarah's charm was wearing thin. Dan Fagan, who less than a year earlier had written that she had a "heart of gold" and was "obsessed with integrity," now said, "The governor has one filter in which she determines policy: How will this make me look?" He accused her of "spending most of her time acting as her own press secretary," and wrote, "This governor does not like to be doubted, challenged or even questioned. And she has shown a propensity to hold a grudge, get even and never forget if you oppose her."

Fagan had not yet reached the point of calling Sarah "the Hugo Chavez of Alaska," but for the first time someone had written in Alaska's only newspaper with statewide circulation that the empress was wearing something less than a full suit of clothes.

In early June, Sarah billed the state for her travel from Juneau to Wasilla for two evangelical events. On June 8 she and Lieutenant Governor Parnell were blessed by Assembly of God pastor Kalnins at the Wasilla sports complex in a ceremony attended by an estimated six thousand people. Kalnins was the minister who had brought Thomas Muthee to Wasilla in 2005 to launch Sarah's campaign for governor.

Kalnins once publicly stated that anyone who criticized President George W. Bush would go to hell. In addition, during the 2004 presidential campaign he said, "I'm not going to tell you who to vote for, but if you vote for this particular person [John Kerry] I question your salvation."

Sarah's other June 8 event was a talk to the graduating class of the Master's Commission program at the Assembly of God church on West Riley Avenue, a street named for the pastor who had baptized her.

For eight thousand dollars a year (with no dating allowed during the first year), students in the three-year Master's Commission program—open to men and women from ages eighteen to twenty-five—were taught "deference to authority, Biblical memorization, prophesy, and miracle healing."

After receiving an honorary diploma, Sarah read from the New Testament Book of Ephesians. Then she told the graduates, "It was so cool growing up in this church and getting saved here." She said, "Just be amazed . . . the umbrella of this church here, where God is going to send you from this church. Believe me, I know what I am saying, where God has sent me from underneath the umbrella of this church." Her sincerity more than made up for her lack of coherence as she spoke of "a spirit of prophecy . . . a spirit of revelation" that, she said, would "bubble over."

This talk came in the midst of the legislative debate about AGIA, and Sarah urged the new graduates to pray for passage of her proposal. "Having grown up here, and having little kids grow up here also," she said, "this is such a special, special place. What comes from this church, I think, has great destiny. What I need to do is strike a deal with you guys as you go out throughout Alaska—I can do my part in doing things like working really, really hard to get a natural gas pipeline. Pray about that. I think God's will has to be done in unifying people and companies to get that gas line built, so pray for that . . . We can work together to make sure God's will be done here."

She then turned her attention to the war in Iraq. "Pray for this country, that our leaders are sending our military men and women out on a task that is from God," she said. "That's what we have to make sure we are praying for, that there is a plan and that that plan is God's plan."

In closing, Sarah recalled the blessing she'd received from Thomas Muthee three years earlier: "You know how he speaks," she said, "and he's so bold. And he was prayin', 'Lord make a way, Lord make a way.' And I'm thinkin', 'This guy's really bold. He doesn't even know what

I'm gonna do, he doesn't know what my plans are.' And he's prayin' not 'Oh Lord if it be your will may she become governor.' No, he just prayed for it. He said, 'Lord make a way and let her do this next step.' And that's exactly what happened."

SARAH'S NEXT STEP, on July 11, 2008, was to fire Walt Monegan. All hell broke loose. At the time, Alaskans knew nothing of Todd and Sarah's years-long attempt to take away Mike Wooten's badge.

Monegan said his dismissal "came out of the blue. If the governor was upset with me for one thing or another, it had never been communicated to me." At first, even he could not believe that Sarah would fire him because he'd said he couldn't fire Wooten.

Sarah's spokespeople offered some mumbo-jumbo about wanting to move the department of public safety "in a new direction," but were unable to say what direction.

On July 17, Halcro reported on his blog what Alaska newspapers had not: that Sarah had axed Monegan because he would not fire a trooper who "was being maliciously hounded by Palin's family. Walt Monegan got fired because he had the audacity to tell Governor Palin no, when apparently nobody is allowed to say no to Governor Palin."

Halcro also disclosed that "confidential material in Wooten's Administrative Investigation file had been released to his ex-wife and her attorney. AI files are strictly confidential and can only be released with the written signature of the trooper . . . no one could explain how the detailed confidential information was released."

At first Sarah denied everything. In a prepared statement, she said, "To allege that I, or any member of my family, requested, received or released confidential personnel information on an Alaska state trooper, or directed disciplinary action be taken against any employee of the Department of Public Safety, is, quite simply, outrageous."

Outrageous, but also true. The next day, Monegan confirmed the allegations in Halcro's blog, saying that not only Todd but also members of Sarah's administration had pressured him. "The new assertions from Monegan . . . conflict with what the Republican governor said earlier in the week," the *Daily News* reported.

On July 21, Sarah said she would welcome an investigation. "I've said all along, hold me accountable. And I'm telling the truth when I say there was never pressure put on Commissioner Monegan." Had anyone in her administration ever tried to make Monegan do her bidding in regard to Wooten? "No, no, absolutely not. No," she said.

She got a brief respite the next day when the statehouse voted 24–16 to approve the state's exclusive contract with and $500 million subsidy to TransCanada. But it was a mark of how far she'd fallen that fifteen house members who had originally voted in favor of AGIA were now against it. One of them, Mike Hawker, an Anchorage Republican, said, "AGIA—I'm a little bit afraid it stands for 'Alaska Goofs It Again.'"

On the same day, Monegan's replacement, Chuck Kopp, acknowledged that a sexual harassment complaint had been filed against him in 2005 and that he'd received an official reprimand from Kenai city officials. He said he'd hugged the female employee in question "three or four times, friend-to-friend," but "I did not kiss her." This contradicted his earlier statement that "There is no history of these types of complaints" and that he'd never received a reprimand.

On July 24 one of Sarah's spokespeople said she'd known about the complaint when she appointed Kopp, but had been told it was unsubstantiated. She had not been aware of the reprimand. "She is concerned, and she's also disappointed," the spokeswoman said. After meeting with Sarah the next day, Kopp resigned.

On July 28 a twelve-member bipartisan panel of legislators voted unanimously to hire an independent investigator to look into "the circumstances and events surrounding the termination of former Public Safety Commissioner Monegan, and potential abuses of power and/or improper actions by members of the executive branch."

A week earlier Sarah had said, "Hold me accountable." Now a spokeswoman said that the governor "doesn't see a need" for the investigation. A *Wall Street Journal* story quoted state senator Hollis French as saying, "This is a governor who was almost impervious to error. Now she could face impeachment."

On August 1 the state senate approved the TransCanada license by a vote of 14–5. In both houses of the legislature, it was Democratic support that allowed Sarah to prevail.

But the same day, legislators hired Steve Branchflower, a lawyer with twenty-eight years of experience as a prosecutor in the Anchorage District Attorney's office, to investigate what was becoming known as Troopergate. In response, Sarah said she would conduct her own investigation, led by her attorney general, Talis Colberg.

Then it got worse. Branchflower had just begun his investigation when Sarah called a press conference on August 13 to admit that, contrary to her earlier denials, one of her aides had called a state police official in February in an attempt to have Wooten fired. It was the worst public moment she'd ever endured.

Talis Colberg, digging through the dirt before Branchflower arrived, had discovered that the state police had recorded the call from Frank Bailey, a longtime loyalist whom Sarah had appointed as director of boards and commissions.

"I do now have to tell Alaskans that pressure could have been perceived to exist, although I have only now become aware of it," she said, with scant regard for the truth. She admitted that in addition to the Bailey call, members of her staff—including her then chief of staff, Mike Tibbles, and Attorney General Colberg—had contacted public safety officials more than twenty times in regard to Wooten. "The serial nature of the contacts could be perceived as some kind of pressure, presumably at my direction," she said.

She released a recording of Bailey's call to state police Lieutenant Rodney Dial. In it, Bailey said, "The Palins can't figure out why nothing is going on. Todd and Sarah are scratching their heads. Why on earth hasn't this—why is this guy still representing the department? From their perspective, everybody's protecting him."

Bailey also told Dial, "My understanding is, you know, Walt has been very reluctant to take any action . . . She really likes Walt a lot, but on this issue she feels like it's, she doesn't know why there is absolutely no action for a year on this issue. It's very, very troubling to her and the family."

Sarah denied knowing anything about anything and dragged Bailey out so he could fall on his sword. He had to tell the press that no one had asked him to make the call and that he didn't know why he'd indicated he was speaking on behalf of Sarah and Todd.

Andrew Halcro wrote, "In Wooten's eight-year career, the only complaints that have been filed against him came from people associated with Governor Palin during a divorce and child custody fight in which they were trying to get him fired so he wouldn't be able to get custody of his children."

Jesse Griffin wrote in his Immoral Minority blog, "I think it is well past time for Alaskans to not allow themselves to be seduced by Palin's dewy eyes and to realize they are dealing with nothing more then [sic] another politician who will use her influence to circumvent rules she feels should not apply to her . . . The bottom line is that Sarah let her desire for revenge get the best of her, and punished an honorable man for not doing what he knew was wrong."

As August waned and Branchflower continued his investigation, Sarah found herself at the low point of her political career. Former supporters, both Democrats and Republicans, turned against her. After promising honesty, transparency, and the highest ethical standards, she found herself accused of lying, cover-up, and actions that seemed, at the least, a grievous ethical breach.

Autumn is a mere blink of an eye in Alaska, and looking beyond it, Sarah would not have been able to see anything other than a long, dark winter of turmoil, acrimony, and discontent. Then, like an angel on a personal mission from her Heavenly Father, John McCain swooped down to tap her with his magic wand.

SARAH BECAME a national sensation overnight. Her September 3 speech to the Republican convention in Minneapolis was hailed as "dazzling" and "electrifying" by a national media that had at first viewed her with skepticism.

In the weeks that followed, she carried the momentum of Minneapolis with her across the country. John McCain's previously moribund campaign pulsed with Sarah's energy. With Todd at her side and her children—especially Trig, the Down syndrome baby—much in evidence, she created a sensation wherever she went. Adoring crowds flocked to her appearances.

Democratic attacks on her lack of knowledge and experience and her inability to answer simple questions were widely viewed as attempts by a panicky East Coast elite establishment to undermine this plainspoken "hockey mom" who personified "real" American values.

Even many in the liberal media were stupefied. For example, while noting that she was a born-again Christian, mainstream media largely ignored Sarah's religious extremism, even after her blessing by Thomas Muthee went viral on YouTube.

Max Blumenthal, writing in *Salon,* The Huffington Post, and elsewhere, and Bruce Wilson, on the Talk to Action website, exposed with penetrating clarity Sarah's close ties to the radical fringe of the Pentecostal movement. Old-line print media, however, seemed to view Sarah's picaresque religious beliefs as a private matter best left unexplored. (In the same way, they shied from reporting on her children, even after Sarah dragged them with her into the limelight and put them to work serving as props for her political career.)

Later in the campaign, Sarah would excoriate Barack Obama for having been a member of a Chicago congregation presided over by the incendiary reverend Jeremiah Wright. But only a week before

McCain chose her, Sarah attended a Wasilla Bible Church service at which the evangelical preacher who'd founded Jews for Jesus said that terrorist attacks in Israel were nothing more than a manifestation of God's displeasure with the Jewish state.

As governor, Sarah worshipped at the Juneau Christian Center, an Assembly of God affiliate whose pastor railed against evolution, saying, "Believe the word of God—you are not a descendant of a chimpanzee." In Wasilla, in addition to Assembly of God and the Wasilla Bible Church, she'd also attended services at Church on the Rock, whose pastor preached, "This nation is a Christian nation! God will not be mocked! Judgment Day is coming. Where do you stand?"

That pastor, David Pepper, described Sarah as "a Spirit-filled believer." He said, "She was very comfortable in the environment of our church. She is very genuine, very authentic." He also said her involvement in the church went "beyond being just an attender" and that "There is definitely a sense of destiny over her life. There's a sense that she is here for a time such as this."

Many evangelicals thought Sarah was the Esther of modern times, comparing her to the Old Testament queen chosen by God to save the Jews from genocide. One of them, Mark Arnold, of Life Covenant Church of Monroe, Ohio, had the chance to meet her during the 2008 campaign and tell her so, an experience he described on his website, Agree in Prayer.

"I got to talk to Sarah Palin," he wrote. "What an awesome time we had . . . I confirmed to her that 'MILLIONS were praying for her and that she was to stand strong and be courageous . . . Be strong . . . stand strong . . . know people are praying . . . be like a bull-dog and don't stop . . . stand strong!' Each time I would say the above information to her . . . she would wink at me and say, '. . . THANK YOU and THANK those who are praying for us . . .' WOW . . . OH GOD . . . YOU ARE AWESOME!"

Arnold believed that the Holy Spirit had called him to deliver a message to Sarah about being Esther. As he approached her, he said in an interview published by *Charisma* magazine in February 2009, "She spun around, looking right at me, and I told her: 'God wants me to tell you that you are a present-day Esther.' She began to cry and shake my hand in an affirming way. She said, 'Yes, I receive that.'"

On September 22, in the midst of the campaign, Mary Glazier prophesied the election of John McCain, but also his death in a terrorist attack that would make Sarah president. Glazier sent out a "WARNING OF IMMINENT ATTACK." She said two of her "trusted intercessors" had received warnings of a terrorist attack that "would cause national mourning." One of them, Glazier wrote, "received the scripture Gen. 50:3, 'A period of NATIONAL MOURNING.' She then saw Sarah Palin standing alone and she was mantled with the American flag . . . I knew she was stepping into an office that she was mantled for."

In mid-October, Sarah did a twenty-minute telephone interview with James Dobson, founder of the Colorado Springs–based evangelical group Focus on the Family. Dobson told her that not only was he praying for her but that he'd just hosted a gathering of more than four hundred "prayer warriors" and that "We were sure asking for God's intervention" in the campaign.

"Well, it is that intercession that is so needed," Sarah said. "And I can feel it, too, Dr. Dobson. I can feel the power of prayer and that strength that is provided through our prayer warriors across this nation . . . We hear along the rope lines that people are interceding for us and praying for us. It's our reminder to do the same, to seek His perfect will for this nation, and to of course seek His wisdom and guidance in putting this nation back on the right track . . . I have to have faith that our message will get out there minus the filter of the mainstream media . . . I have to have that faith that God's going to help us get that message out there."

"My goodness," Dobson said. "If our audience is any indication, they're getting it. There are millions of people praying for you and for Senator McCain."

Evidence abounded that Sarah's extremist beliefs were not only religious but also political. But, again, the mainstream media were too busy swooning to pay attention. Even the disclosure that Todd had been a member of the Alaska Independence Party from 1995 to 2002—he changed his voter registration to Republican only when Sarah decided to run for lieutenant governor—caused little stir.

Sarah herself had spoken at the AIP convention in Wasilla in 2006. As David Talbot of *Salon* reported on September 10, party chairwoman Lynette Clark viewed her as a kindred spirit. "She impressed me so much," Clark said. "As I was listening to her, I thought she sounds like what we've been saying for years."

Salon also disclosed that in October 2007, Clark's husband, Dexter, told delegates at the Secessionist Convention in Chattanooga, Tennessee, that Sarah "was an AIP member before she got the job as a mayor of a small town. But to get along to go along, she eventually joined the Republican party . . . She's pretty well sympathetic [to us] because of her former membership."

In 2008, as governor, Sarah recorded a message of welcome to convention delegates in Fairbanks. She said, "I share your party's vision of upholding the constitution of our great state . . . I say good luck on a successful and inspiring convention. Keep up the good work, and God bless you."

The McCain campaign quickly denied that Sarah had been an official member of the secessionist party, and only Max Blumenthal and David Neiwert of *Salon* investigated her long-standing Wasilla connection to extremists such as Mark Chryson and Steve Stoll.

IN ALASKA, after an initial burst of parochial jubilation that for the first time in history an Alaskan was a candidate for national office, reaction to Sarah's sudden ascent to national stardom was less than effusive. For one thing, she had unfinished business with the state, most important, Troopergate, the tar baby she couldn't shake from her heel. On September 12, legislators voted to subpoena thirteen witnesses, including Todd. The next day, more than a thousand anti-Palin protesters showed up at an Anchorage rally sponsored by a group called Alaska Women Reject Palin. The crowd, wrote the *Daily News,* "appeared bigger than any Anchorage has seen in recent memory."

On September 18 one of Sarah's spokespeople announced that Todd would refuse to testify in the Troopergate inquiry, despite being subpoenaed. The next day, neither Todd nor any of the other witnesses called by the legislative committee showed up at the hearing convened to take their testimony.

Again, on September 26, seven subpoenaed Palin aides failed to appear before the committee. The same day, Attorney General Colberg filed a motion in Anchorage superior court seeking to quash the subpoenas. Despite having said, "I'm happy to comply, to cooperate. I have absolutely nothing to hide. No problem with an independent investigation," Sarah was now stonewalling as hard as she could. Hollis French said, "For over two hundred years, legislatures have exercised their right to oversee the activities of the executive branch. Denying us that authority undermines the basic democratic process."

The next day, more than a thousand protesters, many chanting, "Recall Palin," convened in downtown Anchorage to protest her obstruction of the Branchflower inquiry.

Scant attention was paid to any of this outside Alaska, as Sarah continued to mesmerize national media. But on September 30, columnist Michael Carey wrote in the *Anchorage Daily News,* "Sarah Palin may be making new friends as she campaigns the nation, but at home she's making new enemies." He said that "the bulk of the responsibility for the ugly mess" that was Troopergate "falls on Palin herself, who can't separate her personal life from her professional life."

On October 2, an Anchorage judge denied Colberg's motion to quash the subpoenas, which were now being ignored not only by Todd but by almost a dozen members of Sarah's administration. On

October 5, Colberg announced that seven of the subpoenaed state employees—although not Todd—would testify. Colberg said Todd would respond to written interrogatories.

In his sworn statement Todd acknowledged that he'd waged a personal war against Wooten throughout Sarah's tenure as governor. For the first time he admitted to initiating frequent discussions with Monegan. "We had a lot of conversations . . ." Todd said. "We talked about Wooten possibly pulling over one of my kids to frame them, like throwing a bag of dope in the back seat just to frame a Palin. I had hundreds of conversations and communications about Trooper Wooten over the last several years, with my family, with friends, with colleagues, and with just about everyone I could—including government officials."

On October 8 the state supreme court heard an emergency appeal by Sarah's lawyers asking that the entire Branchflower investigation be shut down. The court denied the appeal the next day, clearing the way for Branchflower to deliver his report. As the *Daily News* wrote, "Within hours of the court ruling, the McCain-Palin campaign looked to discredit the investigator's report without having seen it."

The Branchflower report was made public on October 10. It found that Sarah had, in fact, abused the power of her office by seeking so strenuously to have Wooten fired and by allowing Todd to do the same in his capacity as her quasi-official representative. "Governor Palin knowingly permitted a situation to continue where impermissible pressure was placed on several subordinates in order to advance a personal agenda," Branchflower wrote. Also, she had allowed Todd to use her office "to continue to contact subordinate state employees in an effort to find some way to get Trooper Wooten fired."

The investigator also found that while Monegan's refusal to fire Wooten was clearly a factor in his dismissal, Sarah did have the authority to act as she did because, like Irl Stambaugh in Wasilla, Monegan was an "at will" employee.

Sarah's lawyer denounced the report as a partisan attempt to "smear the governor by innuendo"—despite the fact that the investigation had been ordered by a bipartisan legislative committee.

The next day, extraordinarily, Sarah tried to claim that the Branchflower report had exonerated her. "I'm very, very pleased to be cleared of any legal wrongdoing, any hint of any kind of unethical activity," she said, stopping short of adding that black was white and up was down. She said she'd fired Monegan because he'd displayed a "rogue mentality." Sarah apparently felt that "going rogue" was acceptable only when she did it herself.

In the *Daily News*, columnist Elise Patkotak wrote, "The legislative report comes out concluding Palin broke the state ethics law and she calls that an exoneration. The only thing missing from this circus is a bunch of clowns exiting a small car in the center ring . . . Alaska is in danger of becoming one big national joke, the Dan Quayle of states. Someone should tell our governor that we deserve better than that. Someone should give our governor her brain back."

Alaskans were also incensed to learn that Sarah was not the ethical Snow White she'd pretended to be. On September 9 the *Washington Post* reported that she'd billed Alaskan taxpayers sixty dollars a day for meal money while spending more than three hundred nights at home during her first year and a half as governor. Ex-governor Tony Knowles said, "When you're living at home, you don't pay yourself for living at home . . . it's not right." The paper also disclosed that she'd charged the state more than $30,000 for airfares—as well as billing for meals and hotels—for family members who accompanied her on official trips.

Taking stock of national Republican efforts to sell Sarah as someone she was not, *Daily News* columnist Carey wrote the next day that the GOP, "Like con men in the Old West . . . used a few nuggets to salt a gold mine. Then they went out to sell the mine to gullible suckers who didn't know the difference between a gold mine and a hole in the ground."

As Sarah continued her barnstorming, revival tent, rock star tour of red-state America, Alaskan bloggers such as Andrew Halcro, Shan-nyn Moore, Jeanne Devon, Phil Munger, and Jesse Griffin—people Sarah would later refer to in an *Esquire* interview as "bored, anonymous, pathetic bloggers who lie"—stepped up their campaign to inform America that Sarah was certainly not a gold mine.

Not only bloggers, but published authors such as Nick Jans and Seth Kantner put out informed and trenchant commentary. Jans, a Juneau-based magazine writer, member of the *USA Today* board of contributors, and author of several books about Alaska, wrote in *Salon*:

> Palin is a genuine Alaskan—of a kind. The kind that flowed north in the wake of the '70s oil boom, Bible Belt politics and attitudes under arm, and transformed this state from a free-thinking, independent bastion of genuine libertarianism and individuality into a reactionary fundamentalist enclave with dollar signs in its eyes and an all-for-me mentality.

Author and journalist Seth Kantner wrote from Kotzebue, fifty miles above the Arctic Circle:

> By now the world knows our Gov. Palin is an expert at swishing around in color coordinated this and that, with her makeup, fake Minnesota accent, and her mooseburger and mean-spirited commentary. We can only hope people realize . . . she's a pretty atypical Alaskan, one who is simply skimming the gravy off our hard-earned Alaskan mystique to mix with her varnished nonsense.

As the campaign wore on, McCain advisors lost patience with Sarah's impulsiveness, unbridled egotism, and volatile temper. CNN reported on October 25 that "They have become increasingly frustrated with what one aide described as Palin 'going rogue.' A source said, 'She is a diva. She takes no advice from anyone. She does not have any relationships of trust with any of us, her family or anyone else. Also, she is playing for her own future and sees herself as the next leader of the party.'"

McCain staffers were particularly outraged by what *Newsweek* termed "Palin's shopping spree at high-end department stores." It was reported that she'd billed the Republican Party more than $150,000 for new clothes for Todd and herself. One aide angrily complained to *Newsweek* about "Wasilla hillbillies looting Neiman Marcus from coast to coast."

Sarah later denied the accounts of extravagant shopping, but to Alaskan ears they rang true. "You know that's true," one friend told me in 2010. "I know somebody who was over there. They've got the clothes. They're there. They got them. They joke about it. Sarah's a compulsive spender—for herself. When she had that job with the oil and gas commission down in Anchorage, Todd would be like, 'Fuckin'-A, man, all she does is go to Nordstrom's every goddamned day and buy hundreds of dollars' worth of shit.'"

THREE DAYS before the election, Sarah was pranked by a Canadian radio host who had her thinking she was talking to French president Nicolas Sarkozy.

"I see you as a president one day, too," the fake Sarkozy said.

"Maybe in eight years," Sarah replied.

She refrained from saying that if McCain lost it could be four.

In Phoenix, on election night, Sarah demanded that she be allowed to give her own concession speech. She was furious when denied permission. A week later, she said to Matt Lauer on the *Today* show, "I thought, even if it was unprecedented, so what, you know?"

SARAH'S VICE-PRESIDENTIAL CAMPAIGN made her a national star, but it destroyed her forever in Alaska. Her shrill partisanship (accusing Barack Obama of "pallin' around with terrorists"), her twisting of the truth, her mutation into a grotesque caricature of the woman Alaskans thought they knew, had created an indelible stain.

When she returned, in defeat, in November 2008, succor was in short supply; rancor was not. While Sarah saw herself as on a mission from God, in the minds of many Alaskans, she had made a deal with the devil, trading what she might—or might not—have become as their governor for a garish new identity as the patron saint of the right-wing extremists who would soon coalesce into the Tea Party.

NINETEEN

S EPTEMBER ARRIVES. It's almost time to go home and start writing. I've been the good neighbor I told Todd I would be. I haven't intruded on the Palins' lives in any way. If Sarah hadn't made an issue of it, only the few people I told would have known I'd been living next door since late May. My rent is paid through the middle of September and my trash pickup paid through November. I've talked to the people I wanted to talk to, except for those who were either too loyal or too scared of Todd and Sarah to talk.

The one unanswered question is Trig. Is he really Sarah's child? That question has come up again and again throughout the spring and summer, and usually not because I asked it. Nothing has surprised me more than finding that so many people, even some who like and admire Sarah, have doubts.

At first it seemed outlandish, even indecent, to suppose that Trig might not be Sarah's child. I did not, and I don't. And yet . . . and yet . . . the circumstances surrounding both Sarah's pregnancy and her fifth child's premature birth are very difficult for anyone—especially anyone who has ever become a parent—to understand.

On his *Atlantic Monthly* Daily Dish blog on June 28, 2010, Andrew Sullivan, author, columnist, one-time editor of the *New Republic*, and former Harvard professor, had a long post about why it matters whether Sarah actually gave birth to Trig. Sullivan has been ridiculed, not least in the liberal press, for continuing to care about this, but he makes some cogent points, especially about mainstream media, which—despite Palin's incessant ridiculing of it as "lamestream"—has served as her great enabler, reacting to her every subwoof and tweet as if she were already the influential world leader that their fetishizing of her may someday allow her to become.

Sullivan wrote:

If her giving birth to a Down Syndrome child is a complete hoax, then she's simply psychotic . . . If the scenario is merely a function of deep irresponsibility, an unconscious desire to miscarry her child by extreme recklessness, then the same applies . . .

My real frustration here is with the media who have never questioned, let alone seriously investigated, the story, and who have actually gone further and vouched for its truthfulness and accuracy without any independent confirmation . . .

What's their excuse for not investigating or even asking? Their first is Palin's alleged family privacy. But there is no family privacy once you have deliberately forced an infant with special needs into the bewildering public space . . . and used him as the central prop in the construction of a political identity.

Their second reason for not investigating is that it doesn't really matter. As I am often told by the Beltway crowd, she's never going to be president, she's just a flash-in-the-pan, leave it be, she'll go away soon enough. Well, she hasn't yet, has she? . . . Trig's political salience is obvious, and critical to Palin's brand—in fact, the only thing, apart from her amazingly good looks, that keeps her in the game . . .

If Palin has lied about this, it's the most staggering, appalling deception in the history of American politics. Not knowing which is true for real—and allowing this person to continue to dominate one half of the political divide—is something I think is intolerable. In the end, this story is not about Palin. It's about the collapse of the press and the corrupt cynicism of a political system that foisted this farce upon us without performing any minimal due diligence.

And only Joe McGinniss seems to give a damn.

That was a heavy mantle to have placed upon me. To write about "the collapse of the press and the corrupt cynicism of a political system" was not what I set out to do. Despite Sullivan's conviction that the "story is not about Palin," it is the story of Palin that I am telling.

Having said that, the longer I spend in Wasilla and environs, the more skepticism I encounter about the accounts Sarah has given of her 2007–2008 pregnancy and Trig's birth.

Some people simply accept Sarah's version on faith, the way they believe in heaven and hell. Others are so certain it's a fabrication that they would not accept that Trig was her baby even if she produced a birth certificate and a videotape of the delivery.

Why has there ever been a question? And why do the questions continue? Because:

Through her seventh month, not even those who saw Sarah up close every day saw any signs of pregnancy.

Her story of having her water break in Dallas on April 17 and giving birth to Trig in Wasilla twenty-nine and a half hours later stretches credulity to the breaking point.

She has steadfastly refused to provide the birth certificate or medical records that would document her account.

The first public suggestion that Trig was not Sarah's baby was made by an anonymous poster on the Daily Kos blog on August 29, 2008, the day after McCain named Sarah as his running mate. Two days later, the *Anchorage Daily News* described the post as "a version of a rumor—long simmering in Alaska—that Palin's daughter Bristol was pregnant and the governor somehow covered it up by pretending to have the baby (Trig) herself." The newspaper said, "Palin baby speculation is inescapable at this point."

Sarah's Alaskan spokesman said the rumor wasn't true. How did he know? "The governor's not a liar," he said. By the end of August 2008, however, that was an opinion many Alaskans no longer shared. When it was suggested that making Trig's birth certificate available would put the rumors to rest, the spokesman was appalled. "What a thing to request—prove that this is your baby. I mean, my God, that's horrifying to think that she would have to do that."

She did not. And in Alaska, birth certificates are not public record, so the rumors continued to swirl, fed by publication of numerous photographs that showed Sarah looking distinctly unpregnant only weeks before giving birth to a six-pound, two-ounce infant.

Sullivan, a conservative, posed the following questions on August 31, 2008:

Why would a 43 year old woman, on her fifth pregnancy, with a Down Syndrome child, after her amniotic fluid has started to leak, not go to the nearest hospital immediately, even if she was in Texas for a speech?

Why would she not only not go to the hospital in Texas, but take an eight-hour plane flight to Seattle and then Anchorage?

Why would she choose to deliver the baby not in the nearest major facility in Anchorage but at a much smaller hospital near her home-town?

Why did the flight attendants on the trip home say she bore no signs of being pregnant?

Sullivan then wrote, "It strikes me as likely that there are reasonable answers to these questions . . . and the rumors buzzing across the Internets and the press corps are unfounded and unseemly . . . So please give us these answers—and provide medical records for Sarah Palin's pregnancy—and put this to rest."

But neither answers nor records were forthcoming, from either Sarah or the McCain campaign. Instead, they tried to put the story to rest by announcing that Bristol was pregnant. This proved, they claimed, that Trig could not have been Bristol's child.

Bristol was going to be an unwed teenage mother and, by God, Todd and Sarah were going to parade her around the country as such, because it showed how all-American they were, facing up to difficulties caused by randy teenagers just like any other New Apostolic Reformationist mother and Alaskan Independence Party father.

The media spotlight quickly swung to Bristol and Levi. Because it was only just barely mathematically and anatomically possible that Bristol could have become pregnant with a second child so soon after having given birth to a first, she clearly could not be Trig's mother, which meant that Sarah must be. From that point forward, people such as Andrew Sullivan and various bloggers both inside Alaska and Outside who continued to seek answers to their questions about Trig's birth were exposing themselves as unspeakable boors.

Indeed, as was revealed in the summer of 2010, the predominantly liberal membership of the Washington insider group JournoList quickly circled its wagons to protect Sarah, fearing that a full-scale inquiry into the circumstances of Trig's birth would lead to a right-wing backlash.

"By all accounts she's a wonderful mother . . . Leave this be," cautioned one. Another warned, "Leave the kid alone," as if questions about his birth constituted an invasion of the privacy of Sarah's infant son, rather than a measurement of her credibility.

The majority of the invited subscribers to JournoList favored the election of Barack Obama and therefore evaluated the merits of even asking the question in terms of its presumed effect on his campaign, rather than its journalistic validity.

This was a significant first step toward what Sullivan referred to in the summer of 2010 as "the collapse of the press," a dereliction of duty so absolute—a lamestreaming of itself that occurred long before Sarah coined the term—as to constitute a mad dash toward its own immolation on a pyre of irrelevance.

"This is your liberal media, ladies and gentlemen," Sullivan wrote on July 26, "totally partisan, interested in the truth only if it advances their agenda, and devoid of any balls whatsoever. And people wonder how this farce of a candidate now controls one major political party and could well be our next president."

Legitimate questions were not asked during the 2008 campaign for fear that middle America might perceive them as offensive. But because Sarah refused to release her medical records as the other three candidates had done, the questions did not disappear.

Less than two weeks before the 2008 election, NBC's Brian Williams asked Sarah if she would make the records public. "My life has been an open book," she said. "And my life is an open book today." In typically garbled syntax, she continued: "The medical records—so be it. If that will allow some curiosity seekers, perhaps, to have, oh, one more thing that they can either check the box off that they can find something to criticize, perhaps, or find something to rest them assured over, fine."

But she never released them. Instead, on election eve, the McCain campaign presented a one-and-a-half-page letter from Cathy Baldwin-Johnson, Sarah's doctor, longtime friend, and fervent evangelical. Baldwin-Johnson wrote, "Routine prenatal testing early in the second trimester showed evidence of Trisomy 21 . . . there was no significant congenital heart disease or other condition of the baby that would preclude delivery at her home community hospital. This child, Trig, was born at 35 weeks in good health . . ." The doctor did not confirm either that she had delivered Trig or that Sarah had given birth to him.

In the months that followed the 2008 election, Baldwin-Johnson's refusal to speak to the media and Sarah's refusal to provide simple documentary proof that Trig was her biological child not only kept the rumors alive but led to a network of arcane conspiracy theories reminiscent of the years that followed the assassination of John F. Kennedy.

But one does not have to wear a tinfoil hat to wonder.

As her former security chief and many others have said, Sarah displayed no signs of being pregnant when she traveled to Washington for the National Governors Association meeting February 23–25, 2008. After posing for a group photo on the White House steps and meeting privately with John McCain at the Willard Hotel, she flew back to Alaska, wearing jeans.

Within days of her return, she phoned Mary Glazier and prayed with her for "wisdom and direction."

On March 4, McCain won the Republican nomination. The very next day, Sarah announced that she was seven months pregnant. The child would be born with Down syndrome. Giving birth to such a child would make Sarah the patron saint of the antiabortion movement and would spark fervent enthusiasm within a Christian conservative base that was notably cool toward McCain.

Once again, Sarah found herself in the right place at the right time, and—in this instance—in the right condition. McCain later said Sarah had made a strong impression on him during their meeting. It's not unreasonable to assume that he at least hinted that she was one of the people he'd consider as a running mate if he won the nomination.

It would be worse than unreasonable to assume that he told her that the only thing that would make her a more appealing choice would be if she could somehow give birth to a Down syndrome baby before the Republican convention in September. Yet only eight days later Sarah announced that that's exactly what she expected to do.

Glazier prayed again with Sarah—this time in person, not over the phone—at a Governor's Prayer Breakfast later in March, after she'd announced her pregnancy.

At 9:26 on Monday morning, April 14, Sarah e-mailed a staff member to say she did not want Gary Wheeler or anyone else from her security detail to accompany her two days later when she flew to Dallas to speak at a Republican Governors Conference luncheon.

"First Spouse is available to travel instead," she wrote. Never before as governor had Sarah traveled out of state without her security detail, and she offered no reason for wanting to do so at this time.

Any number of people have observed that it was reckless of Sarah to have traveled to Dallas in her condition. How much more reckless was it to leave behind uniformed security personnel who could have helped to ensure her safety and that of her baby if a medical emergency arose? What could have been her motive for doing so? Was it because, as Gary Wheeler told me, if he'd been there and her water had broken at 4:00 AM on April 17, he would have whisked her to a Dallas hospital as soon as possible, and certainly wouldn't have let her fly to Alaska twelve hours later?

Nobody asked Sarah this question at the press conference she held in Anchorage on April 21, three days after Trig's birth. The atmosphere was celebratory, not inquisitorial.

Describing her time in Dallas, Sarah said, "Felt perfectly fine, but uh, had thought maybe a, a few things were starting to progress a little bit that, that perhaps there was an, an idea there that maybe he'd come a little bit early. So called my doctor at about, uh, four in the morning in Texas, [1:00 AM Alaska time] and, um, I said, 'You know, I'm gonna stay for the day' . . . have a speech that I was determined to give at one o'clock that afternoon."

She was asked if she'd felt contractions.

"Well, not contractions so much . . . nothing real painful but just knowing that, um, it was feeling like I may not, um, be able to be pregnant a whole, another four or five weeks, knowing that it would be not a bother to call our doctor and let her know. . . . We knew to call her and just get her advice."

She was asked if her water had broken.

"Well, if you must know, uh, more of those type of details, but, um—"

"Well, your dad said that and I saw him say it, so that's why I asked," a reporter said.

"Well, that was again if, if I m-must get personal, technical about this at the same time, um, it was one, uh, it was a sign that I knew, um, could lead to, uh, labor being, uh, kind of kicked in there was any kind of, um, amniotic leaking, amniotic fluid leaking, so when, when that happened we decided, okay, let's call her."

She tells the story somewhat differently in *Going Rogue*. "At 4 AM a strange sensation low in my belly woke me and I sat up straight in bed. 'It can't be,' I thought. It's way too early. Moments later, I shook Todd awake. 'Something's going on.' He sat up in bed, instantly alert. 'I'm calling CBJ [Cathy Baldwin-Johnson].' 'No, don't do that. It's only 1 AM in Alaska.' I didn't want to call anyone yet. I just wanted to take stock and see whether this baby was really coming. I also wanted time to pray and ask God silently but fervently to let everything be okay. Desperation for this baby overwhelmed me."

Desperation for the baby overwhelmed her? She wanted to ask God to let everything be okay? The best way to ensure that everything will be okay in a high-risk obstetrical situation when the amniotic sac ruptures and fluid starts leaking is to get to a hospital as quickly as possible.

In many ways, Sarah was better off in Dallas than she would have been in Alaska. Dallas has at least five world-class hospitals and medical centers equipped with neonatal intensive care units and personnel who specialize in high-risk births. Even without her security detail, Todd could have taken her to either the University of Texas Southwestern Medical Center, Methodist Dallas Medical Center, Baylor University Medical Center, Medical City Dallas Hospital, or Presbyterian Hospital of Dallas. Safely ensconced in any one of them, Sarah might have found her "desperation for this baby" less overwhelming. But, according to *Going Rogue*, it faded quickly, even without medical attention.

"Over my protests, Todd called CBJ. I told her that I felt fine . . . We agreed that I would stay in contact with CBJ through the day. I'd take it easy, give my speech, then catch an earlier flight back to Alaska. I still had plenty of time."

Did she? Sarah's age alone put her into the high-risk category for childbirth. She was carrying an infant whose Down syndrome made him high-risk as well. In addition, she'd already had two miscarriages. In addition to that, the rupture of her amniotic sac prior to her thirty-seventh week of pregnancy indicated that she'd give birth prematurely.

So why would she think she had plenty of time? Perhaps more to the point, how could Dr. Baldwin-Johnson assume she did? How could any competent physician, awakened by a 1:00 AM phone call from a patient thousands of miles away who said she was leaking amniotic fluid not have insisted she go immediately to a hospital for evaluation? How could she have allowed Sarah to risk infection, or worse, by continuing with a full day's worth of normal activity and travel?

In *Going Rogue*, Sarah writes that in those predawn hours her only thought was for the welfare of Trig: "Please don't let anything happen to this baby," she prayed. "It occurred to me, once and for all: I'm so in love with this child, please, God, protect him! I had fallen in love with this precious child. The worst thing in the world would be that I would lose him."

But in the next sentence she writes that she "absolutely did not want to cancel my speech and disappoint the folks at the conference."

So she did nothing for the next nine hours and then made a speech at 1:00 PM. Actually, nobody knows what she did during those nine hours. Did she order room service breakfast? Did she take a hot bath? Did she go shopping?

In any event, surely now, after her speech, she'd go to a hospital, at least for examination and evaluation. She couldn't even consider putting her unborn child at grave and unnecessary risk by flying back to Alaska without first being seen by a physician. Just as surely, her loving and attentive husband couldn't let her even entertain such an idea.

Todd had the whole morning to make arrangements for Sarah to receive medical attention as soon as she finished her speech. He had the governor of Texas within arm's reach. The finest obstetricians in Dallas would have lined up to ensure the safest possible delivery of Sarah's premature Down syndrome baby.

Instead, Todd used his BlackBerry to e-mail Sarah's aides Frank Bailey, Kris Perry, and Ivy Frye, using the subject line "Her speech kicked ass." The message: "Awesome man!!!! She rocks!!" He made no mention that her water had broken ten hours earlier and that she was apparently about to deliver her baby a month before its due date.

In *Going Rogue,* Sarah writes, "I reached Todd at the exit and he eyed me with a grin. 'Love this state, but we can't have a fish picker born in Texas.'"

In her April 21 press conference, Sarah said, "Called my doctor before I got on the plane to say, 'Yeah, we think that we will come home a few hours early,' and, uh, she said, 'Okay, well, call when you, when you land and I'll check you out.'"

If that conversation occurred as Sarah said it did, some might feel that at best Dr. Baldwin-Johnson displayed poor judgment. In a telephone interview with a *Daily News* reporter on April 21, her only public comment about Trig's birth, Baldwin-Johnson said of the patient whom she hadn't examined and who had not been examined by any doctor in Dallas, "Things were already settling down when she talked to me. I don't think it was unreasonable for her to continue to travel back."

So, almost twelve hours after her amniotic fluid had started to leak, Sarah began a journey that involved a flight from Dallas to Seattle, a change of planes and a two-hour layover in Seattle, a flight from Seattle to Anchorage, and then a drive from Anchorage to Wasilla. It would be at least a ten-hour trip, barring delays.

"Digest that for just a second," Dr. Jeffrey Parks, a Cleveland, Ohio, surgeon, later wrote.

A 43 year old woman carrying a child with known Down's Syndrome, in her eighth month of pregnancy voluntarily embarked upon a transcontinental adventure to give [a] speech. Then, after noticing some cramps and the passage of amniotic fluid, she went ahead with her speech and, instead of proceeding directly to the nearest Dallas high risk pregnancy center, boarded a four hour flight to Seattle. Then she hung out in the Seattle airport lounge for a while and took a connecting flight to Alaska. Then she drives to Wasilla. Finally, she decides to seek medical attention at a local Wasilla hospital, a facility lacking a NICU [neonatal intensive care unit] and other high risk specialists. That's her story . . . Palin willfully and wantonly placed herself and her unborn child in tremendous danger by flying cross country with amniotic fluid running down her legs . . . What kind of mother would take a risk like that with her child, let alone a high risk, premature one?

There are some who think her entire story is a fabrication, that she was never pregnant but had arranged to have a Down syndrome baby presented to her at the Mat-Su Medical Center in order to advance her political career. That baby wasn't due until mid-May, so Sarah felt free to make an April speech in Dallas. When she suddenly received word that the Down syndrome baby was coming prematurely, she hurried back to be there when, or soon after, it arrived.

A friend saw Sarah briefly the night before she gave her speech in Dallas. He and Todd had been to a Dallas Mavericks basketball game and he stopped by Sarah's hotel room after the game to say hello and wish her well. "I patted her belly," he told me in March of 2011. "I didn't feel a baby kick, but to me she seemed obviously pregnant."

No flight attendant on either of the two Alaska Airlines flights Sarah took back to Anchorage the next day, however, even noticed she was pregnant, much less leaking amniotic fluid. Nor did the man who talked to her in the Alaska Airlines lounge at the Seattle airport between flights. He later sent her an e-mail that said, "Yesterday evening as I was flying back to Juneau from a business trip in Seattle, I had the pleasure of chatting with you and your husband Todd in the Alaska Airlines boardroom. It seemed as though you were engrossed in a book so I spoke mostly with Todd and tried not to intrude on your opportunity to relax. Little did I know that you were in labor at the time. I'm impressed that you were gracious enough to speak with me even though you both obviously had much more important things on your mind."

Andrew Sullivan's Daily Dish described Sarah's story in detail to eight leading U.S. obstetricians. "While none would say that this pregnancy could not have happened," he wrote, "all of them said it was one of the strangest and unlikeliest series of events they had ever heard of and found Palin's decision to forgo medical help for more than a day after her water broke and risk the life of her unborn child on a long airplane trip to be reckless beyond measure."

Was she deliberately trying to kill her baby before it was born? Given Sarah's religious beliefs, that would make her a cold-blooded murderer, a far more serious charge than that she chose to advance her political career by means of a hoax that, for years to come, would leave her caring for a Down syndrome child that wasn't hers.

Is it even barely possible that the pregnancy story was cooked up in a hurry after Sarah met with John McCain, and that Trig was obtained, indirectly, from a pregnant woman who felt herself unable to care for a special-needs child? That concept is so abhorrent, the level of cynicism it would require so impossible to imagine, that surely no rational person could believe it. Sullivan, an eminently rational man, isn't saying he believes it, but he does point out, "Without the Down Syndrome pregnancy, Palin would not have had the rock-star appeal to the pro-life base that contributed to her selection."

I DIDN'T COME to Alaska in a quest for "the truth about Trig." Maybe Sarah has already told it, as outlandish as her story is. Maybe she did get to be seven months pregnant with no one noticing, and maybe she did have a good reason for suddenly deciding to go to Texas without her customary security detail, and maybe everything was just as she's described it, and maybe Trig is Sarah's child.

In that case, on April 17, 2008, she and Todd were guilty only of gross negligence and a level of irresponsibility that put the life of their unborn child at severe and deliberate risk. Why? Because you can't have a fish picker born in Texas.

I don't know. I do know that I found a remarkable number of fair-minded, "commonsense" Alaskans who've known Sarah for many years who do not believe that Trig is her child.

This surprised me. I would raise the question, expecting to be told that doubts about Trig were preposterous. Time and again, however, I found a deep and abiding skepticism. Thus, it does not seem irrelevant to point out that in regard to Trig, as with so many other aspects of Sarah's life, those who know her best believe her least.

It is perhaps the most blistering assessment of her character possible that many Wasillans who'd known Sarah from high school onward told me that even if she had not faked the entire story of her pregnancy and Trig's birth, it was something she was eminently capable of doing.

TIME TO go home. Sarah and Joe Miller and Glenn Beck are staging some sort of September 11 extravaganza in Anchorage, but I don't feel the need to stay for that, because I've already seen Sarah perform.

That was in The Villages, a Florida retirement community north of Orlando, during Thanksgiving week 2009. It was part of the book tour for *Going Rogue,* the tour that she pretended to be doing by bus but actually did most of by private plane, hopping on the bus only in time to hop off again at the next destination, waving Trig around like an American flag until everyone got the news footage and stills they needed.

I flew into Orlando and drove to The Villages the night before Sarah arrived. I had dinner with my friend Ray Hudson, who had come up from Fort Lauderdale. Ray is from Newcastle, England, and played for Newcastle before jumping to the North American Soccer League in the 1970s, where, playing for the Fort Lauderdale Strikers, he became one of the league's stars, alongside the likes of Johan Cruyff, Franz Beckenbauer, and Pelé. Ray now does the color commentary on soccer matches for Gol TV, mostly from La Liga, in Spain. His verbal flair, which combines raw passion with Shakespearean flights of poetic imagery, has made him a cult figure among soccer fans in the United States. Believe me, you have never seen Barcelona play if you haven't heard Ray Hudson do the commentary on one of their matches.

The Villages is a sprawling agglomeration of private homes and condos surrounding a couple of ersatz "town squares," to which retirees can drive their cars and golf carts and shop without fear of being mugged. Everything about it is artificial, designed to "recapture" the feel of an America that never existed, but one that many wealthy whites in their seventies and beyond would like to think they remember. In its utter syntheticness and absolute devotion to Republican homogeneity, it seems the perfect venue for Sarah. In fact, during the 2008 campaign an estimated sixty thousand people turned out at The Villages to hear her speak, the largest crowd she had drawn anywhere in America during her run for the vice presidency. The Villages simulates real life precisely as Sarah simulates genuine concern for the future of our nation.

After dinner, Ray and I walk over to the Barnes and Noble at which Sarah will sign books for the first five hundred people in a line that is already forming, although she's not scheduled to arrive until 2:00 PM the next day. The mood is congenial and relaxed. These are pilgrims who have reached the very walls of Mecca. Many, in their lawn chairs and canvas recliners, stay awake through the night by reading aloud from *Going Rogue*.

Ray and I opt for an early night so we can be back out among the worshippers by 5:00 AM. By then, even in a drizzle, many hundreds have gathered, and Barnes and Noble employees are telling those who join the end of the line that already they're too late: the five hundred magic wristbands that will permit entry to the store in the afternoon have all been distributed.

A gray dawn breaks gradually over the asphalt, on which thousands of folding chairs now sit. But many in the crowd—at least two thirds of which is made up of people older than me, at sixty-six—are too energized to be still, and shuffle slowly back and forth, expectant.

"I hear she's gonna speak before she goes in to sign."

"Yeah, see that podium? That's for her. She's gonna do an interview with Gretchen what's-her-name from Fox."

"Gretchen Van Susteren?"

"No, the other one. The blond one."

"They're all blond."

My camera battery dies just before the Sarahbus arrives. She emerges, holding Trig. Once the TV cameras and still photographers have had their fill, she hands him off to an assistant, who soon puts him down on the asphalt parking lot and lets him crawl. The lot is covered with broken glass, cigarette butts, and old chewing gum, and Trig is barefoot. Eventually Piper comes along and puts him in a stroller.

This is almost the full monty, family-wise. Chuck and Sally and old Aunt so-and-so, plus Piper and Trig. Chuck and Sally work the crowd. Leaving Trig in the stroller, so does Piper. She's eight years old and has the fake smile of a ten-term congressman. For some reason this sticks with me as the saddest sight I see all day.

Eventually Sarah mounts the podium and does her thing. "There's something very special about this place," she says. "You're all so energetic and inspiring and encouraging." There are maybe a thousand people in the parking lot. They wave signs and hold their copies of *Going Rogue* in the air and cheer.

Then Sarah does her interview with the blond Fox Gretchen, whose last name turns out to be Carlson. Can this be right? Don't they have a guy named Tucker Carlson? Can there be two Carlsons at Fox? Are they related? I'll have to ask Roger Ailes. As Sarah chats with Gretchen, their backs to the crowd, a makeup woman is making up Piper so she can join them. That is almost as sad as seeing her work the line.

Up close, Sarah radiates energy, just as the crowd's enthusiasm energizes her. "She loves to have people adore her," a longtime Alaskan friend of hers once told me. "Who doesn't, right? But Sarah feeds off it like a bear in a berry patch." If so, she's clearly come to the right place. I look at the eyes of the people in the crowd as Sarah speaks: these people are besotted with love, they live only to worship, they are having a religious experience. I have no doubt that if she put her mind to it, she could have half of them speaking in tongues.

But once she goes inside to sign, the toll taken by the long night and morning becomes evident. We're suddenly all just a bunch of old farts standing around a parking lot in funny clothes with nothing to do, Ray and me most definitely included.

As we walk out of the parking lot, I overhear occasional snatches of conversation. A sturdy, white-haired white woman dressed in red, white, and blue says to a companion, "I would love for her to get to the White House so bad. We need an American like us there."

That's no more than a predictable racist comment from a resident of a central Florida retirement community. The comment that gets me—and I hear it a dozen times if I hear it once—is "She's so real."

She's so real. Sarah Palin, whose every word and gesture is the product of carefully constructed and well-maintained artifice, is hailed for being "so real." Truly, as P. T. Barnum apparently never said, there is a sucker born every minute—and a disproportionate number of those over sixty-five seem to have made The Villages their home.

I don't need to see the Sarah show again, especially not with the odious Glenn Beck involved.

• • •

I LOVED every minute of my time in Alaska this summer. The new friends I made will be friends for the rest of my life. Walt Monegan, Sharyn Moore and Kelly Walters, and J. C. McCavit all give me smoked salmon to take home, and another friend gives me three pounds of Kaladi Brothers coffee.

I throw a terrific farewell party on the night of Saturday, September 4. I know it's terrific because Verne Rupright and Kelly are still debating constitutional issues in my kitchen at 2:30 AM when Verne's wife calls and tells him to get home. He needs to rest up for his 2011 mayoral campaign against Levi Johnston.

My only regret is that I never got to meet the woman next door.

TWENTY

I WAS IN ALASKA the day before Election Day 2008, researching my story about AGIA and the gas pipeline for *Condé Nast Portfolio* magazine. Because I was staying at the Captain Cook Hotel in Anchorage, it was a simple matter to go to the lower lobby, where a second Troopergate report was to be released.

Alarmed by what they accurately sensed would be a withering report from Stephen Branchflower, the state personnel board, whose members were hired by and could be dismissed by the governor, had enlisted Anchorage attorney Tim Petumenos to conduct a separate Troopergate investigation.

Unsurprisingly, Petumenos found no wrongdoing on Sarah's part. What everyone overlooked at the time, but what Anchorage attorney C. Donald Mitchell pointed out in an *Alaska Dispatch* article the next summer, was that Sarah, who had refused to testify during the Branchflower investigation, may have committed perjury when questioned under oath by Petumenos.

Both Sarah and Walt Monegan gave sworn testimony to Petumenos. Monegan described the January 2007 conversation with Sarah in Juneau during which he'd said, "Ma'am, I need to keep you at arm's length with this," warning her that it was inappropriate for her even to raise the question with him of firing Wooten.

Sarah denied that the conversation had occurred. Petumenos wrote, "Governor Palin . . . testified under oath that this is not a failure of recollection on her part since the nature of the conversation as described is such that she would have remembered having it."

In other words, one of them was lying. For Sarah to have lied under oath would have been an impeachable offense. Under the Alaska constitution it was the duty of the state senate to determine whether such an offense had been committed.

During the winter of 2008–2009, as Sarah resumed her duties as governor, the senate showed no inclination to impeach, but as Mitchell pointed out, the question remained very much alive and may have been a significant, if overlooked, factor in Sarah's decision to resign the following summer. "If Sarah had decided to stay for her full term," Mitchell wrote, "the perjury issue would have circled back on her."

Even absent such an explosive allegation, the state Sarah came back to on Election Day was not the one she'd left two months earlier, at least in its attitude toward her. In the *Daily News,* Tom Kizzia quoted Kate Troll, executive director of the Alaska Conservation Alliance: "All the alliances she used to get things done have been shattered. She comes back to unknown territory."

From her first days back, it was clear she did not want to stay. Reporting to work at her Anchorage office three days after the election, Sarah pretended she still cared.

"Good to be here, good to be here," she chirped. "A lot to do, as every day is a full day here in the governor's office, so, ah, anxious to get to talk to the folks who have been holdin' down the fort and workin' real hard also, but, ah, you know, it's gonna be busy days here, just like it was busy days on the trail, 'cause bein' the governor's a full ti . . . a full time . . . in addition to bein' a candidate. Now, of course, we get to concentrate just on . . . one of those."

As I wrote in *Portfolio,* "The last three words—'one of those'— emerged with jaws so tightly clenched that it wouldn't have been surprising to see a broken molar pop out."

During her speech to the Republican convention in September, Sarah made the bizarre claim that Alaska had already begun "a nearly $40 billion natural gas pipeline." She repeated the statement during her debate with Joe Biden, saying, "We're building a nearly $40 billion natural gas pipeline, which is North America's largest and most expensive infrastructure project ever."

But the state was not building any such thing. All AGIA had done was commit Alaska to paying $500 million to a foreign company that had neither gas nor access to gas and was under no obligation ever to lay a single piece of pipe.

So many excited utterances, so many false claims, so many words and actions now waiting to haunt her. From her first day back as governor, it was obvious she wanted out.

Also, in the aftermath of her failed vice-presidential campaign, a number of those who'd worked with her "on the trail" began to talk. Shopping sprees, temper tantrums, ignorance of issues, emotional instability—handlers began airing the dirty laundry. "I never asked for anything more than maybe a Diet Dr Pepper once in a while," Sarah said in response, but the words didn't ring true.

She said the charge that she'd thought Africa was a country, not a continent, was "taken out of context" and that it was "cruel, mean-spirited, it's immature, it's unprofessional and those guys are jerks . . . It's not fair." She did not, however, deny it.

She did deny that she'd changed. "If there's criticism that all of a sudden I've . . . become an obsessive partisan, then it's not accurate." Maybe she was right about that. Maybe she'd been an obsessive partisan from the start and the only change was that she'd finally stopped pretending that she wasn't.

In an interview conducted in her house on Lake Lucille, Sarah lashed out against "misinformation." Asked for an example, she said, "Some of the goofy things like who was Trig's mom. Well, I'm Trig's mom and do you want to see my medical records to prove that?" But once again, no medical records were forthcoming.

"My life is in God's hands," she told CNN in mid-November. "If he's got doors open for me . . . I'm going to go through those doors." But Sarah herself—establishing a pattern that would become more marked as time passed—was opening her own door only to those she could trust not to ask hard questions. She turned down interview requests from Oprah Winfrey, Barbara Walters, George Stephanopoulos, and Charlie Rose (although she would do Winfrey's and Walters's shows at the time of *Going Rogue*'s publication), while agreeing to talk to Wolf Blitzer, Larry King, Bill O'Reilly, Sean Hannity, Greta Van Susteren, and Glenn Beck.

Her selective postelection image rehabilitation campaign prompted Zane Henning, the oil field worker from Wasilla to whom I spoke in the summer of 2010, to file a new ethics complaint, citing the November 10 interview with Van Susteren conducted in Palin's governor's office. "The governor is using her official position and office in an attempt to repair her damaged political image on the national scene," he charged.

Meanwhile, with Todd and Sarah back, state police were receiving so many calls threatening harm against Mike Wooten that officials took him off patrol and reassigned him to desk duty in Anchorage.

Nothing was going right for Sarah. On November 20 a photo op built around her pardoning a Thanksgiving turkey provoked widespread glee when video showed birds being bloodily slaughtered directly behind her as she spoke. "It's unfortunate, because it's been a rough fall, and this was meant to be a lighthearted event," one of Sarah's spokespeople said.

Alaskans for Truth, the group that sponsored the second local anti-Palin rally of the fall, called for the legislature to censure Sarah for breaking state ethics laws, to hold hearings regarding possible perjury by her and Todd in connection with Troopergate, and to seek contempt charges against Todd for ignoring the subpoena that required him to testify in person.

It was only Outside that people still seemed glad to see her. On December 1 she campaigned with Georgia senator Saxby Chambliss, who was involved in a runoff election, and was met by adoring throngs of Republicans wearing PALIN 2012 T-shirts.

Back home, thorny budget issues loomed as a result of the price of oil plummeting from $145 to less than $40 a barrel within four months. Worse, there were calls for Sarah to release the sworn testimony she'd given to Petumenos. On October 24, the day she'd answered his questions under oath, Sarah had promised to make the deposition public. Now she refused. A spokeswoman said, "The matter is closed. We are moving forward now, not looking back."

But doing so was not as easy as saying so. Andree McLeod went to court in Anchorage seeking e-mails that Sarah had refused to release on grounds of "executive privilege." Although not a state employee, Todd had been copied on many of the e-mails Sarah was trying to withhold. "The state can't cloak these communications in secrecy when the governor and her staff have broken the chain of custody by sharing them with a mere private citizen," McLeod said.

As winter arrived, the price of oil continued to fall. Even the news that Bristol had given birth to Tripp on December 28 was marred by simultaneous reports of Levi's mother's arrest for selling Oxycontin. The eight hundred dollars Sherry Johnston got for her pills was dwarfed by the reported $300,000 Bristol received for giving *People* an exclusive first look at her son.

As Alaska celebrated the fiftieth anniversary of its statehood on January 3, there was little question that Sarah was less a part of its future than its past. On January 27, only a week after the state legislature opened its 2009 session, Sarah showed where her priorities lay by announcing the formation of a political action committee, SarahPAC. Nonetheless, she told reporters the next day, "I'm not going to leave Alaska . . . I'll rarely travel outside Alaska . . . We're a little bit more parochial here, which is good, it keeps you grounded." She then flew to Washington to speak at the elite Republican Alfalfa Club Dinner and to meet privately with a new cadre of national political advisors.

With the state facing a budget deficit of more than $1.5 billion, Sarah became conspicuous by her absence from Juneau. On February 6, 2009, the state senate voted 16–1 to find Todd and nine members of Sarah's staff in contempt for ignoring their subpoenas. The resolution, however, did not call for punishment, because all those subpoenaed eventually delivered sworn statements in writing.

Four days later attorney general Talis Colberg, who had tried to quash the subpoenas, resigned. "He just explained that it is a tough environment right now," Sarah said. No wonder Todd was happy to be back on his snowmobile for the 2009 Iron Dog race.

Alaskans learned on February 17 that Sarah would have to pay income tax on the thousands of dollars she'd taken in per diem expenses while living in Wasilla. A spokeswoman for her formerly open and transparent administration said, "The amount of taxes owed is a private matter."

Two days later Sarah announced that she finally intended to do something to help Natives in the Lower Yukon region of western Alaska, many of whom—hit by a perfect storm of high fuel prices, a poor fish harvest, and an extended spell of subzero temperatures— were finding it impossible to feed their families.

The villagers' plight had come to statewide attention in January through a letter sent by Nick Tucker of Emmonak to various Alaskan media sites. For a month, Sarah tried to ignore the emergency. Her small-government vision apparently did not allow for state aid to people who were on the verge of freezing or starving to death. Only when she arranged for help from a private source—in this case, Samaritan's Purse, an evangelical Christian organization directed by Reverend Franklin Graham, the son of Billy Graham—did she involve herself.

Sarah and Graham had been courting one another since she was first elected governor. Both in 2007 and 2008 (when he was joined by Mary Glazier on the dais), Graham spoke at Sarah's Governor's Prayer Breakfast, an annual event staged by a group whose website says it believes that "God directs the affairs of Man and is the ultimate authority over human events."

Especially with television cameras rolling (as she demonstrated again in 2010, when she accompanied Graham on a brief but well-publicized drop-in on Haiti), Sarah was apparently quite comfortable in the presence of a preacher who in 2001 had described Islam as "a very evil and wicked religion."

Accompanied by the ever-faithful Sean Parnell and a Samaritan's Purse television crew, Sarah and Graham and right-wing Anchorage evangelical minister Jerry Prevo flew to the Alaskan villages of Russian Mission and Marshall on February 20. Sarah handed out chocolate chip cookies, while Graham provided more substantial fare, accompanied by religious pamphlets.

Seeking to avoid what she feared might be a confrontation with Nick Tucker, Sarah and her entourage gave Emmonak a wide berth. The industrious Tucker, however, hitched a ride on a bush plane and flew the 125 miles to Russian Mission in order to talk to Sarah in person.

Her combination of condescension, evasiveness, platitudes, and non sequiturs made for one of the most awkward meetings with a member of the voting public that Sarah had ever had. It was captured on handheld video and later, with accompanying transcript, made available by Sarah's least favorite Alaskan bloggers, including Mudflats, Progressive Alaska, and Immoral Minority.

Despite being offered a chocolate chip cookie, Tucker—who had told Sarah, "I don't do politics. I come from the heart and the sorrow of our people"—was offended by Sarah's words and attitude. In a follow-up letter to rural newspapers, he said, "I am outraged . . . I felt like Governor Palin treated Emmonak with most disregard and disrespect by not coming here where it all started . . . Here, I had a person whom I voted for and who turns around and stabs us . . . Is it not embarrassing enough to have to cry out, let alone be put down by our state leadership? I think all rural Alaska deserves an apology and never to be treated like this again . . . I am an open man, but I feel insulted myself and on behalf of our rural Native villages."

A week later Sarah settled one of the ethics complaints against her by agreeing to reimburse the state $6,800 for nine trips her children took with her in 2007 and 2008. Sarah being Sarah, however, she would not admit she'd done anything wrong. In a written statement she said, "This is a big state and I am obligated to . . . keep Alaskans informed and meet with them as much as I can . . . At the same time, I am blessed to have a large and loving family, and the discharge of my duties should not prevent me from spending time with them." The next day, she said she'd also repay the state for the cost of bringing her three daughters to the starts of the 2007 and 2008 Iron Dogs to watch their father.

In mid-March she angered Alaskans anew by rejecting almost $300 million in federal stimulus funds that had been set aside for the state, including $170 million for education, a move that critics said was designed to enhance her standing among conservatives nationally at Alaska's expense.

A few days later she said she intended to bolster her personal finances by creating a fund through which the public would be able to help pay the legal fees she incurred while defending herself against the growing number of ethics complaints against her. Of ten already filed, six had been dismissed, one was settled, and three were pending. She said she owed her Anchorage lawyers more than $500,000. In a written response to questions put to her by the *Daily News,* Sarah said, "With the political blood sport some are playing today, only the independently wealthy or those willing to spend their income on legal fees . . . can serve."

AGIA was getting nowhere and achieving nothing but increased indebtedness for Alaska. In conjunction with the price of oil, natural gas prices had plunged almost 50 percent since Sarah had charmed the legislature into approving her proposal to give TransCanada $500 million of Alaskan taxpayers' money for nothing more than a hope and a prayer that the company might one day think about building a pipeline.

On March 21, Paul Jenkins predicted in the *Anchorage Daily News* that AGIA would become "a train wreck of monumental proportions." Going a step further, he asked whether Sarah actually wanted a gas line. "If the dragons were slain," he wrote, "wouldn't she then have to be governor, with all the grinding minutiae that entails? What would she use to fuel the populism she hopes will catapult her into national office? No war, no enemies, no glory and no whipping boys is a poor recipe for her style of us-against-them populism."

On the same day, "her-against-us" protesters staged yet another demonstration in Anchorage, this time decrying Sarah's rejection of the federal stimulus funds they felt Alaska needed. The protest took place outside the city's public library, as legislators met inside to hear from constituents who objected to Sarah's refusal to accept the nearly $300 million that the Obama administration was offering to the state.

One protestor held a sign that read simply, MAMA GRIZZLY, YOU FORGOT YOUR CUBS. Inside the building, to raucous shouts and applause, an Anchorage special education teacher said, "Our governor has chosen to pander to her political pipe dream . . ."

In the midst of this chaos, Sarah took time for a long talk on the phone with Rick Joyner, a Third Wave proselytizer and founder of MorningStar Ministries, of Charlotte, North Carolina.

Two years earlier, Joyner, who was closely linked to a militant dominionist movement called Joel's Army, had prophesied the imminent coming of the kingdom of God. "At first, it may seem like totalinarianism [sic]," he said, describing "a point of necessary control while people are learning."

Joel's Army, which the Southern Poverty Law Center has described as "an Armageddon-ready military force of young people with a divine mandate to physically impose Christian 'dominion' on non-believers," was led by Todd Bentley, founder of Lakeland Revival, a charismatic Christian church based in Florida.

Bentley has defined the mission of Joel's Army: "To aggressively take ground for the kingdom of God under the authority of Jesus Christ, the Dread Champion . . . The trumpet is sounding, calling on-fire revolutionary believers to enlist in Joel's Army . . . Many are now ready to be mobilized."

Bentley was a protégé of Rick Joyner, who described him as "a man of exceptional theological depth" and who praised his "impartation of faith, power and fire." Assembly of God pastor Kalnins used Joyner's writings in his Master's Commission program and led students on a pilgrimage to Joyner's church in Charlotte. During the 2008 presidential campaign, MorningStar's "head of prophecy," Steve Thompson, headlined a conference at the Wasilla Assembly of God.

In a video released on March 25, 2009, Joyner did not say whether he and Sarah had discussed the mobilization of Joel's Army during their extended conversation. He did say, "Democrats are extremely threatened by her, and I believe rightly so. I believe there is a spiritual authority and a calling on Governor Palin that is extraordinary . . . I believe she has a national calling on her life . . . When I first saw her on television, I felt right away, 'I am listening to the President of the United States.' . . . I want the Lord's leadership . . . We can't allow the media to win with Sarah Palin."

BUT NOT EVEN prayer warriors could prevent the filing in late March 2009 of yet another ethics complaint, this one accusing Sarah of using her office for personal profit by appearing at the start of the Iron Dog the year before wearing clothes that bore the logo of the company that sponsored Todd.

This one, filed by blogger Linda Kellen Biegle, pushed Sarah even further over whatever edge she'd been clinging to. Sarah's prepared response asked, "Are Alaskans outraged, or at least tired of this yet?" The statement said, "Another frivolous ethics charge . . . This would be hilarious if it weren't so expensive for the state to process these accusations and for me to defend against these bogus harassments."

Sarah did not address the question raised by the complaint: How much had Todd's Iron Dog sponsor, Arctic Cat, paid Sarah to appear at the start of the race sporting the company logo? And if they hadn't paid her directly, to what financial extent had they sponsored Todd, with the understanding that, when the right time came, Sarah would be a walking, talking example of product placement?

In 2007, Arctic Cat had paid Todd $7,500 in return for his using one of their machines in the Iron Dog. How much more was it worth to the company in 2008 to have Sarah, as governor, parade around in Arctic Cat gear? Neither Sarah nor the company would disclose the amount.

What was later recognized as Sarah's parting slap to Alaska's face came on March 26, when she nominated her former lawyer, Wayne Anthony Ross, to succeed Colberg as state attorney general. The *Daily News* described Ross as "a gun rights advocate who blazes around town in a red Hummer with the personalized tag WAR."

A member of the board of the National Rifle Association, Ross had helped to found the antiabortion group Alaska Right to Life and had served as honorary cochairman of Sarah's gubernatorial campaign. He was well known for his opposition to "rural preference," a policy that gave Alaskans who practiced a subsistence lifestyle greater hunting rights than those granted to people who, like Chuck Heath, hunted for sport.

The Alaska Federation of Natives was quick to oppose the nomination. The organization's cochairman said, "It almost looked like she was rubbing our face in Anthony Ross's appointment. Like rubbing our faces on the ground, saying, 'Here, take this.'"

The legislature opened confirmation hearings for Ross on April 8. He was confronted immediately with a 1993 letter to the state bar association in which he called homosexuals "degenerates."

During the third day of hearings, Ross was asked about his allegedly having said in a 1991 talk to an Anchorage group called Dads Against Discrimination, "If a guy can't rape his wife, who's he gonna rape? There wouldn't be an issue with domestic violence if women would learn to keep their mouth shut." Ross heatedly denied having made the remarks, adding, "Anybody said that to me, we'd have a little confrontation because that's a bunch of crap."

Under further questioning about his use of words such as *immoral, degenerates,* and *perversion* to describe homosexuals, Ross said, "I hate lima beans. I never liked lima beans. But if I was hired to represent the United Vegetable growers . . . would I tell you if I disliked lima beans? No, because my job is to represent the United Vegetable Growers."

Meanwhile, as the hearings continued, Sarah publicly feuded with Levi Johnston. "We're disappointed that Levi and his family, in a quest for fame, attention and fortune, are engaging in flat out lies, gross exaggeration, and even distortion," Sarah's chief spokesperson, Meg Stapleton, said.

Dan Fagan wrote, "Imagine that. Someone in a quest for fame, attention and fortune, engaging in flat out lies, gross exaggeration, and even distortion. I wonder if Stapleton knows anyone else like that."

On April 13, at the start of the final week of the 2009 legislative session, Sarah's once-steadfast allies in the Democratic Party broke with her publicly, issuing a statement that said, "She is putting her national political ambitions ahead of the needs of Alaska."

It was not a fresh complaint. During the 2008 session, legislators had taken to wearing "Where's Sarah?" buttons to highlight her frequent absences from Juneau and her disengagement even when she was there.

"Where is Sarah Palin?" state party chairwoman Patti Higgins asked now. "She is going to be halfway across the country, she's at a right-to-life fundraiser . . . We need a full-time governor." Her chief of staff responded, "We did not anticipate that the governor's political opponents would want their hands held in the final hours of the session."

Sarah herself was at an antiabortion banquet in Evansville, Indiana, where, the *Evansville Courier and Press* said, she "was besieged . . . by people urging her to run for president in 2012." The story quoted a security guard as saying, "Some people would just shout it out, and you'd see others just asking her. I heard it two or three times a minute . . . She'd just smile and wave. She was very gracious. Never once did I see her say or do anything that made her look less than sincere, like rolling her eyes when no one was looking."

A political scientist at the University of Southern Indiana called Sarah's appearance "the first major event of the 2012 presidential campaign."

SHE DIDN'T NEED Alaska anymore, and Alaska no longer needed her. Wayne Anthony Ross said that, as attorney general, one of his tasks would be to stop "having barbs thrown at the governor all the time."

The legislature threw a barb his way on April 16, rejecting his appointment by a vote of 35–23. It was the first time in Alaskan history that someone nominated to head a state agency had been rejected.

Just how far Sarah's stock had fallen in the state was made clear by a Paul Jenkins column in the *Daily News* on May 3. "There are signs of frustration and anger," he wrote. "People already are wondering whether she will, or should, consider running for governor next year. She could lose."

That was a risk she had no intention of taking.

On May 12 she announced that she'd signed a multimillion-dollar book deal with Rupert Murdoch's HarperCollins publishing company.

She said the book would give her a chance to tell her story "unrestrained and unfiltered." HarperCollins announced that the book would be co-published for the Christian market by its subsidiary Zondervan.

In early June she went to New York to make a speech, lead a parade, and attend a Yankees game. Then she went to Washington to attend a Republican fund-raising dinner. She was interviewed by Fox News, CNN, and NBC.

Life Outside seemed far more appealing than the prospect of spending the summer on the shores of Lake Lucille surrounded by a swelling chorus of critics whom, in her binary way, she called "haters." As Howard Bess said, in Sarah's world, "everything and everyone is either good or evil."

Economist Gregg Erickson went binary in the *Juneau Empire*, writing that Sarah was "either a cynical hypocrite or delusional." In a June 22 editorial, the newspaper said, "If it wasn't noticeable before, it is now painfully obvious: Alaska is no longer big enough for Sarah Palin . . . Governor Palin needs to decide soon what she's going to do with the next year: run the state of Alaska or run for national office."

ON THE AFTERNOON of July 3, standing in her backyard, on the shore of Lake Lucille, Sarah announced her decision: she would resign as governor before the end of the month. The speech in which she made her announcement was so jittery, incoherent, and just plain daffy that many who heard it feared for Sarah's mental and emotional health. Almost everyone—not only her growing bevy of critics, but even the dwindling band of true believers—felt it signaled the end of Sarah's political career.

They were wrong. She had no intention of disappearing. She knew that, unencumbered by the demands of the governorship, she'd be free to pursue the office she'd had in mind even before she became mayor of Wasilla: the presidency of the United States.

TWENTY-ONE

T HE TIME has come to strike the tent.

That may seem like a strange thing to say in the last chapter
of a book about the star performer of the circus. But no matter how
much my book sales might benefit from a Palin presidential campaign
in 2012, I sincerely hope that the whole extravaganza, which has been
unblushingly underwritten by a mainstream media willing to gam-
ble the nation's future in exchange for the cheap thrill of watching a
clown in high heels on a flying trapeze, is nearing the end of its run.

The sheer giddy *spectacle* of Sarah has mesmerized the media for
far too long. Quitting her job as Alaska's governor enabled Sarah to
make the jump from politician to full-time celebrity. Her new status
meant that it no longer mattered what she did or said—the mere fact
of her doing or saying it made it news. The same was true for other
members of her family. And even for people whose only connection to
her was that they'd briefly lived in her neighborhood.

Thus, my moving out of the house next door to hers in September
2010 became national news. "Joe McGinniss is packing his bags and
notebooks and leaving Sunday for his home in Massachusetts to write
the book he has been researching on the former governor and GOP
vice presidential candidate," an Associated Press story reported.

I moved in, I moved out: nothing newsworthy happened in between. But Sarah could not get over the fact that I'd been there at all. At the start of an October 1 telephone interview, right-wing radio host Mark Levin asked her, "By the way, did that jerk next door leave yet?"

"He left," she said. "Just in time. We had a big windstorm, too, and half the fence fell down. So he left and we're gonna hopefully get back to normal . . . the *freak.*"

Even six weeks later, on the premiere of her TLC series, *Sarah Palin's Alaska,* she was still obsessing about me. The first episode opens with Sarah seated at a table on the patio outside her house, wearing a yellow jersey and scribbling in a notebook.

In a voice-over, she says: "Where I like to do a lot of my writing and researching—especially on a beautiful day—is outside, on our slab, where I get to take in the beauty of the lake."

Then Todd approaches and says, "Gettin' some work done?"

Sarah answers in a whisper: "Yeah."

Todd: "So, ah, you comfortable up here?"

Sarah (sotto voce): "I am if you want to peek around the corner and see if he's over there."

We don't see Todd actually peeking. The next shot is of Sarah, wearing a blue top (indicating that this part was filmed on a different day), saying, "Our being here certainly has changed this summer"— cut to a shot of my house, taken from the lake—"because of this new neighbor."

Then we have a closeup of my deck, with my American and Alaskan flags hanging from the railing. And lo and behold, there, sitting on a chair reading a book, is someone whose face has been intentionally blurred but who looks a lot like me.

Cut back to the opening scene on the patio.

"Yeah, he's probably over there," Todd says.

"Do you want me to look?" Sarah says.

"No, that's okay."

"You need to drill a little tiny hole there, a peephole, and let me look through and see where he is," Sarah says.

The next shot shows Todd by the lake, saying, "Our summer fun has been kind of taken away from us because of a new neighbor next door, who's writing a hit piece on my wife. I mean, life's about bein' productive, but these people want to seek and destroy."

Then it's back to Sarah (yellow top) and Todd on the slab. Sarah says, "He doesn't need to be seein' what I'm writing and reading, right?"

"Yeah," Todd agrees. She pats him affectionately on the leg.

"Todd and his buddies got out there and built a fourteen-foot-high fence, and I'm very thankful for that," blue-top Sarah says. "By the way, I thought that was a good example, what we just did, others could look at and say, 'Oh, this is what we need to do to secure our nation's border.'"

Then we see Todd and yellow-top Sarah get up from the patio table. Sarah says, "I want Piper to play on the other side of the house, too, okay?" As they walk away, Sarah says in a voice-over, "I think it's an intrusion and an invasion of our privacy and I don't like it."

Back to blue-top Sarah: "Some reporters have said I was overreacting, and I wanted to ask them, 'How would you feel if some dude who you knew was out to getcha'"—then a cut to yellow-top Sarah on the bed of a pickup truck on the other side of house—'moved in to keep you away from *your* kids? How would you feel?'"

About twenty minutes later in the episode, Sarah returns to the subject again. As she and Todd and Piper are walking from the lake to their house after a floatplane trip, she says, in voice-over, "And Piper spies, right there in the next-door neighbor's yard, our neighbor." This is followed by the same shot used earlier of me reading a book on my deck.

"He's an author who's writing a book about us," Sarah continues, "and Piper whispered to me as we were comin' up the lawn, 'Mom, that neighbor's out there, he's watchin' us, he's watchin' us.'"

The camera shows Sarah and Piper walking up the lawn.

"Where is he?" Sarah asks. "Are you gonna wave to him? We'll just keep walkin'." Then she asks, "Is he takin' pictures?" Although I never took a picture of any member of the Palin family, Piper nods. She seems already aware of how she's supposed to respond, regardless of the truth. Sarah walks faster, with an exaggerated stride. "Don't give him the pleasure of takin' a picture."

Then we're back to blue-top Sarah, facing the camera. She says, "I would think, really, at the end of the day, he's gonna be bored to death if that's all he has to do is observe our normal, kind of boring family and our activities, but"—then a cut for the third time to the same shot of me reading—"it's just none of his flippin' business."

The scene—if that's what we can call such a spliced-together mish-mash of voice-over and footage taken at different times—ends by re-turning to the shot of yellow-top Sarah, Todd, and Piper walking toward their house.

"He was stuck inside, writin' an ugly book," Sarah says to her nine-year-old daughter. "See, we one-upped him, Piper, we had a good day. And he's stuck in his house." She and Piper exchange a high five.

A NUMBER of reviewers of *Sarah Palin's Alaska* commented on the irony of Sarah complaining about my intrusiveness even as she in-vaded her own children's privacy by thrusting them in front of TLC cameras in return for $250,000 per episode. Others, however, swal-lowed the bait whole, failing to recognize that "reality" television is to reality as love handles are to love.

Particularly credulous was Janet Malcolm, writing in the *New York Review of Books*:

Palin, who is both narrator and star of the series, performs arduous and sometimes even dangerous feats of outdoorsmanship to dem-onstrate the conservative virtue of self-reliance. In the episode in which she struggles for a foothold on a vertiginously steep glacier at the foot of Mt. McKinley in eerily beautiful and vast Denali National Park, she knows that no government handout is going to help her. She isn't even sure God will help her, though she cries out to Him and His Son, "Oh God. Help me, Lord!" . . . She is tied by a rope to a guide above her and her husband below, but she can't seem to make progress on the rock. The guide gives her instructions, but she can't follow them. "I don't know what I'm going to hold on to here. . . . What about my legs? Where do I put 'em?"

Forty-five minutes later (as a subtitle tells us) she is still clinging to the rock, helpless to take the next step up. "That's so much worse than I ever thought it would be," she groans. Finally, through a great effort of will, she manages to heave herself up to the pinnacle. "I don't think that I have been that scared or that challenged in a long time," she says, *and we believe her. The episode has a realism not often seen in reality TV* [emphasis added].

"We" believe her? Maybe not quite all of us. Longtime Alaskan and former rock climber Phil Munger wrote on his Progressive Alaska blog, "The rock climbing episode was simply awful. . . . Her whining and self pitying was horrid."

Author, photographer, and guide Stewart Green, who has written nineteen books about rock climbing, reviewed the "sorry episode" for About.com. He wrote, "If there are three things that climbers can agree about, they are these: We don't like made-up climbs to make someone look good; we don't like anyone faking it; and we don't like having BS tossed around about our beloved sport."

Sarah, he wrote, "groaned and cackled and whined with a cat-claws-on-blackboard-voice all the way up the route. Her stiff boots were not rock climbing shoes. . . . Her pants were way too tight and restricted her leg movement. . . . Another huge problem with the episode was that Sarah Palin, husband Todd, as well as the climbing guide were not wearing climbing helmets. Tsk tsk tsk. Very bad form and a very bad idea . . . I seriously doubt that the 'Bumpit' that Sarah wears while climbing would protect her noggin from falling boulders."

Thus, contrary to what the gullible Malcolm wrote, most of us were *not* taken in by Sarah's histrionics. Malcolm also fell for a more disturbing ploy that involved Trig and his future as a Down syndrome child.

"There is another passage in *Sarah Palin's Alaska* that stands out . . . for its emotional truth," she wrote. "It takes place in a native village called Eluk, where Todd Palin's Eskimo cousin Ina has set up a summer 'fish camp.' . . . In Ina's kitchen, Sarah and Ina cut up fish and have an intimate women's talk"—as if women ever have "intimate" talks when surrounded by cameras, boom mikes, slithering cables, and milling television technicians.

Ina has a Down syndrome twelve-year-old. After talking to her, Sarah confides to producer Mark Burnett's cameras and a television audience of millions, "Getting to meet our little cousin there . . . kind of gives me a look at ten years from now." Malcolm writes that Sarah "is devastated by the look into the future. . . . We see her breaking down and beginning to cry, and we cry with her. At this moment . . . she is a woman one pities and sympathizes with and, yes, even admires."

I can only speak for myself and not for "one," but I don't think I'm alone in being revolted by the cynicism of choosing to parade severely disabled children in front of television cameras for monetary and political gain.

The eight-episode series was stuffed to the gills with hokum and tripe. In the *New Yorker,* Nancy Franklin wrote, "Nearly every . . . moment comes across as calculated . . . and we find out nothing about Alaska that we didn't learn in elementary school. I know that some Americans think Palin is stupid, but I never realized that she thinks *we're* stupid."

A reviewer in the English *Telegraph* wrote, "Various people called things like Truck and Trog, Troop or Trib or Troll wander about, walk-on players in this risible woman's delusional pitch for power. Alaska looked very fetching though. It was a bit like being on a spectacular holiday marred only by the worst travelling companion imaginable."

The *Guardian* observed that Sarah, "freed from her political brief of standing on the far-right talking rubbish, is just this incredible force for boredom. It's like a magic trick; she can take an observation that is already inherently boring, then make it 10 times more boring with unenlightening statistics, a Newspeak vocabulary and this ghastly cheerleader delivery. . . . The truth is, there's nothing to see but a tedious, narrow-minded, pedantic, uncurious person. And some snow."

Even before the show aired, Republican strategist Karl Rove expressed doubt about the wisdom of a prospective presidential candidate displaying herself on "reality" television. "There are high standards that the American people have for [the presidency]," he said, "and they require a certain level of gravitas. People want to look at the candidate and say, 'That candidate is doing things that gives me confidence that they are up to the most demanding job in the world.'"

I have no reservations about saying that in the history of American politics, no candidate for national office has ever displayed *less* gravitas (that is, high seriousness, substance, a dignified demeanor) than Sarah Palin.

Over the course of *Sarah Palin's Alaska,* she became such a caricature of herself—in one episode cavorting, giggling, and pouting with the queen of reality television's housewives, Kate Gosselin—that by the time it was over she'd all but removed herself from the 2012 political equation. She earned millions of dollars, but she paid a fatally high price in credibility for every dollar.

• • •

THEN CAME TUCSON. On the morning of Saturday, January 8, 2011, a gunman shot and killed six people and wounded thirteen others in a supermarket parking lot as Democratic congresswoman Gabrielle Giffords held an outdoor meeting with voters. The prime target was Giffords, who was shot point-blank in the head.

Within hours, news reports revealed that Giffords' congressional district was among twenty that Sarah's political action committee had targeted with gunsight crosshairs early in 2010. "Let's take back the 20, together! Join me today," Sarah wrote below a map showing the districts of twenty House democrats she wanted targeted for special attention in the 2010 elections.

As early as March 2010, Giffords had told people that the use of crosshairs made her uneasy. "We're on Sarah Palin's 'targeted' list, but the thing is that the way she has it depicted, we're in the crosshairs of a gun sight over our district," she told an interviewer. "When people do that, they've got to realize that there are consequences to that action."

Her observation left Sarah unfazed. More than two months after Giffords won reelection, the map with the crosshairs remained up on the SarahPAC website.

Thus, when a demented twenty-two-year-old Tucson resident named Jared Lee Loughner attempted to assassinate Representative Giffords with a shot to the head and opened fire on others in the crowd, people made the obvious connection to Sarah's crosshairs map and to her militant rhetoric ("Don't retreat, reload!"), which had been stirring the passions of millions of gun-toting right-wingers since 2008.

Sarah was outraged that anyone would think she should bear any responsibility for Loughner's actions. She called Roger Ailes, president of Fox News, on Sunday, January 9, the day after the shootings. In itself, this was unusual. Months would go by without Ailes speaking to Sarah directly. He had hired her and unleashed her and left her largely on her own ever since, knowing that whatever trajectory her broadcasting career followed—whether she soared back into contention for the Republican presidential nomination in 2012 or crashed and burned—she'd produce ratings that translated into revenue. Contrary to public perception, Ailes was far more concerned about Fox News's bottom line than about the future of the Republican party.

Sarah demanded that Ailes immediately clear airtime on Fox so she could go live with a national broadcast disclaiming any responsibility for the shootings.

He refused. Ailes could see that already the story was turning, as it became evident that Loughner was a lone lunatic, not affiliated with the Tea Party or with any right-wing militia, and that his obsession was with Representative Giffords, not with Sarah Palin.

Ailes advised Sarah to hold her peace. It would do her no good to insert herself into a tragic tale that had nothing to do with her. He said he would not clear airtime on Fox, nor would he permit her to use the equipment in the home studio Fox News had built for her so she could record a statement about the shootings.

By Monday, Ailes's prudence seemed justified, as mainstream media opinion coalesced around the view that it was unfair to blame Sarah for a deranged gunman who'd never shown the slightest sign of even knowing who she was.

But Sarah couldn't leave well enough alone. On Tuesday, January 11, the day before President Obama flew to Tucson to visit Giffords in the hospital and to speak at the memorial service for the victims, Ailes, in his office at Fox News headquarters in New York, received an unsettling report.

A Fox executive told him that Sarah was renewing her demand for airtime. She wanted to broadcast a statement the next day. She was determined to speak out. She felt that she, too, was a victim of the shootings.

Ailes was unequivocal. He would not let her appear on Fox—

especially not on the day of the memorial service!—in an attempt to make the story about her. He was stunned by her tastelessness and lack of judgment.

Sarah could not accept no for an answer. Denied access to Fox News, and even denied the right to use her Fox studio, Sarah read and recorded a ghost-written statement anyway, using her personal video equipment.

On Wednesday, January 12, the day of the memorial service, with President Obama en route to Tucson, Sarah went public with her response to the Tucson tragedy, releasing a video on Vimeo and posting her statement on her Facebook page. Not even Roger Ailes was going to muzzle this pit bull.

Sarah's post-Tucson plunge into the pool of Narcissus proved to be, by several light years, the worst political blunder she'd ever made.

After some boilerplate expressions of sorrow for those who'd been killed or wounded in the shootings, Sarah stressed that there was one victim as yet unnoticed: herself. She condemned "the irresponsible statements from people attempting to apportion blame for this terrible event" (i.e., anyone who said her crosshairs targets could be an incitement to violence).

She said, "Acts of monstrous criminality stand on their own. They begin and end with the criminals who commit them, not collectively with all the citizens of a state, not with those who listen to talk radio, not with maps of swing districts."

Then she added, "Especially within hours of a tragedy unfolding, journalists and pundits should not manufacture a *blood libel* that serves only to incite the very hatred and violence they purport to condemn. That is reprehensible [emphasis added]."

What observers found reprehensible was Sarah's use of the term *blood libel.* Throughout history, the phrase has referred to the false accusation that Jews murdered Christian babies so as to use their blood in religious rituals.

Sarah, whose grip on historical fact is less than secure, clearly hadn't the slightest idea of the term's origins. Quite likely, neither did whoever wrote the speech. Conservative law professor Glenn Reynolds had invoked it in a January 10 *Wall Street Journal* opinion piece, and there's no reason to think that anyone in the Palin camp knew that "blood libel" was anything more than a handy new phrase that Reynolds himself had coined.

Denunciation of Sarah's attempt to equate her post-Tucson plight with the ugliest effects of anti-Semitism through the ages was quick and widespread. Jack Cafferty's response on CNN was typical: "Sarah Palin may have done herself in. The tragedy in Tucson, Arizona, presented an opportunity for Palin to reach beyond her base and strike a note of unity. It was her chance to say something that showed she was capable of true leadership. . . .

"Before Palin opened her mouth, there was a good deal of sympathy for her. Many believed it was wrong to drag her into the debate. But then she spoke. And it was just awful. Defiant and inflammatory, Palin invoked the historically painful term 'blood libel' in attacking the media."

In the days that followed, Sarah received the sort of history lesson she'd just as soon have skipped. Reaction was so strong and so unanimously adverse that she did something she'd never done before: she shut up.

THREE MONTHS PASSED. Her uncustomary silence eventually caused mainstream media to adopt a new meme: Sarah was finished. She was done.

In *Newsweek,* Howard Kurtz asked rhetorically, "Is Sarah Palin Over?" His answer was such an emphatic yes that a couple of days later he was doing a live Internet chat about "the end of the Sarah Palin phenomenon." Even neoconservative Bill Kristol, who had first legitimized her with establishment right-wingers, began to distance himself. "I thought she had a real chance to take the lead on a few policy issues, do a little more in terms of framing the policy agenda. I don't think she's done that," Kristol said.

But as those who'd come to understand her character suspected, Sarah wasn't retreating, she was reloading. She was never going to just fade away. Her silence in the wake of the "blood libel" fuss was strategic, as she waited for the impact of the Tucson shootings and her disastrous response to fade.

In May, she bought a $1.7 million house in Arizona, in order to be more centrally located in anticipation of the 2012 Republican primaries. She also announced her "One Nation" bus tour, which she described as "part of our new campaign to educate and energize Americans about our nation's founding principles, in order to promote the Fundamental Restoration of America."

Unlike on her *Going Rogue* book tour in 2009, Sarah didn't bring Trig this time. He had turned three, and was no longer quite so easy to wave around in front of adoring throngs as if he were a loaf of heaven-sent manna bread.

In addition, more and tougher questions about Trig's birth were being asked on blogs, and, shielded by anonymity, more Wasilla residents were coming forward with statements that contradicted Sarah's version of events. One persistent allegation was that Sarah had had a tubal ligation after Piper was born and could not ever have become pregnant again.

Sarah may have felt it was time to distance herself from Trig. So she brought Piper on the first leg of her bus tour. Even that turned sour, however, as in appearance after appearance the ten-year-old displayed a petulance that made her misery clear to all who saw it.

Sarah kicked off her "campaign to educate and energize Americans about our nation's founding principles" on the back of a Harley at a Memorial Day motorcycle rally in Washington, D.C.

In New York, she ate bad pizza in Times Square with Donald Trump, whose personal plan for the "Fundamental Restoration of America" involves high-rise hotels, condos, and gambling casinos named after himself in Las Vegas and Atlantic City.

Then it was on to Boston, where in response to a question about who Paul Revere was, Sarah said he was "he who warned, uh, the . . . the British that they weren't gonna be takin' away our arms, uh, by ringin' those bells and, um, by makin' sure that as he's ridin' his horse through town to send those warnin' shots and bells that, uh, we were gonna be secure and we were gonna be free . . . and we were gonna be armed."

As I wrote on my blog that night:

Were Sarah's version correct, the U.S. might still be a British colony today. We certainly wouldn't have won the Revolutionary War.

First of all, Sarah: Revere wasn't warning "the British" of anything. He was warning the rebels *about* the British army's nighttime advance.

Second, the whole point of Revere's ride from Boston to Lexington (his destination was Concord, but he didn't make it) was that it was *secret.* Because the Middlesex County countryside was rife with British supporters, Revere virtually *whispered* his warnings that the King's forces were crossing the Charles River on the night of April 18–19, 1775, to launch an attack upon the American rebels.

Ringing bells and sending warning shots while on a clandestine mission? To warn *the British* that they *"weren't gonna be takin' away our arms"*? Was *this* the version of American history that Sarah learned in Wasilla public schools, and as the daughter of her schoolteacher/father Chuck Heath?

From Boston, Sarah traveled to New Hampshire, where she upstaged Mitt Romney on the day he formally announced his candidacy for the Republican nomination. Then she flew home to Arizona, having once again displayed her ability to wrap the mainstream media around her finger.

In the *Los Angeles Times,* James Rainey expressed the new conventional wisdom, writing that he found Sarah "fascinating" and quoting in support a *Politico* editor who called her "arguably the most electrifying presence in American politics."

Suddenly, it was the summer of 2008 all over again. Justifying the frenzied, mile-by-mile coverage of what was essentially a six-day non-event orchestrated by a noncandidate for public office, Rainey wrote, "At some point writers, editors and producers have to give their audiences a dose of what they are interested in."

The *Politico* editor Charles Mahtesian was more candid. "There's a mutual codependency in the relationship," he said. "Neither side can live without the other."

SO THAT'S WHAT it has come down to as America prepares for the 2012 presidential campaign: our mainstream media reduced to a level of helpless codependency, in which its willing suspension of disbelief in regard to Sarah requires that it not look at or listen to her too closely, for fear that it might discover something it can't ignore.

Sarah Palin practices politics as lap dance, and we're the suckers who pay the price. Members of our jaded national press corps eagerly stuff hundred-dollar bills into her G-string, even as they wink at one another to show that they don't take her seriously.

What should never have been more than a freaky sideshow performed on a carnival midway was transformed by John McCain's desperation into what many still seem to see as the greatest show on earth.

Actually, it's long past time to strike the tent.

ACKNOWLEDGMENTS

I would like to thank Dennis Holahan for so many things that it would be impossible to list them in the space allotted here. Suffice it to say that for the past ten years he has done so much to help me, in so many ways, that it's not an overstatement to say that I doubt I could have written this book without his friendship, guidance, and unflagging support.

As was the case thirty-five years ago when I lived in Alaska to research *Going to Extremes,* dozens of Alaskans opened their hearts and homes to me during my return visits over the past three years. Many of their names appear in the text of this book. I hope they are already aware of my gratitude and affection.

There are others, both in Alaska and elsewhere, whom I'd like to thank, but so many of them—for fear of harassment by supporters of Sarah Palin—have asked me not to mention them by name that I'll simply tell them all here how grateful I am and that I'll convey my appreciation in a more personal way to each and every one as soon as possible. I wish it could be otherwise, but I have to respect the wishes of those who have expressed the desire to remain unnamed.

Among the exceptions are:

David Larabell, my agent at The David Black Literary Agency. It used to be that an agent made the deal, wished you well, and went on to the next piece of business. Dave Larabell is not like that. He has been with me every step of the way, providing everything from editorial guidance to the contractual restructuring that enabled me to research this book as deeply as I needed to. In addition, in 2009, when I'd just about given up on the notion of writing about Sarah Palin, it was Dave Larabell who persuaded me of her ongoing relevance to the American political scene.

Matthew Martin, vice president and associate general counsel at Random House, Inc., and David Drake, senior vice president and executive director, publicity, of The Crown Publishing Group.

Jenna Dolan, the best copyeditor I've ever had the pleasure of working with. If you don't like the book, don't yell at her; she is not responsible for the content. In fact, though she may not have received public thanks for it, she copyedited Sarah Palin's second book.

Geoffrey Dunn, author of *The Lies of Sarah Palin: The Untold Story Behind Her Relentless Quest for Power.* Such generosity of spirit from the author of a contemporaneous book about the same subject as my own is something I've never encountered before.

Russell A. Baer, DDS, and Martin Marcus, DDS, of University Associates in Dentistry of Chicago. People ask me why I went all the way to Chicago for dental implants. My smile should provide the answer. And thanks also to Lisa A. Uyehara, M.D.

The most important exception is my wife, the brilliant, beautiful, and fearless Nancy Doherty, whose editorial assistance—and so much more—has once again proved priceless.

ILLUSTRATION CREDITS

pp. 1, 8: Joe McGinniss

p. 10: Mapping Specialists, Ltd.

p. 25: © Sports Illustrated/Getty Images

p. 76: Tom Kluberton

p. 78: AP

p. 116: Joe McGinniss

p. 158: Abe Alongi

p. 183: Reber Stein

pp. 184, 188: Joe McGinniss

p. 189: Howard Cheezem

pp. 205, 212: *Doonesbury* © G. B. Trudeau. Reprinted by permission of Universal Press Syndicate. All rights reserved.

p. 206: Mark Thiessen/Associated Press

p. 286: Joe McGinniss